The Betrayal of Witness

The Betrayal of Witness

Reflections on the Downfall of Jean Vanier

Edited by
STANLEY HAUERWAS
and HANS S. REINDERS

CASCADE *Books* · Eugene, Oregon

THE BETRAYAL OF WITNESS
Reflections on the Downfall of Jean Vanier

Copyright © 2024 Wipf and Stock Publishers. All rights reserved. Except for brief quotations in critical publications or reviews, no part of this book may be reproduced in any manner without prior written permission from the publisher. Write: Permissions, Wipf and Stock Publishers, 199 W. 8th Ave., Suite 3, Eugene, OR 97401.

Cascade Books
An Imprint of Wipf and Stock Publishers
199 W. 8th Ave., Suite 3
Eugene, OR 97401

www.wipfandstock.com

PAPERBACK ISBN: 978-1-6667-7230-2
HARDCOVER ISBN: 978-1-6667-7231-9
EBOOK ISBN: 978-1-6667-7232-6

Cataloguing-in-Publication data:

Names: Hauerwas, Stanley, 1940–, editor. | Reinders, Hans S., editor.

Title: The betrayal of witness : reflections on the downfall of Jean Vanier / edited by Stanley Hauerwas and Hans S. Reinders.

Description: Eugene, OR : Cascade Books, 2024 | Includes bibliographical references.

Identifiers: ISBN 978-1-6667-7230-2 (paperback) | ISBN 978-1-6667-7231-9 (hardcover) | ISBN 978-1-6667-7232-6 (ebook)

Subjects: LCSH: Vanier, Jean, 1928–2019. | Arche (Association)—History. | Sex crimes—Religious aspects—Christianity. | Psychological abuse—Religious aspects—Christianity.

Classification: BX2347.8.M4 B48 2024 (paperback) | BX2347.8.M4 B48 (ebook)

VERSION NUMBER 041124

Contents

Contributors | vii

Introduction | xi
—Stanley Hauerwas and Hans S. Reinders

Chapter One
Sitting at the Table with a Sinner: Christian Witness and Truthfully Remembering Jean Vanier | 1
—Jason R. Greig

Chapter Two
Against Living Saints | 18
—Keith Dow

Chapter Three
Considerations for an Evolving Vision of Identity and Witness | 37
—Anne Masters

Chapter Four
Who Wants to Be Vulnerable? On Vulnerability beyond Vanier | 56
—Talitha Cooreman-Guittin

Chapter Five
Putting Aside Charisma for Charism: A "New Springtime" for L'Arche | 71
—Pia Matthews

Chapter Six
Disabling Virtue | 89
—Patrick McKearney

Chapter Seven
A Mixture of Light and Darkness: Accounting for My Vanier | 104
—Hans S. Reinders

Chapter Eight
Hidden in Plain View | 120
　—Benjamin S. Wall

Chapter Nine
On Remaining in God's Story as Passion | 137
　—Hans G. Ulrich

Chapter Ten
Jean Vanier: A Paradox for Cancel Culture | 150
　—Medi Ann Volpe

Epilogue
Needing Vanier: A Brief Confession | 164
　—Stanley Hauerwas

Contributors

Talitha Cooreman-Guittin is professor of pastoral theology, religious education, and homiletics at the University of Freiburg (Switzerland). She coedited two volumes on disability theology for the *Journal for Disability & Religion* (2021) and in the *International Journal for the Study of the Christian Church* (2022). Among her publications on theology and intellectual disability are "Could Adam and Eve Have Been Disabled? Images of Creation in Catholic Religious Education Textbooks in France" in the *Journal of Disability & Religion* (2018) and "Growing in Humanity: On Vulnerability, Capacitation, and Encounter in Religious Education: A Christian Practical Theological Approach" in *Religious Education* (2019).

Keith Dow started his career in direct support work with persons with cognitive impairments and joined the Organizational and Spiritual Life team at Christian Horizons in 2006. In 2019 he received his PhD in theological ethics from VU University Amsterdam for the thesis "Call, Recognition, and Response: Loving My Neighbor with Intellectual Disabilities." He authored *Formed Together: Mystery, Narrative, and Virtue in Christian Caregiving*. Dow is on the core council of the Institute on Theology and Disability and cochairs the Religion & Spirituality Interest Network of AAIDD.

Jason R. Greig is a lecturer in disability studies and philosophy at King's University College in London, Ontario, Canada, and accompanies people with cognitive impairments in Kitchener, Ontario, Canada. In 2015 he authored *Reconsidering Intellectual Disability: L'Arche, Medical Ethics, and Christian Friendship* through Georgetown University Press. He has authored numerous articles on theology and disability, including "Discipleship at God's Pace: Living a Christian Timescape in L'Arche," and "The Slow Journey Towards Beatitude: Disability in L'Arche," and "Staying Human in High-Speed Society."

Stanley Hauerwas is professor emeritus of theological ethics at Duke University where he held the Gilbert T. Rowe chair for more than twenty years. In 2000 he was invited to deliver the Gifford Lectures, leading to *With the Grain of the Universe* in 2001. Among his numerous publications are *Sanctify Them in the Truth: Holiness Exemplified* (1998), and *Living Gently in a Violent World* (with Jean Vanier, 2008). His latest publication is *Fully Alive: The Apocalyptic Humanism of Karl Barth* (University of Virginia Press, 2023).

Anne Masters, PhD, FAAIDD, is the director of the Office for Pastoral Ministry with Persons with Disabilities for the Archdiocese of Newark. She did her doctorate at VU University Amsterdam in 2020 from Vrije Universiteit for her thesis, "Who Do You Say That I Am? Overcoming the Marginalization of Individuals with Intellectual and Developmental Disabilities in the US Catholic Church." Masters is past president of its Religion & Spirituality Interest Network of the AAIDD. Recent published works include "Rethinking Charity" and "Considering a Case for Rights and Charity."

Pia Matthews lectures in theology, philosophy, bioethics, and medical law at St. Mary's University Twickenham and Allen Hall Seminary, London. She is a faculty member of the Mater Ecclesiae College, London. Matthews has written extensively on disability and theological and philosophical anthropology. Her books include *Pope John Paul and the Apparently "Nonacting" Person*; *God's Wild Flowers: Saints with Disabilities*; and *Discerning Persons: Profound Disability, the Early Church Fathers and the Concept of the Person in Bioethics*. Matthews's daughter, Paula, has complex and profound disabilities.

Patrick McKearney is an assistant professor in the department of anthropology at the University of Amsterdam conducting research on people with intellectual disabilities in the UK, India, and Italy. His recent articles on disability, care, ethics, and religion include publications in *Social Analysis*, *Ethnos*, and *JRAI*. He has also edited two special issues on cognitive disability in *The Cambridge Journal of Anthropology* and *Medical Anthropology*.

Hans S. Reinders is professor emeritus of ethics at VU University Amsterdam where he taught from 1995 to 2016. In 2010 he edited *The Paradox of Disability: Responses to Jean Vanier and L'Arche Communities from Theology and the Sciences*. He authored many publications on disability, theology, and ethics with a focus on L'Arche, including "Being with the Disabled: Jean Vanier's Theological Realism" in 2012, and "Transforming Friendship: An Essay in Honor of Jean Vanier" in 2015. With Cristina Gangemi he coauthored "Does L'Arche Need Another Saint?" (2022).

Hans G. Ulrich is professor emeritus of systematic theology at the University of Erlangen (Germany). In his many publications he has focused particularly on Christian ethics, strongly influenced by his admiration for Martin Luther's work. His thesis on Nietzsche was published as *Anthropologie und Ethik bei Friedrich Nietzsche: Interpretationen zu Grundproblemen theologische Ethik*, 1975. Among his most influential works is *Wie Geschöpfe leben: Konturen evangelischer Ethik*, 2005.

Medi Ann Volpe is a Catholic moral theologian and mother of four children, including a daughter with Down Syndrome, and currently serves as director of research at Wesley House, Cambridge. Her work explores the intersection of ecclesiology and spiritual formation, with a special interest in discipleship and Christian identity of people with intellectual disabilities. She is the author of *Rethinking Christian Identity* (2013), and has published in journals and handbooks, including the *International Journal of Systematic Theology*, *Modern Theology*, and the *Oxford Handbook of Catholic Theology* (which she coedited with Lewis Ayres). She also serves on the board of the *Journal of Disability and Religion*.

Benjamin S. Wall is a priest and theologian in residence at Church of the Redeemer in Greensboro, North Carolina, doing work on the intersection of disability, mental health, and Christian theology. He has been a professor at several institutions of higher education and was a mental health professional for over ten years. He authored *Welcome as a Way of Life: A Practical Theology of Jean Vanier* and has published many articles on disability, theology, and ethics with a focus on L'Arche, hospitality, and ethics of social care provision.

Introduction

Stanley Hauerwas and Hans S. Reinders

This is rightly a sad book. None of the authors who wrote one of its chapters did so without the desire to avoid or at least hesitate as to what they must say. Perhaps this puts the matter too clearly since it seems to indicate they all knew what had to be said. We know that was not the case. Some had to write their essay while being unsure what can truthfully be said about Jean Vanier's destructive behavior—not so much with regard to the facts that have been established, but rather because there are questions that remain, even though the most important facts are known. Partly because there are things about Vanier's inner life we still don't know and never will, and partly because what we do know is beyond our comprehension. It is to their credit that those who have written these essays refrained from any simplistic account of Vanier's story.

Presumably the readers of this volume will know that story, but if this is not the case, or it is only known to some extent, here is a short summary. Jean Vanier, who was the venerated founder and leader of L'Arche, died in May 2019 at the age of ninety.[1] Within a year after his death the news came out that he had sexually abused six women as their spiritual counselor. L'Arche International published a report in February 2020 that laid out the facts as they were then known.

It concluded that the testimonies of the six women were considered reliable and that it could not be denied Vanier was rightly accused of sexual

---

1. For readers not familiar with the story: L'Arche is a place where adults with and without intellectual disabilities are building a community by living and working together. They are seeking connections of friendship that go beyond caring/helping relationships. L'Arche was founded by Jean Vanier in 1964.

abuse. It was added that nothing indicated that he had also abused persons with intellectual disabilities. Also announced was an investigation into the circumstances and background of the practice of sexual misconduct in order to lay out all the relevant facts with regard to Vanier's behavior. Crucial to this investigation would be what could be found in personal archives and correspondence about how he himself accounted for his sexual misconduct.

The results of this investigation were published in January 2023. It confirmed that Vanier was guilty of sexual abuse, and that he was a central figure in a small, sect-like group that adhered to an obscure kind of mystical theology that supposedly justified its practices. It had already been subject to investigation by the Roman Catholic Church in 1952, and was finally condemned as heretical in 1956, eight years before Vanier in 1964 started the first house of what was to become L'Arche.

The origin of this mystical theology was developed by a priest and professor of theology by the name of Thomas Philippe who Vanier considered his spiritual mentor since his early twenties. Philippe managed to mix up his desire for unification with the divine with his desire for sexual gratification. In the early 1950s he initiated Vanier in his practices, with a few others, and taught them they were blessed to be advanced in Christian spiritual life to the full satisfaction of body and mind. It was a sect-like group in that they considered their knowledge to be incomprehensible for both the hierarchy in the church as well as for the people at large, which meant it had to be kept a secret.

This explains why the contributors to this volume, like most of Vanier's public connections, had no knowledge of the man's history of sexual transgression before February 2020. Even those who regarded him as a friend were largely unaware of what was going on in his life. For Vanier and his inner circle these connections were in fact part of a public audience that was carefully attended to with talks, retreats, interviews, and books. There had been some rumors regarding Thomas Philippe before L'Arche got started, but Vanier had silenced them by making publicly known that he had severed his ties with him. Consequently, many of his admirers did not consider it a story worth pursuing. It was a blatant lie. When the truth came out finally, it appeared that after Philippe had been condemned and removed from his post by the church, Vanier took the lead in organizing that he would stay connected with his group, and acted as one of his closest allies until the man's death in 1991.

As a consequence, most of those who have written the chapters of this book are people who cannot help but feel that they have been betrayed by Vanier. Such a stance may suggest they are judgmental, and subject to the reflex of abandoning the man, as is common in what nowadays is known as "cancel culture." Had he just betrayed them personally, it would have been bad and painful but probably not as devastating as the fact that he betrayed the witness to a truly Christian existence that he was believed to embody. Frankly, Vanier was believed to live the Gospel. This attitude speaks from the pathos that shapes the prose of the authors' reflections in this book. They are struggling and deeply devastated, making it impossible to take pleasure from what they must say if they are to be truthful in what must be said.

For most of us Vanier was once a sign of hope in a cynical world. Accordingly, his was no ordinary betrayal. The authors had to tell the truth about his secret life, however, first and foremost to themselves and then to their neighbors. This task was especially painful for those who have been among his deepest admirers and closest friends. Their admiration came from seeing Vanier as someone who knew how to live his life in a morally coherent way. God knows we live in a time of moral confusion. It is not that we are bad people, but we are aware of the fact that most of our lives are deeply incoherent. We hope there will be at least some people who have a moral integrity enabling them to live their lives in a way that can be called good. Many of us longed to have the confidence that Vanier's was such a life. We were desperately wrong.

Vanier's behavior was bad enough as it was. What makes the truth about his life especially hard to swallow is that he wrapped his sexual aggression in pietistic language, which suggests he may actually have assumed he was doing something "good." God knows how deeply our lives are gripped by conditions that lead to self-deception. Absent friends capable of telling us the truth, self-deception can become a way of life. Vanier had such friends but he maintained a careful secrecy to keep them at a distance, while the friends of his inner circle were incapable of seeing the truth about what they were doing. A reminder that sin is not only something we do but a power that holds us captive.

Vanier was clearly a prisoner of that power, which kept him from seeing the full truth of what he was doing. The extensive praise for the good work he did may well have prevented him from recognizing the contradiction in the heart of his life. Facing the numerous facts that proved this contradiction, the Study Commission that investigated his story did not consider it its task to list all the good things he has done. Rightly so, we think, because an unambiguous message was needed about his destructive behavior. The commission's report sends that message. But this doesn't mean, of course, that these good things did not happen. The common response to Vanier's demise has been one of shock and outrage, which indicates that most of his admirers had known a different man.

For many it is important that Vanier was a Christian in a time and place when Christianity is seen by many as intellectually and morally inadequate. There is nothing self-evident about being a Christian anymore, if there ever was. It is not that Christians no longer believe in a way that was once considered a given. Rather the challenge nowadays is that being a Christian does not seem to make much of a difference for how Christians live. We all need witnesses who in word and deed teach us the difference. We thought Vanier to be such a person. Many Christians saw his life as a form of hope against despair. Such a hope was shattered by his sexual violence.

It is our hope, however, that these essays are a sign of hope. To let Vanier's destructive behavior destroy the good work of L'Arche would be a tragedy. The challenge is to know how to go on without the denial either of the wrong that was done or of the good that was done. We need to know how to tell the story of L'Arche without a "hero" or, as several of the authors of these essays suggest, without a charismatic founder. The challenge is to remember the center of L'Arche has always been the core members, not Jean Vanier.

But let there be no mistake. The authors of these essays remain challenged by Vanier's strange life. There is simply no denying he had a gift in his ability to be with and enjoy those who are intellectually different. Those of us who think there is some connection between a person's character and their behavior cannot help but find Vanier a challenge, which explains why the authors started their conversation resulting in this collection years before the Study Commission's report from January 2023. Much of the information it brought out did not change but only intensified the challenge, mainly because Vanier seemed to be a person of extraordinary moral character who could be trusted without reserve, until we found out that he was devious. We suspect he never understood himself to be such, which is one of the reasons his life turned out to be so destructive.

We think readers will find these essays to be informative and probing, but they are not arranged to produce a cumulative conclusion. Though the contributors have different levels and kinds of experiences with L'Arche, each in their distinct way is well acquainted with Vanier's work as with the story of his demise.

As editors, we decided to refrain from the habitual introduction by means of a brief description of each of the chapters. But we will identify a few of the themes and topics that they have in common, be it that the authors present them from different angles. We wanted each contributor to speak in his or her own voice. Most of them are personally involved in being inspired by the theology of L'Arche as it has been publicly espoused by Vanier, in various ways and to various degrees, which inevitably requires space for a personal response. That the overall result shows overlapping observations, questions, and arguments is also inevitable.

A major theme is biographical. Authors observe that there have been two sides to Vanier that do not seem to be reconcilable, but is that final for how he will be remembered? A second theme concerns his theology. It looks at Vanier's version of Catholicism and his adherence to the mystical theology he learned from Thomas Philippe. Another key topic is his understanding of vulnerability with regard to persons with intellectual disabilities and how that shaped the space for expressing their individuality. The overwhelming role of Vanier's presence and the weight of his views raise questions about the position of assistants and the willingness to take their problems seriously. Several contributions consider the social ramifications of Vanier's vision for the leadership of L'Arche as a community.

As some of the authors of this volume testify, Vanier had the gift of intimacy. It was assumed he could be trusted. His mode of negotiating the relations with those around him seemed to be the exemplification of kindness, all of which makes his behavior all the harder to understand or remember. These authors suggest that as hard as this may be, the memory of what happened is crucial if L'Arche is to have a future "after Vanier" at all. Crucial for such a remembering is the challenge of a forgiveness that cannot be cheap.

The Christian faith is a force that can free the soul of falsehood, but that same power can be transformed and destroy the soul. Put differently, Christianity is a faith constituted by convictions that can transform lives, but exactly because of their significance those same convictions can result in distorted forms of life.

The Study Commission's report is rightly named *Control and Abuse* (2023). It has undoubtedly shown that the disgusting behavior of Thomas Philippe and Jean Vanier was there at the outset of L'Arche. Nonetheless it is also true that there was much going on in L'Arche homes that was unequivocally good. How to acknowledge and distinguish good from evil in Vanier's life and work is a challenge for the future that is not easily met. The contributions in this book are an attempt to help us to see the difference.

Chapter One

Sitting at the Table with a Sinner
Christian Witness and Truthfully Remembering Jean Vanier

Jason R. Greig

What Now?

So were my thoughts on the morning of February 22, 2020, after I read the "Summary Report" on the allegations of sexual misconduct by Jean Vanier.[1] I was not shocked; while I was profoundly disappointed (and more than a little angry) at Vanier, the claims appeared consistent with previous allegations made against Thomas Phillippe, his spiritual father. For someone who had used his written work constructively and been inspired by it through living in L'Arche, I found myself wondering: what do I do now with this person and his work?

On the one hand, I was deeply dismayed by not only the harm Vanier inflicted on the women who testified about the manipulation he exercised in their relationships. I was equally demoralized that the wrongdoing was done under the guise of a heterodox form of bridal mysticism, which Phillippe had been indicted for years earlier by the Roman Catholic Church and his Dominican order. Manipulating women sexually was horrible enough, but

1. L'Arche International, "Summary Report."

to justify it by way of the Christian mystical tradition seemed particularly egregious. Even if one wanted to give Vanier as much of the benefit of the doubt as possible, the report illustrated a severe abuse of power, where Vanier appeared to never admit to the gravity of his acts.

Yet I also could not forget the man beyond the acts. Personally, Vanier's life and work had inspired me to write about Christian theology in the context of cognitive impairment, leading me to spend a significant portion of my life in L'Arche being transformed by relationships with persons considered to be intellectually disabled. But Vanier's impact was much greater than me and my own work. Thousands of lives were impacted by his work, whether it was those labeled as intellectually disabled who had been "liberated" from institutional life, or the multitude of persons inspired to share life with those persons and witness to a new way of living peace in the world. A brilliant speaker and preacher, Vanier captivated audiences with a message proclaiming the value and giftedness of the lives of people with cognitive impairments, and founded L'Arche as a new form of peace community in a world driven by power and violence. Vanier offered a philosophical and theological anthropology, grounded in his relationships with people considered intellectually disabled, that could challenge deformed visions of the human and provide insights on how our cultures could become more hospitable to all of those understood as "other."

What do I do now with these two sides of Jean Vanier? Can they in fact be held together? Can constructive aspects of Vanier's life and work still be retrieved? Should they be retrieved? These questions related about much more than simply what to do with my own scholarly work. What would now be the place Vanier had in L'Arche's historical and ever-evolving story? Were any of his insights and public philosophizing relevant or acceptable for ecclesial communities and theological reflection? Or was everything about Vanier now inherently corrupt and best left forgotten? What was the witness that L'Arche and the church were now called to offer in regards to Vanier? In short, how was L'Arche, the church, and the theological community to *remember* Vanier going forward? For it seemed to me that the proper way to answer many of these questions depended a great deal on how exactly Vanier was to be remembered.

In this essay I will draw upon the theological reflection of Miroslav Volf in an attempt to describe what a "right remembering" of Jean Vanier might look like. Based upon his own experience of interrogation, Volf argues that a truthful remembering of wrongdoing and wrongdoers requires that immoral acts not be whitewashed, but also need to be seen in the context of the whole life of the wrongdoer. Practicing this kind of remembering in the context of Christian community affirms the humanity of the wrongdoer, and helps maintain the ultimate end of condemnation not as punishment but repentance and reconciliation. When the community of those who surrounded Vanier remember this way, Vanier is seen as a "sinner" who requires both challenge but also engagement, just as Jesus encountered the "sinners" in the Gospels. By refusing to completely expel Vanier from fellowship with the faithful, those most implicated in his life's work can both denounce his hypocrisy and affirm how the Holy Spirit worked through him to reveal the truth and love of God.

As I have intimated in this introduction, this chapter will not reside solely on an "academic" or "objective" domain. While I will engage in theological reflection, this essay will also involve aspects of *confession*. Like many others, my own relation to Vanier's work was never purely an intellectual one, but also involved the spiritual and the human. I never claimed Vanier as a personal "friend." Yet through his presence in L'Arche, as well as the place his writings have had in my own spiritual growth, I believe that I have at least a limited responsibility to both critique Vanier truthfully and grudgingly not banish him from the larger Christian community that has formed me in following Jesus.

This essay has three main audiences. First, I write to the theological community, particularly those who have drawn upon Vanier's work (constructively and critically) in theological reflection. We are all implicated in Vanier's life to varying degrees, and thus have a particular role to play in what to do with his writings and their place within the Christian theological tradition. Second, I write to the wider ecclesial community. Vanier's works have inspired churches and congregations in various ways in their desire to create communities of Gospel witness. While this relationship to Vanier's work may need to be challenged, I believe that a truthful remembering of Vanier might not only assist in keeping aspects of his work valuable for a Christian witness in the world, but also offer potential resources for how the church can reflect upon wrongdoing in a church both holy and sinful. Third, I write to communities and members of L'Arche throughout the world. Like many others, my own experience of sharing life and faith in L'Arche communities has formed me in a vision of the Gospel that has transformed my own life and vision of faith. While I am not officially a member of L'Arche today, I have a certain interest and investment in seeing the movement flourish and live the Gospel. As a long-time L'Arche colleague once said to me, while many L'Arche assistants may leave and not be *in* L'Arche, many stay forever *of* L'Arche. As someone not in but *of* L'Arche, I believe that the movement can benefit from a truthful remembering of Vanier, not merely as a matter of dealing with trauma but as a possible way forward in clarifying its mission and witness in the world.

Forgiveness: Is It Possible? Advisable?

Related to right remembering is the theology and practice of Christian forgiveness. Can Vanier be forgiven? Should he be forgiven? While a fundamental aspect of Christian life, the practice of forgiveness is profoundly challenged by egregious wrongdoing. For theologians like Miroslav Volf—who has written extensively about forgiveness and reconciliation in the context of violence and ethnic cleansing—forgiveness cannot be easily foregone, even in the context of the "unforgiveable." "Forgiving the unrepentant is not an optional extra in the Christian way of life; it's the heart of the thing."[2] Mennonite theologian Gayle Gerber Koontz argues strongly that the church can be a place that both stands by victims of abuse *and* accompanies perpetrators to repentance and a new way of life.[3] In the light of clergy sexual abuse, Stephen Pope and Janine Geske claim that victims have a right to morally legitimate anger, and that this does not have to preclude the possibility of forgiveness as an authentic willing of the good of the offender.[4]

Yet forgiveness in the context of abuse is not without major problems. The demand for victims to forgive can easily remove their moral agency,[5] and relegating forgiveness to a "private" binary of victim-perpetrator can ignore institutional complicity in forms of abuse.[6] Forgiving too quickly or easily can even be a form of power wielded over victims, with the exhortation to forgive being a way to exercise (damage) control over a situation.[7] Alice MacLachlan points to the "gendered" dimension of forgiveness, which often includes associations with "soft" virtues like patience and care. When forgiveness is advocated or practiced unthinkingly, it can too easily lead to the highly negative forms of "self-sacrificing" that have traditionally oppressed women and rendered them silent.[8] In the specific case of Vanier, countenancing forgiveness becomes particularly difficult. Vanier's death before the release of the allegations means that some form of "confession" from him is now impossible. In addition, there appears to be significant evidence that even when confronted by victims and L'Arche structures about these allegations, Vanier remained stubbornly "unrepentant."

---

2. Volf, *Free of Charge*, 209. For more from Volf on Christian forgiveness and reconciliation in the context of violence, see his *Exclusion and Embrace*, ch. 3; see also Volf, "Social Meaning," and Volf, "Forgiveness."

3. Koontz, "Seventy Times."

4. Pope and Geske, "Anger."

5. Horsfield, "Forgiving Abuse."

6. Arms, "When Forgiveness."

7. Koontz, "Seventy Times," 145.

8. MacLachlan, "Practicing," 192–93.

In the light of these concerns, I will not argue or advocate for the possibility of forgiving Vanier. I may draw upon thinkers who see forgiveness and reconciliation as the *telos* of remembering, but my focus will remain with right remembering. While I remain agnostic on whether Vanier can ultimately be forgiven, I hope that the reflections offered here might assist in some way in a conversation on forgiveness and a truthful telling of his relationship to L'Arche, the church, and the women he manipulated.

Remembering Rightly

As mentioned earlier in regard to theologies of forgiveness, Miroslav Volf has written extensively on how to come to terms with egregious acts of violence in the context of the Christian's tradition's call to reconciliation and peace. In *The End of Memory: Remembering Rightly in a Violent World*, Volf continues this work, this time with a focus on his own experience of abuse in the context of communist Yugoslavia.[9]

Summoned to compulsory military service in the fall of 1983, authorities quickly understood Volf as a potential "national security threat" for having such things as a wife from the US, theological training in the (capitalist) West, and being the son of a pacifist Christian pastor. After a period of time where fellow soldiers clandestinely spied on him and attempted to lure him into "subversive" discussions, Volf was called in for a "conversation" with "Captain G." Captain G. showed Volf his foot-thick file of "evidence" that Volf was indeed a spy, with the possibility of eight years in prison for his "crimes." For the following months Volf was regularly interrogated, which included threats of imprisonment if he did not admit his guilt and tell them what he "knew."

While the attention he received gave him a certain sense of importance, nothing occupied his mind more than fear. "Though I was never physically tortured, I was firmly held in my interrogators' iron hand and completely dependent on their mercy. They could do with me anything they wanted."[10] Volf did not so much fear possible imprisonment as the overwhelming power that his interrogators had over him, a power he felt as patently "evil." "I was trapped and helpless, with no ground of my own on which to stand.

---

9. I do not use Volf's reflections on the harms of suffering from interrogation as a way to equate them with the harms suffered by the women Vanier manipulated. In drawing upon Volf, I wish more to use interrogation as "analogous" to, rather than an exact similarity with, Vanier's wrongdoing.

10. Volf, *End of Memory*, 6.

Or from which to resist. Trembling before the false gods of power, I was something all right. But as a person, I was nothing."[11]

After what Volf terms the "mid-level form of abuse" perpetrated against him ended, Volf wished to move on with his life and leave his horrible experience behind. Yet Volf found that his mind "was enslaved by the abuse I had suffered."[12] Knowing the call he felt from Christ to "love his enemy," Volf could not stop feeling "cold, enduring anger that even vengeance, if it were possible, would not alter."[13] The compulsion to react to Captain G.'s evil with revenge lingered for Volf, and forced him to ask himself if he could hold to enemy love even if he had undergone more overt forms of torture.

Yet Volf could not let go of Christ's command to love the enemy, even the interrogator who inflicted tremendous psychological harm on him. Thus, Volf's task then became how to negotiate the place that Captain G. held in his imagination. This task entailed not simply whether to remember what his interrogator had done to him, but "*how to remember rightly.*" "How should I remember abuse as a person committed to loving the wrongdoer and overcoming evil with good?"[14]

What does Volf see as the requirements to remember wrongdoing rightly as a Christian? Firstly, Volf emphasizes that whitewashing or relativizing crimes is *not* a truthful way to proceed. Simply to name acts as wrongdoing is justifiably to condemn them as evil. Volf reflects that he could have dissolved Captain G. into an evil "system," but that would have relieved his interrogator of all responsibility. However, the key for Volf lies in the *why* and the *how* of condemnation. In the Christian tradition, reconciliation and conversion guide the purpose of condemning others in their wrongdoing. According to Volf, this *telos* at the heart of calling out wrongdoing does not mean foregoing any forms of possible punishment and not calling people to account for their egregious acts. Yet to condemn rightly also means that the goal is not purely retributive but ultimately includes the desire for a restoration of a relationship that has been damaged by wrongdoing.

Secondly, Volf understands that remembering truthfully requires remembering *justly*. Remembering justly demands being truthful about an experience and situation of wrongdoing, both by the wrongdoer and the person being wronged. For example, Captain G.'s framing of the interrogation as "conversations" tried to justify the harms committed against Volf's person. To (mis)remember this way not only masks the injury but

---

11. Volf, *End of Memory*, 6.
12. Volf, *End of Memory*, 7.
13. Volf, *End of Memory*, 7–8.
14. Volf, *End of Memory*, 11.

misrepresents the situation unjustly. At the same time, Volf states the moral obligation on the part of the wronged person to remember truthfully. When victims remember unjustly, they risk merely retaliating and reacting to wrongs and perpetuating the memory of the conflict. Remembering truthfully "is to render justice both to the victim and the perpetrator and therefore to take a step toward reconciliation."[15] Just remembering gives the events and people involved in them due credit, whereas an untruthful remembrance not only does injustice to persons but also risks perpetuating further violence.

Thirdly, Christian right remembering means understanding the evil acts of perpetrators in the context of their whole lives. In the face of egregious wrongdoing, it is tempting to reduce the whole of a person to their worst deeds. Understanding the perpetrator this way could even be "truthful," but for Volf it is not enough. If Christians are called to truly *love* their enemies, their wrongdoing cannot be remembered in isolation from a person's overall character.

"Those who love do not remember a person's evil deeds without also remembering her good deeds; they do not remember a person's vices without also being mindful of her virtues."[16] Remembering in this way seeks not to evade the wrongdoing and the harms committed, but to remember the other as made in the image of God and thus ultimately called to repentance and reconciliation.

Even as he outlines a Christian right remembering of wrongdoing and wrongdoers, Volf has no illusions about the stakes involved. The attempt to remember not only the vices but the virtues of wrongdoers risks denying the ultimate claims of justice. "For those who see the world in simple moral terms—with clearly divided camps of the righteous, deserving vindication, and wrongdoers, deserving punishment—any talk of grace and reconciliation seems sentimental, even immoral."[17] Volf experienced his own rebellion at the prospect of loving Captain G., and understands the seeming impossibility of setting aside revenge in a secular world. He writes:

> The letting go of memories of wrongs strikes us as immoral, unhealthy, dangerous—to top it off, impossible. This seems immoral because giving up on such memories breaks faith with victims and whitewashes perpetrators; unhealthy because memories of evils suffered and committed are deemed essential to our identity, and it is claimed that their disappearance would

---

15. Volf, *End of Memory*, 56.
16. Volf, *End of Memory*, 64.
17. Volf, *End of Memory*, 111.

wreak even greater havoc on our psyches than their painful presence; dangerous because the absence of such memory of misdeeds leaves no deterrent for future perpetrators and seduces potential victims to let down their guard; and finally, impossible because major events in our lives remain indelibly inscribed in our memories and continue to be operative in subconscious memory even if they disappear from conscious memory.[18]

According to Volf, the only way to undergo and embody the cost of right remembering comes through placing it within the Christian story. "From the Christian standpoint, to remember *rightly* wrongs that we have suffered is to remember them through the lens of the memory of Christ's death and resurrection."[19] Remembering rightly means not only following Jesus's commands, but of living into a future where healing and liberation can occur. In the "new world" of the Gospel, the past no longer must remain a prison of guilt but can be transformed into a future where peace reigns and relationships are reconciled. "Remember wrongs so that you can protect sufferers from further injury, remember them truthfully so as to be able to act justly, and situate the memories of wrongs suffered into the narrative of God's redemption so that you can remember in hope rather than despair."[20]

In the new world of the Gospel, remembering rightly is never a purely individualistic event, but is inherently *social*. For Volf, persons never remember alone but always with others, thus making the church crucial in right remembering. "My soul was at stake in the way I remembered Captain G., but I was not left to remember him on my own. I was (and still am) part of a community of memory—a Christian church—that from the start framed my memories."[21] As a first-hand recipient of violence, Volf understood the difficulty of "being a Christ" to Captain G. in his memory. The church became vitally important as the place that could not only hold him in his trauma, but also show and practice truthful remembering when he could not. "Communities of sacred memory are, at their best, schools of right remembering—remembering that is truthful and just, that heals individuals without injuring others, that allows the past to motivate a just struggle for justice and the grace-filled work of reconciliation."[22]

---

18. Volf, *End of Memory*, 143.
19. Volf, *End of Memory*, 103–4.
20. Volf, *End of Memory*, 115.
21. Volf, *End of Memory*, 17.
22. Volf, *End of Memory*, 128.

Remembering Vanier Rightly?

So where does this leave us in the context of Jean Vanier's severe wrongdoing? How are we to now remember him truthfully? We can begin by assessing Vanier in the light of the characteristics of right remembering Volf outlined in regards to his experience of interrogation.

Condemning Rightly

To remember Vanier rightly means not attempting to whitewash or relativize his wrongdoing. In this way, condemnation of his acts is more than appropriate. While there is potential value in trying to unearth Vanier's psychological history as a way to explain his actions, this should never be as a way to make him into a "victim," which reduces his own responsibility. However, as Volf maintains, the *why* of condemnation is crucial to keep in mind. Certainly, Vanier's misdeeds should be condemned in order to say that such manipulation of women is a moral evil. But Volf also wishes to add that condemnation in this instance must also have the goal of coming to terms with a relationship that has been damaged. As mentioned earlier, the fact that Vanier has died makes this more than complicated with the actual women he manipulated. Yet what about the theological community, Vanier's friends and colleagues, and L'Arche as a whole? The persons in these groups can also offer condemnation—but with the goal of coming to terms with Vanier's place in their lives and work.

Just Remembering

As difficult as it might be to be just to Vanier in this instance, just remembering demands it. While we lack his direct first-person testimony, remembering justly requires a certain discipline in rendering what we know of how he experienced events. Importantly, this listening to Vanier does not have to mean questioning or denying the testimony of the women who have brought accusations forward. A moral obligation exists to justly remember their telling of events, and listen with the deepest respect to the harms they claim to have suffered. However, Vanier and the victims are not necessarily the only persons involved in remembering. One could argue that those of us who stand at a distance in the "aftermath" of the events have as much a stake in remembering truthfully as the parties involved. It is more than tempting in our current (western) cultural context to use hyperbole to comment and reflect upon wrongdoing; it may even be an understandable response emanating from an experience of trauma. But is it a *just* remembering? Does it give proper due to everyone involved?

Remembering in the Context of a Whole Life

Arguably an element of "just" remembering requires remembering Vanier's wrongdoing in the context of his wider work and life. The temptation to turn Vanier into a "monster" may be understandable and perhaps even "truthful" in a certain sense, but does this categorization truly capture a Christian response to an encounter with the "other"? According to Volf, remembering Vanier's wrongdoing can happen *alongside* remembering all he did to liberate people with cognitive impairments from institutional life, as well his proclaiming the gift of their lives in cultures who could only perceive them through the lens of "defect" and "regret." Note my emphasis here on remembering misdeeds *alongside* the virtues of wrongdoers. Truthful remembering does not exist in a binary of one or the other, but remembers them *together*. In cultures where good and evil exist as discrete entities, and where one must fall wholly on one side or the other, remembering in this way can be extremely difficult. But for Volf, this is the only way to remember as people who have *all* been created by a loving God, and who all contain sparks of the divine within (even if those sparks remain latent).

Just as for Volf the faith community is crucial in being able to do this work of right remembering, so it is in Vanier's situation. The demands involved in remembering Vanier truthfully can appear impossible when we remember alone. Only by belonging to communities that consistently remember truthfully can we even begin to walk alongside Vanier's virtues *and* evildoing. My own experience of living in L'Arche included much in remembering the whole of people's lives rather than focusing on isolated parts of them. This kind of right remembering could be hard enough when living with persons radically different than oneself. To remember truthfully in the context of vile wrongdoing can easily feel beyond individual human capacity. This is why community—especially those who would have been considered in Vanier's closest and most intimate circle—is so important. Through being part of a body that commits itself to practicing right remembering, individuals can both feel free to exist on a spectrum of remembering and trust that together justice and love can happen.

Excursus: On Biblical "Sinners"

So how should we then remember Vanier in a truthful and Christian way? I propose that as Christians—whether "theologians" or "lay people" or whatever designation you want to name—and as (persons *in* and *of*) L'Arche we remember Vanier as a "sinner." To remember Vanier this way requires noting the potential problems that come with this approach. The religious label of "sinner," although widely acknowledged as a historical feature of the Christian tradition, can be widely and amorphously defined. In the context of Vanier's wrongdoing, a further problem with using "sin" and "sinner" language is that it can relativize the significance and severity of Vanier's immoral acts. If, as the Apostle Paul claims, *all* have sinned and are in need of repentance and redemption, making Vanier a "sinner" risks placing his wrongdoing on par with any and all forms of "sin." In this way, important distinctions between the degree of wrongdoing can be evaded or ignored, thus making it all too easy to whitewash Vanier and either forget or exonerate him.

One way to mitigate against the dangers of this kind of relativizing lies in specifying the kind and degree of sin being discussed. In Vanier's own Roman Catholic tradition, the distinction of "mortal" sin could be employed. As sin that "destroys charity" and "turns [humanity] away from God," mortal sin, if not confessed and repented, potentially causes "exclusion from Christ's kingdom" and even possible "eternal loss."[23] While this kind of categorization may be helpful in delineating the severity of Vanier's misdeeds, it arguably does not provide enough guidance on the proper way to respond to and accompany this kind of "sinner" (particularly after their deaths). In addition, while such language fits within a particular Roman Catholic context, its applicability to other theological traditions and communities outside of a religious milieu makes these distinctions less than useful.

A potentially more robust way in which to put being a "sinner" lies in its Gospel context. A consistent claim (and often accusation) against Jesus in the Synoptics Gospels is the amount of time he spends openly with "sinners" (Matt 11:19; Mark 2:15–17; Luke 7:34; and Luke 15:1–2). For those of us who have grown up practicing and reflecting in the Christian tradition, such associations tend to slide down our backs. Many understand Jesus's fellowship here as an illustration of his compassion and solidarity with marginalized people. That these accusations in the Gospels usually come from Pharisees assists our siding with "sinners" as "victims"; two thousand years

---

23. Catholic Church, *Catechism*, §1856, 1859, 1864.

of understanding the Pharisaic movement as the real "enemies" of Jesus easily justifies us into thinking that the Pharisees must be patently wrong, and that Jesus's association with "sinners" must mean that those people so labelled are unjustly accused.

These theological assumptions can easily prevent us from fully appreciating the depth of the scandal Jesus created and maintained by his fellowship with "sinners." In the Greco-Roman world, a *hamartolos* or the *hamartoloi* connoted a strong sense of erroneous and condemnatory behavior, and consistently maintained a derogatory meaning, if not being used as a term of actual abuse.[24] In relation to the Psalms, "the title 'sinner' implies unremitting recalcitrance, and permanent opposition to God and to God's people."[25] While the profile of sinners in the LXX and Second Temple Literature varies widely, a common characteristic perceives "sinners" as "enemies" and "outsiders" to Israel, and as a stark contrast to the "righteous."[26] By the time of the Gospels, "sinners" represented "those who sinned willfully and heinously and who did not repent," those who "flagrantly and persistently disobeyed the law,"[27] and those who "signify apostates and heinous, willful sinners who do wrong without conscience."[28] Far from the innocuous miscategorization of being victimized people, to be labelled a "sinner" in ancient Palestine was to be associated with people engaged in serious evildoing. While many have projected the historical accusation of "oppressive legalism" on the Pharisees for singling people out as "sinners," biblical scholar Paul Trebilco asserts that the vast majority of people in Palestine—including those labeled as the *am ha-aretz*, or the "people of the land"—would have agreed with the Pharisees' condemnatory view. "Given that 'sinners' are presented as outsiders in *everyone's opinion within the Jewish world*, with virtually all groups being portrayed as agreeing about who could be labelled 'sinner,' and not just the Pharisees, then it seems most likely that the connotation of the term is 'flagrant law-breaker' since virtually all other Jews would have agreed that such people were outside the covenant, and so were 'sinners.'"[29]

Take the example of the "tax" or "toll collectors" (*telōnes*) mentioned in the Synoptics, the term the Gospel writers commonly use (especially Luke) in connection with the "sinner" designation. Like similar contemporary misperceptions of a "sinner" in the Gospels, it is easy to see the

---

24. Trebilco, *Outsider Designations*, 113.
25. Roth, *Blind*, 116. For an example, see Ps 50:16–22.
26. Trebilco, *Outsider Designations*, 114.
27. Sanders, *Jesus and Judaism*, 177, 180.
28. Holmén, "Sinners," 575.
29. Trebilco, *Outsider Designations*, 124.

"toll collectors" as relatively harmless players, or perhaps even see them as marginalized persons who Jesus befriends and liberates. A closer historical look at who the *telōnes* were and what they did complicates this assessment drastically. *Telōnes* were essentially "tax farmers" who purchased the right to collect the taxes in a certain region. Their job consisted in recuperating what they had paid out, with everything they collected as "extra" understood as personal "profit." The vast majority of people had no idea what the "correct" amount of taxes were, and were thus left at the whim of whichever toll collector they met that day. In Palestine, the vast majority of *telōnes* would have been Jews, which could result either in accusations of collaboration with Roman oppression—in those areas governed directly by Rome—or, arguably the more common claim, of being inherently greedy and dishonest by robbing people of their (already subsistent and meagre) income. Thus, it should come as no surprise that toll collectors were universally despised, with visible displays of wealth being particularly galling. In this context, most people in ancient Palestine would have understood "toll collectors" not as "victims" but as *perpetrators* of gross injustice.

Relatedly, one might then begin to understand the "grumbling" (Luke 19:7) and dismay related by many regarding Jesus's presence with these "sinners." Certainly, some stories illustrate "sinners" who appeared to "repent" in a manner consistent with Jewish theology and practice: Levi "left everything" and followed Jesus (Luke 5:28), and Zacchaeus offered to repay his profits (and then some) from those he stole (Luke 19:8). However, there is no indication that *all* "tax collectors and sinners" Jesus associated with actually "repented." If that were indeed the case, why would anyone object to his associations and meetings with these people? There were lots of calls by Jews in Jesus's time for the "wicked" and "evildoers" to turn back to God and live a just and righteous life (e.g., Isa 1:27; Ezek 14:6; 18:30; Hos 14:1; 2 Esd 7:133; Sir 17:25). Jesus departs from the general Jewish consensus by putting much less emphasis on the need for conversion *first* and *foremost* before associating with "sinners." This did not mean that Jesus condoned the wrongdoing and evil these people may have committed. Instead, Jesus was willing to associate with people *while they were still "sinners."* For a believer in ancient Palestine who wanted to live in the righteous path of God, Jesus's approach was highly unusual if not ludicrously irresponsible.

Yet Jesus was not merely willing to associate with "sinners," but is often mentioned *eating* with them. To share a table and eat with someone in ancient Palestine was akin to entering into a covenant with them, and denoted them as fellow "insiders" and "friends." This covenant making came with particular rights and responsibilities of the parties involved, and assumed either a maintenance or elevation of status for each member. To involve "sinners" in a covenant was inconceivable; the general religious approach to "sinners" was either segregation from them[30] or exclusion from fellowship, especially at table.[31] Not only did Jesus violate the former by associating with "tax collectors and sinners," but he openly shared a table with them. By doing so, Jesus contradicted his own tradition's practice of dealing with sinners and embodied a new way of conceiving of God's reign. "When Jesus announced the kingdom and *then* ate with sinners, he was saying that these sinners were included in the kingdom whose inauguration he was proclaiming. He was entering into a covenant-like relationship and accepting them as part of his kingdom community, even though they were sinners who should have been excluded."[32]

Jean Vanier as "Sinner"

What difference does it make to understand Vanier as a "sinner" in the context of Jesus and the Gospels? Remembering Vanier as a "sinner" means not mean relativizing, evading, or ignoring the "flagrant law-breaking" he perpetrated. Responding compassionately like Jesus does not mean making Vanier into a marginalized "victim," but understands him truthfully as someone who disobeyed God and deviated from the path of righteousness. At the same time, imitating Jesus means not necessarily segregating ourselves from Vanier and his "sin" but fully engaging him, to the point where we are willing to "eat" with him, even while he remains "unrepentant." This does not require us to "forget" or condone Vanier's evildoing, just as the Gospels give us no indication that Jesus condoned the greed and complicity of the toll collectors of his time. Jesus's practice calls us to continue a relationship with Vanier—even one as intimate as fellowship around a table—in the midst of the misgivings, anger, and loathing we may feel about him.

When we can stay in that difficult and demanding relationship with Vanier, we place ourselves in a position where we can not only come to greater clarity about his wrongdoing, the institutional factors that aided the harms he committed, and the problematic aspects of his thought; just as importantly, we can also begin to come to peace with the place Vanier has in our story, whether it be the personal stories of those who encountered him, or more corporate stories such as L'Arche or the Christian theological tradition. In this way, Vanier becomes, whether we like it or not, "our"

---

30. For examples, see Ps 1; Sir 12; Pss; Wis 3; 1 En 97:4; 1QS 5:1–2.

31. See Is 25:6–8; 65: 13–14; Jub 22:16; 1 En 62: 13–14; 2 En 42:5, 2; Bar 29:3–4; 1QSa. 2:11–22.

32. Trebilco, *Outsider Designations*, 126.

sinner, where we relate to him less as "us" versus "them" than see him as part of the "we," the people we have become through engagement with his work and life.

As difficult as it might be to sit with Vanier at a (metaphorical and/or eschatological) table, doing so in the spirit of Jesus might not only assist us in coming to terms with the egregious acts he committed. When we can understand Vanier as part of the "we" we have become, we open ourselves to potentially seeing him as someone the Holy Spirit used to reveal God's peace and justice for the world. Vanier could then take his place with the parade of historical people of faith who have both sinned greatly *and* been instruments of God's truth. Consider the biblical figure of Abraham. As the founder of Judaism and (arguably) the "father" of Christianity and Islam, few historical figures have so embodied what a faithful response to God's call looks like. Yet it does not take long upon reading his story to see that Abraham was no hagiographical "saint." Ponder his lying about Sarah being his sister rather than his wife (Gen 12:10–26; 20:1–18).[33] Two times he lies in order to save his own life, with the consequence that he makes both the Pharaoh and Abimelech susceptible to the charge of adultery. To make sure the reader understands Abraham's guilt, both "pagan," non-Israelite monarchs rebuke Abraham—with Abraham giving totally inadequate responses—and are both justified before God. Yet this wrongdoing does not remove Abraham as the patriarch and progenitor of the future nation of Israel. As Claus Westermann asserts, the ancient narrator wants to say that "Abraham can still be an intercessor despite his guilt; for all his shortcomings and limitations he can still invoke God's saving power for others without himself being exalted thereby."[34] One could say that Genesis offers a truthful account of the father of Judaism: man of faith *and* egregious sinner. God's work can even be accomplished through one so ambiguous and mixed as Abraham.

Conclusion

Might the same be true of Jean Vanier? I have argued that facing directly the grievous allegations against Vanier presents theologians, the church, and L'Arche with an opportunity to witness to what Miroslav Volf calls "right remembering." Truthfully remembering Vanier does not thoughtlessly defend his actions or whitewash or ignore the harms he perpetrated. Yet

---

33. One could also discuss his complicity in the expulsion and oppression of Hagar and Ishmael. For an analysis that includes Abraham's role, see Trible, *Texts of Terror*, ch. 1.

34. Westermann, *Genesis*, 329.

condemning Vanier's evildoing *rightly* means justly remembering it and places his misdeeds in the context of the broader story of his life. I contend that a right remembering of Vanier in a Christian context means seeing him as a (grievous) "sinner," with the full weight and gravity that the Gospel accounts assume. Understanding Vanier as a "flagrant law-breaker" means letting go of the pristine, "saintly" image of Vanier as one who could do no wrong, what the theologian Brian Flanagan understands as the truthful ecclesial practice of "a-hagiography."[35] However, just as Jesus "ate and drank" with "sinners," so the church and L'Arche can embody for the world what a truthful engagement with "deplorable" people looks like.

Certainly, right remembering is much more a *process* than a single event. I have no illusions that such a practice can happen quickly and easily, and that it must be forced on anyone. Remembering in the way Volf outlines requires a patience and discipline of listening (to all parties) that is demanding and costly. Engaging with Vanier and his egregious acts is no different, and must be practiced in a way that also respects people's feelings of trauma, betrayal, and hurt.

Yet when this kind of truthful engagement with Vanier can occur, not only will we embody Jesus's own response to the "sinners" he encountered (and still encounters). At the same time, "eating" with Vanier might also assist in clarifying the aspects of his life and work that remain valid tools for living in community and the Christian life. In this way, we can witness to how the Holy Spirit can breathe through the most unlikely and despicable characters to reveal the truth of God's love and grace—even through one like Jean Vanier.

Bibliography

L'Arche International. "Summary Report." February 22 2020.
Arms, Margaret F. "When Forgiveness Is Not the Issue in Forgiveness: Religious Complicity in Abuse and Privatized Forgiveness." In *Forgiveness and Abuse: Jewish and Christian Reflections*, edited by Marie M. Fortune and Joretta L. Marshall, 107–28. New York: Haworth, 2002.
Catholic Church. *Catechism of the Catholic Church*. Ottawa: Canadian Conference of Catholic Bishops, 1994.
Flanagan, Brian P. *Stumbling in Holiness: Sin and Sanctity in the Church*. Collegeville, MN: Liturgical, 2018.
Holmén, Tom. "Sinners." In *Encyclopedia of the Historical Jesus*, edited by Craig A. Evans, 575–77. New York: Routledge, 2008.

---

35. Flanagan, *Stumbling*, 107. See also Dow, "Against Living Saints."

Horsfield, Peter. "Forgiving Abuse: An Ethical Critique." In *Forgiveness and Abuse: Jewish and Christian Reflections*, edited by Marie M. Fortune and Joretta L. Marshall, 51–70. New York: Haworth, 2002.

Koontz, Gayle Gerber. "Seventy Times Seven: Abuse and the Frustratingly Extravagant Call to Forgive." *Mennonite Quarterly Review* 89 (2015) 129–52.

MacLachlan, Alice. "Practicing Imperfect Forgiveness." In *Feminist Ethics and Social and Political Philosophy: Theorizing the Non-Ideal*, edited by Lisa Tessman, 185–204. Dordrecht: Springer, 2009.

Pope, Stephen J., and Janine P. Geske. "Anger, Forgiveness, and Restorative Justice in Light of Clerical Sexual Abuse and Its Cover-up." *Theological Studies* 80 (2019) 611–31.

Roth, John S. *The Blind, the Lame, and the Poor: Character Types in Luke–Acts*. Sheffield, UK: Sheffield Academic Press, 1997.

Sanders, E. P. *Jesus and Judaism*. London: SCM, 1985.

Trebilco, Paul. *Outsider Designations and Boundary Construction in the New Testament: Early Christian Communities and the Formation of Group Identity*. New York: Cambridge University Press, 2017.

Trible, Phylis. *Texts of Terror: Literary-Feminist Readings of Biblical Narratives*. Philadelphia: Fortress, 1984.

Volf, Miroslav. *The End of Memory: Remembering Rightly in a Violent World*. Grand Rapids, MI: Eerdmans, 2006.

———. *Exclusion and Embrace*. Nashville: Abingdon, 1996.

———. "Forgiveness, Reconciliation and Justice: A Theological Contribution to a More Peaceful Social Environment." *Millenium* 29 (2000) 861–77.

———. *Free of Charge: Giving and Forgiving in a Culture Stripped of Grace*. Grand Rapids, MI: Zondervan, 2005.

———. "The Social Meaning of Reconciliation: Forgiveness and Reconciliation." *Interpretation* 54 (2000) 158–72.

Westermann, Claus. *Genesis 12–36: A Commentary*. Translated by John J. Scullion. Minneapolis: Augsberg, 1985.

Chapter Two

Against Living Saints

KEITH DOW

The saint. What sort of saint? No one has ever seen a saint. For the saint remains invisible, not by chance, but in principle and by right.

Jean-Luc Marion[1]

When Jean Vanier entered the room, it was buzzing with grace. It was as if the air was buoyed in warmth. Across the room, sensing the presence of someone holy, our friends and housemates—L'Arche "core members," people with intellectual disabilities—turned their faces toward the gentle giant with a broad steady smile and tufts of white hair. He had a slight bend to his back, as if his posture had adjusted over time to look into the faces of those smaller than him, which was almost everyone.[2]

THIS IMPRESSION OF JEAN Vanier was published less than a year before revelations of his serial sexual abuse came to light. Florer-Bixler was not alone in associating Jean Vanier with sanctity or holiness—being "set apart" in some way for God's work in the world. Mother Teresa called him "a most saintly man" and Pope Francis referred to him as a "next door saint."[3] Fr. James Martin, editor at large at *America* magazine, penned,

---

1. Marion, "Invisibility of the Saint," 703.
2. Florer-Bixler, "Vulnerable at the Core," 12.
3. Study Commission, *Control and Abuse*, 177, 178.

Jean Vanier showed us, like few people ever have, the overwhelming power of gentleness. Not only in his ministry with the disabled but in his voice, his demeanor, his very presence. During his life there was no one I thought more deserving of the title "living saint."[4]

In early 2020, nearly a year after Vanier's death, allegations of his coercive sexual abuse over several decades were verified.[5] Many who had met him or had been shaped by his speaking and writing were shaken. How could someone who eloquently put into words the dynamics of human vulnerability and interdependence—who was interpreted to embody these values in his physical presence—have engaged for so many years in sexual abuse and spiritual manipulation?

Perceiving "Sainthood"

Despite championing "going down the ladder" of success and power to be with "the poor," Jean Vanier did not embody *compassionate descent*.[6] He may have foregone particular career options to build community with people with intellectual disabilities but carried power and social capital—along with his parents' funding—into these spaces.[7] He was a persuasive speaker and author with a PhD in philosophy; a tall, well-respected Canadian who was older than most people who joined L'Arche. Members of his close circle, despite referring to themselves as "les tout-petites" (the little ones), prized intellectual sophistication and credentials.[8] Before long, Vanier had amassed a wide following and vast audiences.[9]

Vanier's physical stature seemed to communicate not only a towering intellect but the humility to "stoop" to the level of those around him. His presence embodied what people thought of as the L'Arche mission. Yet, as

---

4. Dulle, "Jean Vanier," para. 8.

5. Study Commission, *Control and Abuse*, defines sexual abuse as "an unjust use of power of a sexual nature which causes harm to the person who is subjected to it" (503) and confirmed that at least twenty-five women were involved in sexual abuse or a transgressive relationship with Jean Vanier (508).

6. McKearney, "Disabling Virtue."

7. Study Commission, *Control and Abuse*, 123. The report indicates that not even the L'Arche initiative could "be described as humble, small, or without strategic ambition" (377), and was a project where Vanier was "eager to take and remain in control" (384). See also references to social effects (154) and the registers of legitimization of his authority relationships (458–59).

8. Study Commission, *Control and Abuse*, 47.

9. Study Commission, *Control and Abuse*, 137.

Patrick McKearney observes, misinterpreting L'Arche communities as places for the nondisabled to give up social status to be with the disabled only "works by treating the nondisabled as in a genuinely hierarchically superior position to begin with."[10]

The question remains: If Jean Vanier was more sinner than saint, why the apparent "aura of sanctity"?[11] In answering this question, this chapter draws on Jean-Luc Marion's "The Invisibility of the Saint" to argue against identifying *living saints* and to consider related implications for community theology and practice. Marion observes that to call someone a saint, "one must have access to the concept of holiness, must have an experience of sanctity, and must probe the other's heart."[12] I work through these criteria as a framework to critique Jean Vanier's reception as a living saint and the risks that arose from this reception.[13] Vanier's confused conception of sin, confession, and forgiveness rendered a theological world where holiness was *inevitable* rather than *invisible*—where Vanier could not be considered as anything *except* a saint. In this world, evil was inconceivable and unspeakable. I close with a reminder that all that glitters theologically is not gold; an exhortation to seek instead the chaotic stories of actuality in which harsh beauty and disturbing truths are revealed.

Errors of Intuition: Probing Hearts?

People are easily fooled when we judge one another based on appearances. As early as a hundred milliseconds after meeting someone, we have formed an opinion that we tend to only confirm from there.[14] Those with "body capital"—in many contexts, cisgendered white males who are tall, conventionally beautiful, and convey intelligence—fare well in these initial assessments. Taller-than-average, able-bodied men are routinely selected or

10. McKearney, "Disabling Virtue," 92. Following The Study Commission in *Control and Abuse*, Vanier's martyr complex more likely arose from his sacrifice of a priestly vocation because of his close and continued association with Thomas Philippe. Vanier was considered a "fanatical disciple" of Philippe, a heterodox priest and sexual abuser who Vanier stubbornly defended as an unrecognized saint. This, despite the Catholic Church placing punitive restrictions on Philippe due to his abhorrent mystico-sexual theology (Study Commission, *Control and Abuse*, 81, 133, 101, 143).

11. Study Commission, *Control and Abuse*, 598.

12. Marion, "Invisibility of the Saint," 703.

13. Without claiming access to the *concept* of holiness as such, Marion's working definition of holiness is that it "generally defines the setting apart that distinguishes what belongs to the divinity in opposition to what remains in the world," a kind of godly distinction or exceptionality (Marion, "Invisibility of the Saint," 707).

14. Willis and Todorov, "First Impressions."

elected as leaders and statesmen.[15] The inverse is also true. Those with less perceived body capital—people marked by stigma or those who are marginalized due to race, gender, orientation, culture, or ability—face barriers in accessing social advantages.

We unconsciously attribute moral goodness and positive intent to those we believe to be wise, intellectually capable, and able. People with disabilities become unquestioned villains and scapegoats in stories that shape public consciousness.[16] When awed by stature, reputation, education, and apparent virtue, we are quick to look for the best and to not suspect the worst. Others' true characters remain hidden from us (*invisible*) despite these often-unchallenged intuitive beliefs, for good or evil. In the descriptions above, Jean Vanier conveyed a peculiar combination of stooped height, interpreted by many as a humble leader or "gentle giant" who captured a hidden-yet-manifest paradox of holiness.

The ineptitude of human character intuition confirms the impossibility of *"probing the heart of another,"* one of Marion's criteria for assessing sainthood. No one can determine the virtue of others, "precisely because they remain inaccessible to all other egos."[17] Holiness is even *less* accessible than virtue, "as it is not only a matter of gaining access to or judging the other's intelligence or any other competence, which is first brought to bear on universal or particular objects that can be shared by any other intelligence."[18] To attribute virtuous action to someone else based on perceivable data (how they look, behave, act, the effect of their action, etc.) is already problematic. Then, *even if* one had access to the concept of holiness, to assess it in another without knowing their interior life is preposterous. One cannot point to specific, quantifiable data to verify such an assessment. In the same way that no human being can see God's face and live (Exod 33:20), holiness, "insofar as it only manifests itself as invisible, inasmuch it cannot become an object for the intentionality of a gaze."[19]

---

15. Pierre Bourdieu first popularized "body capital" (also referring to it as "physical capital" and "embodied cultural capital") to give expression to the sense that our bodies, and society's reception of them, can obtain us certain goods, services, respect, etc. See Bourdieu, "Sport and Social Class"; Bourdieu, *Distinction*; and Bourdieu, "Forms of Capital." For information regarding height and body capital, see Lindqvist, "Height and Leadership." Also see Stulp et al., "Tall Claims?"

16. Onyx, "Five Common Harmful Representations."

17. Also, "The aporia of intersubjectivity, at least of intersubjectivity understood according to intentionality, applies above all to judging the other's holiness." (Marion, "Invisibility of the Saint," 705).

18. Marion, "Invisibility of the Saint," 705.

19. Marion, "Invisibility of the Saint," 708.

Looking foolish is not the only fallout of misplaced sanctity. The authority and status granted to Vanier helped make his psychological hold on others possible. His perceived holiness silenced those whom he manipulated. As one witness described, "I was like frozen, I realised that Jean Vanier was adored by hundreds of people, like a living Saint, that he talked about how he helped victims of sexual abuse, it appeared like a camouflage."[20] To speak ill of the holy is taboo. Systems of power and privilege are sustained by faulty perception and erroneous intuition *en masse*. As Pia Matthews acknowledges, the "authoritative power surrounding Vanier turned out to be one of the major barriers to transparency and truth."[21] Unquestioned sanctity and unchecked spiritual acclaim only further silenced Vanier's victims and other witnesses.

Egos and Idolatry

I and many others who work with or care for people with intellectual disabilities were tempted to esteem Jean Vanier as a witness to kinds of experiences that shape us. He seemed to translate holy moments of encounter into writing and story; to eloquently express the revelations that come from sharing life in diverse community. Vanier was self-aware of "this gift of Speech."[22] Marion cautions against the idolatry of transference in these moments, however. We commit self-idolatry when we gesture at our own holiness by praising another, more recognizable "saint" or exemplar. "We know perfectly well that no one can say 'I am a saint' without total deception," yet *holiness by association* may belie a subconscious attempt to avoid this charge.[23] We all seek to be heard, understood, and loved. At times, we may seek to reinforce our own value or closeness with the divine by proclaiming the virtue or holiness of another.

This guise of holiness was perpetuated by Vanier himself, who believed his vocation was special and set-apart. It was taken up by L'Arche's belief that Vanier's mandate was bestowed "from above."[24] His approach invoked "the register of singularity, predestination and mystery" and was wrapped in "supernatural legitimacy."[25] He regularly interacted with others recognized as living saints, now canonized, who helped to promote his own figure and

20. L'Arche International, "Summary Report," 6.
21. Matthews, "Putting Aside Charisma," 74.
22. Study Commission, *Control and Abuse*, 146.
23. Marion, "Invisibility of the Saint," 704.
24. Study Commission, *Control and Abuse*, 120, 288.
25. Study Commission, *Control and Abuse*, 120.

reputation.[26] Vanier also used this "halo effect" to draw people into the work of L'Arche and to groom potential victims. For some, "Jean wants you to do it" became the call of God.[27]

Identifying Vanier as set apart by God has always been a self-defeating narrative. Care providers and those who support people with intellectual disabilities are often classified as a unique class of people, capable of superhuman abilities to meet needs and embody resilience. "Oh, good for you. I could never do that!" is a refrain commonly heard by direct support professionals. "God had a special plan for you" or "God must have known you could handle it" are the types of sentiments that caregiving parents hear regularly. Laura MacGregor speaks to the challenge of receiving these kinds of sentiments as mother to a medically complex child (Matthew):

> Being told that God had hand picked me for this difficult journey only increased my sense of spiritual confusion. . . . Community members often assured me that I was uniquely equipped for the challenge of parenting Matthew, a strategy that served to silence my story and lead me to question my faith.[28]

Putting Jean Vanier on a divine pedestal further entrenched the perception that living in community with, or being a caregiver to, people with intellectual disabilities is a specialized and holy calling reserved for those who are uniquely gifted. These beliefs and statements become a way for people to "opt out" of joining in the work or offering to provide much-needed support or respite to families and caregivers.[29]

In *Freedom Is a Constant Struggle*, Angela Davis reflects on the tension of individual and collective action by protesting the "heroic individualism" of figures such as Nelson Mandela and Dr. Martin Luther King, Jr. "It is essential to resist the depiction of history as the work of heroic individuals in order for people today to recognize their potential agency as a part of an ever-expanding community of struggle."[30] When caregivers and support systems are in tragically short supply, praising singular "heroic individuals," or living saints, further *sets apart* care work as the domain of elite or

---

26. Study Commission, *Control and Abuse*, 187.

27. Study Commission, *Control and Abuse*, 430. Messages such as "Jesus chooses you" or "calls you for these graces of love" become means of drawing Brigitte and others into transgressive or abusive relationships with Vanier (583).

28. MacGregor, "Present Absence," 131.

29. McKearney references this in the context of L'Arche, "You know a lot of people idealize L'Arche, and think the assistants are very good. But sometimes that's more a way to keep your distance from it than anything" (McKearney, "Disabling Virtue," 93).

30. Davis, "Progressive Struggles."

divinely chosen individuals. Instead, care is a fundamental societal need. In diverse ways, we are all called to be part of valuing this work and engaging in it as we are able. The "heroic demand" of caregiving quickly becomes a self-fulfilling prophesy: as fewer people take on more responsibility with decreasing resources, care work does become unsustainably difficult.

Theological Deception in Three Acts

Naming someone a saint "presupposes that those who assert and define [sanctity] claim to know what holiness means, hence they claim to experience it and consequently to incarnate it themselves."[31] This quasi-idolatry involves deceiving oneself. Worse, however, is the total deception that sanitizes and sanctifies *all* behavior so that anything besides holiness is inconceivable. In the following pages I argue that this theological deception, which reached its diabolical depths in one-on-one manipulation and sexual abuse, also ran through Vanier's public theology.[32]

Vanier preempted challenges to his holiness by questioning himself, yet shifted the very concepts of sin, confession, and forgiveness. The resultant theological landscape leaves little possibility for distinguishing the *holy* from the *horrific*. The question becomes not whether someone has access to the concept of holiness, as Marion suggests, but whether witnesses can speak to anything besides.

Sin and Brokenness: Shifting Language

Jean Vanier was quick to relay his own fallibility. "He endlessly underlines his poverty, his misery, and this insufficiency of his seems to become a ruse of harmlessness and innocence," yet it "also becomes a means of seduction."[33] Vanier's expression of fears, doubts, and anxieties—along with his simple dress and humble accommodations—made him seem human and relatable. However, "far from making J. Vanier invisible . . . [these indicators of poverty] increase his prestige and reinforce admiration for him."[34] Humility, self-deprecation, and presumed poverty further validated Vanier's sanctity

---

31. Marion, "Invisibility of the Saint," 704.

32. Jacques Maritain was not wrong when writing on Thomas Philippe that "the devil is romping around in this incredible affair" (Study Commission, *Control and Abuse*, 192). A victim of Philipe also wrote, "It was as if God had turned into the devil" (554). In this chapter I refrain from super-spiritualizing in the direction of the diabolical where possible.

33. Study Commission, *Control and Abuse*, 233.

34. Study Commission, *Control and Abuse*, 460.

in people's minds.[35] He wrote simply, "I still have a lot to do to clear up the mess inside of me, and maybe others, too, have work to do."[36] At a time when "sin" is seldom used and rarely defined, "mess" might seem to better capture *missing the mark*.[37] In Vanier's public writings, though, he either shifts "sin" toward a nebulous spiritual concept or he makes transgression so human that it is difficult to condemn.[38] Consider his interpretation of the woman caught in adultery in John 8. "To understand [the story], we have to understand what sin is."[39] A promising start, yet he immediately spiritualizes it. "To sin is to cut ourselves off from Jesus."[40] Further, "When Jesus says, 'Go and sin no more,' he is actually saying, 'Go and remain in my love.'"[41] For Vanier, the problem is not the sinful actions or the effects of sin, *per se*, but failing to remain in relationship with Christ. One's relationship with Jesus is understood to "cover over a multitude" of sins and makes harm—such as that caused by spiritual, psychological, and sexual abuse—inconceivable or incoherent.[42]

---

35. In this way, Vanier seemed to dodge the contradiction of a self-professed holy person: "someone who lays claim to sanctity disproves it in him- or her-self." This is not only due to the sin of pride, but "because holiness is (indicatively, descriptively) unaware of itself. . . . The false prophet, like the false saint, always stands out conspicuously by the fact that this affirmation (of holiness) may never be questioned" (Marion, "Invisibility of the Saint," 704).

36. Vanier, "Seek Out the Weak," 18.

37. According to Google's Ngram Viewer, "sin" and "evil" are beginning to make modest gains since a low point in the 1980s. Their usage is still relatively low in contrast to previous centuries.

38. In Study Commission, *Control and Abuse*, the theme of confusion is prominent. With respect to sexual sin, "it is a great confusion that covers his vocabulary, his way of writing" (35). Vanier's way of expressing things without going into details helped support "an illusion of shared omniscience" (455). He played "hide and seek with words" in intertwining his mystical/public theology (816) and more generally: "J. Vanier's discourse proves to be elusive, disjointed and not very credible at a rational level" (795).

39. Vanier, *Befriending the Stranger*, 77.

40. Vanier, *Befriending the Stranger*, 78.

41. Vanier, *Befriending the Stranger*, 78.

42. Alluding here to 1 Peter 4:8. In this chapter I focus on Vanier's public theology, yet much more could be explored in relation to his private mystico-sexual beliefs, traces of which can be found in a 1956 letter to his parents, where he writes "if one only looks at Jesus' heart—if one puts one's face against Him, everything then becomes good" (Study Commission, *Control and Abuse*, 81). The deeper layer of this, of course, is the adopted Marian beliefs of T. Philippe. Victims were told that sin was no longer possible in the area of sexual purity thanks to "a special choice of the Most Holy Virgin" (251). This language and theology leads to the conviction that the abuser(s) can do no wrong and the fault must lie with the victim somehow (597).

Abstracted from specific actions and the devastating impact of sinful behavior, "sin" simply reveals the weakness or brokenness of the human condition and should be immediately covered by love. Concluding *Community and Growth*, Vanier writes, "We will only find peace when we discover that our setbacks, depression, and even our sins can be an offering and a sacrifice, and so open the door to the eternal."[43] Here human difficulties *and sins* are reframed as an offering that deepen one's connection to the divine.

Returning to the woman caught in adultery, Vanier's words seem more palatable in the biblical context. The woman was being called to account rather than any men. No witnesses stepped forward to accuse her after Jesus's challenge that the one who was without sin step forward to throw the first stone.[44] The onlookers may have even been about to stone the woman for being a victim of rape. Perhaps Jesus did have something else in mind when he said, "Go and sin no more." Maybe, as Vanier adds to the original text, "Jesus looked at her and loved her with tenderness."[45]

Jean Vanier, however, was not a first-century Middle Eastern woman caught in a patriarchal legal system. His context matters as well. Here, we find that Vanier's approach to authority is "marked by the absence of any consideration of the social, economic, and symbolic differences between people."[46] Reconstruing sin as a reminder to love and stay connected to Jesus, within asymmetric power dynamics, can result in the worst kind of deception—outfitting the wolves of the world in sheep's clothing. Conceiving sin as "brokenness," "mess," and "weakness" undermines evildoers' agency and culpability. No longer a choice, sin becomes a natural, understandable, and easily forgivable expression of someone's circumstances.[47]

In this way, it became possible for Vanier to talk openly about his "mess" without inviting suspicions of worse transgressions. In *hyper-spiritualizing* sin as related only to one's God-relationship or *humanizing* sin

---

43. Vanier, *Community and Growth*, 328.

44. John 8:7.

45. Study Commission, *Control and Abuse*, 739.

46. Study Commission, *Control and Abuse*, 481. The report notes Vanier's "blindness to inequalities of all kinds" (482).

47. Vanier wrote (in Brown and Vanier, "After Morgentaler"), "Sexual abuse . . . can deeply hurt people and even kill their hearts. . . . So quickly the sexual urge can become an addiction; it can get out of control, and be used for one's own excitement and pleasure and desire to possess and to control people without respect for them" (para. 28). Rather than addressing agency and accountability for this abuse, he deflected to, "This urge also flows from a deep cry of loneliness" (para. 30). His answer, as such, was an exhortation to "help people discover who they really are, their value, their interior beauty and their gift, their sacredness—as well as their weakness—and how to accept others as they are" (para. 46).

by making it merely another aspect of human brokenness, Vanier lays the theological framework that makes it inconceivable to talk openly about, let alone condemn, his abusive actions over several decades. In *Befriending the Stranger,* Vanier exhorts readers to see Jesus "in the violence and the anguish that are beyond your control."[48] This advice is nothing more than spiritual bypassing and evasion of accountability as Vanier perpetuates abuse against the women who come to him for spiritual accompaniment.[49]

Relating everything to spiritual love obfuscates the need for truth, accountability, justice, and restitution in the "here and now." As the *Control and Abuse* report unearths in detail, the ongoing influence of Vanier's spiritual director Thomas Philippe (himself a perpetrator of sexual abuse) is evident here. Even in Vanier's public writing, we read echoes of Philippe's words, "When one arrives at perfect love, everything is lawful, for there is no more sin."[50]

Vanier wove a web of words whereby his own evil faded into silence. When confronted by a woman he had abused, she recounts "he told me: I thought it was good." Then, when challenged by her husband, "[Vanier] didn't understand and all he could say was that the husband was unreasonably angry."[51] The theological landscape Vanier inherited, adapted, and perpetuated rendered it inconceivable for others to articulate or demand justice for his sins.

Confession, Love, and Justice

Jean Vanier's spirituality diverged sharply from that of his father. Georges Vanier was a dedicated Christian, but "for a long time his religious practice was 'inspired more by fear than by love.' . . . He only took communion two or three times each year, immediately after going to confession, for fear of not being pure enough to partake of his Lord."[52] George's beliefs rose out of Jansenism, "where law, duty, and the fear of hell prevailed."[53] Jean's mother Pauline—his primary influence in meeting and journeying with Thomas Philippe—helped Jean to understand his faith differently, "to perceive

---

48. Vanier, *Befriending the Stranger*, 64.

49. One of the strategies of abusers through this time has been to spiritualize women's objections and difficulties "in an excessive manner," especially evident in G. Adam's approach (Study Commission, *Control and Abuse*, 537).

50. L'Arche International, "Summary Report," 8. For T. Philippe, "there was just love, which demanded total freedom" (Study Commission, *Control and Abuse*, 573).

51. L'Arche International, "Summary Report," 6.

52. Interview with Jean Vanier, November 22, 2013. Constant, *Jean Vanier*.

53. Study Commission, *Control and Abuse*, 695.

communion not as a reward for moral purity but as a necessary support in weakness."[54]

A similar emphasis is found in the preface Vanier wrote to Paul Farren's book on confession. Here, Vanier admits that laws are necessary but "somewhere along the line in the history of the church, people have become more centered upon obedience to laws than upon this relationship of love with a person, with Jesus; more centered upon justice than upon love."[55] Vanier shares Farren's interpretation of the practice of confession "as a meeting of love and as a renewal of friendship. Confession can become, then, a beautiful way to grow in love."[56] It is only building on Vanier's reframing of "sin" that confession could be understood simply as "a beautiful way to grow in love." This is a kind of confession that permits being pronounced "right" without any real accountability, justice, or restitution for wrongs committed. Vanier was committed to a "new law of divine Love," yet his beliefs meant that he was "trapped by the absolutization of a Love that excluded, for him, any idea of Evil."[57]

Vanier contrasts justice and love rather than seeing justice as a necessary component of loving action. He writes of institutional confession,

> It has been such a grace and gift over these years in community to verbalise my sins and to ask for forgiveness of a priest who listens and says "I forgive you." . . . I don't have to hide my guilt anymore. We can only really love our enemies and all that is broken in them if we begin to love all that is broken in our own beings.[58]

This passage reinforces a desire to "love all that is broken in our own beings" instead of seeking accountability and justice. Sin is reframed as brokenness, and Vanier moves directly to claiming forgiveness from a priest without offering restitution to those whom he has wronged. Just as speaking generally about his "mess" attempts to camouflage and evade his abusive actions, so "confessing" to a priest means, for him, "I don't have to hide my guilt anymore" while carrying, in public silence, abusive behavior to his deathbed.

---

54. Constant, *Jean Vanier*, 57.

55. Farren, *Confession*, 7. Vanier does not neglect justice entirely: "True authority is exercised in the context of justice for all, with special attention to the weakest people, who cannot defend themselves and are part of the oppressed minority" (Vanier, *Community and Growth*, 207).

56. Farren, *Confession*, 8.

57. Study Commission, *Control and Abuse*, 170, 722.

58. Vanier, *Community and Growth*, 37.

Forgiveness: Expected or Extraordinary?

Where sins are believed to reveal only a broken spiritual relationship with Jesus or to reflect understandable human failings, confession means meeting with a priest who conveys the love of Jesus and helps confessors to love all that is broken within themselves, without necessarily seeking justice or restitution. In this context, forgiveness becomes an expected and anticipated transaction to bypass wrongdoing in community life.[59]

In 1956, Father Paul Philippe wrote of his shock regarding the lack of condemnation of Thomas Philippe's serial sexual abuses: "I was very awed by the reaction of those involved, by Jean Vanier, the people from l'Eau Vive and the nuns from Bouvines.... They knew, and they wanted to cover up everything, 'not to judge.'"[60] Vanier's 2015 letter regarding his mentor conveys this:

> I cannot judge Fr. Thomas. God alone can judge. Jesus is merciful and he forgives in his love. When I am in the place of "I do not understand" and "non-judgment," I am at peace—without searching to know more—dwelling in Jesus who is at the heart of L'Arche and at the heart of my life. This said, in thinking of the victims and their suffering, I want to ask forgiveness for all that I did not do or should have done. Only forgiveness will mend the breaches in the hearts and the communities.[61]

Later, after challenged for his lack of a clear condemnation of Fr. Thomas's actions, Vanier offered a stronger letter and again asks for forgiveness from the victims.[62] His call for "non-judgment" leaves little room for accountability through justice. Paradoxically, it also makes his request for forgiveness nonsensical. There is both nothing to forgive *and* forgiveness is expected.

Vanier's public letters mirror his prior contradictory approach to his mentor in 1959. He thought of Philippe as an "unfairly condemned saint," yet demanded that mercy triumph over judgment.[63] The practical impact of Vanier's forgiveness-without-judgment enabled Thomas Philippe's continued access to vulnerable people: "The Dominican archives establish conclusively that Vanier was made aware of the reasons for Philippe's censure,

---

59. The approach I analyze here in Vanier's public theology mirrors his private dialogue and correspondence, which is "on the whole exempt from any confession of feelings of sin or guilt" (Study Commission, *Control and Abuse*, 233). His victims note that "he keeps asking forgiveness, but he's never said he's sorry" (631).

60. L'Arche International, "Summary Report," 9.

61. Vanier, "2015 Letter," 2.

62. Vanier, "2016 Letter," 1.

63. Study Commission, *Control and Abuse*, 128–29.

and yet Vanier persisted in keeping in close contact with him, facilitated his inclusion in various L'Arche homes, and ensured that his spiritual practices were resumed."[64]

Vanier's emphasis on love over justice, a move that puts love and justice at odds, results in "forgiveness" as a necessary transaction following transgression rather than a gift that can be extended or withheld. In one breath he asks for forgiveness and, in the next, he pontificates that this is the only way to "mend the breaches in the hearts and the communities."[65]

To readers acquainted with images of God as a menacing, angry judge, Vanier's emphasis on forgiveness might feel like a relief. Yet Vanier proclaimed the need for forgiveness not as one who had been wronged but from a place of power, as someone who had wronged others. Just as confessing one's sins had been reframed, so "forgiveness" has shifted from being an extraordinary call from God to followers of Christ to being an expected transaction within community life.[66] No longer a gift that may be given or withheld by victims, it is expected by Vanier as a community leader. Or as Jason R. Greig describes, "The demand for victims to forgive can easily remove their moral agency."[67]

Where actual, culpable evil is rendered incoherent, forgiveness is expected yet supposedly unnecessary. This is the self-contradictory world Vanier attempts to create to avoid accountability. In this world there is no sin, only a relationship with Jesus and human weakness. There is no need to understand, judge, or make restitution; only to practice confession and forgiveness. Sainthood becomes the only linguistic possibility, everything paradoxically both permissible and forgivable.

---

64. Higgins, "Light Extinguished," 14.

65. Vanier similarly emphasized forgiveness in *Befriending the Stranger* as the cornerstone of L'Arche communities, "we need to become men and women of forgiveness" (Vanier, *Befriending the Stranger*, 75). Later, "To forgive and to be forgiven; to liberate and to be liberated; isn't that the goal of our lives?" (*Befriending the Stranger*, 82). Also, "Community is the place of forgiveness" (Vanier, *Community and Growth*, 37).

66. My intent is not to question the role of forgiveness in the life of a Christian disciple, but rather to ask what role it served in Vanier's theology. Jesus is clear on the need to forgive: "For if you forgive other people when they sin against you, your heavenly Father will also forgive you. But if you do not forgive others their sins, your Father will not forgive your sins" (Matt 6:14–15, NIV). Jesus, Paul, and John all command and commend forgiveness often. Some examples, Paul: Eph 4:32; Col 3:13. Jesus: Mark 11:25; Matt 6:14–15; Matt 18:21–22; Luke 6:37. John: 1 John 1:9.

67. Greig, "Sitting at the Table," 4.

Valorization of Vulnerability

Drawing on Jean-Luc Marion's phenomenological paradox of sainthood, this chapter began by questioning the instinctive, embodied way people assumed we might "probe the heart" of Jean Vanier. Vanier's physical appearance was interpreted as indicative, or reflective, of that of a "living saint." In a quasi-idolatrous attempt to express our own *experience of sanctity*, many may have felt that Vanier relayed something experienced as holy in caregiving encounters. Finally, Vanier's theological vocabulary of sin as brokenness, confession, and forgiveness made culpable evil unthinkable and unspeakable. Rather than express the *concept of holiness,* this theological world attempts to make anything *apart* from holiness incoherent.

Our final consideration of Marion's criteria also relates to the concept of sainthood. He observes, "When a group or a faction declares someone a saint, their definition is restricted to what this group or that faction (and thus their respective ideologies) imagine as holiness, that is to say, their particular fantasy of perfection."[68] Where, then, did Vanier's teaching find its appeal and its power? Vanier promoted a *valorization of vulnerability* that seemed to provide a reprieve from fantasies of perfection based on economic productivity, strength, and body capital. Brokenness and messiness came to express not the devastating effects of human sin but our vulnerability in a world that often feels outside of our control. Our ability to identify sin and abuse became the casualty of a desire to see people only as beautiful and broken, not as moral agents capable of predatory behavior in situations of asymmetrical power.[69]

Even without conflating sin and brokenness, valorizing vulnerability *qua* vulnerability entrenches power structures that keep vulnerable persons at risk of abuse. "Vanier's discourse on authority never mentions either an awareness of inequalities within communities, or—*a fortiori*—an interest in reducing them."[70] Without attending to *precarity,* fewer resources are invested in critiquing and dismantling systems that impose vulnerability on marginalized bodies. Valorizing vulnerability undermines the influence of complex power dynamics. It overshadows the powers of contribution of those labeled "vulnerable." It discounts the destructive power to harm, hurt,

---

68. Marion, "Invisibility of the Saint," 704.

69. In "Considerations for an Evolving Vision," Anne Masters reminds us of the importance of paying attention to *precarity* in relationships with power differentials. Similarly, in "Who Wants to Be Vulnerable?" Talitha Cooreman-Guittin seeks to nuance our notions of "cute" or "positive" vulnerability—important work that is being done but has historically been repressed by the dominance of views like Vanier's.

70. Study Commission, *Control and Abuse,* 482.

or abuse that exists in relationships of power differentials, such as in Vanier's "accompaniment" sessions. We need narratives that complexify vulnerability rather than simply valorizing it.[71]

One of the tragedies of defining people by their vulnerability is that we undermine the diverse gifts they bring to their communities. This may seem absurd given the emphasis Vanier placed on the gifts and contribution of people in L'Arche. Reducing vulnerable people to being "the poor," though, deprived people of their individuality and complexity.[72] In Vanier's writing, people with disabilities "are almost faceless, as if their main function was to reflect the face of the Christ or valorise L'Arche's work."[73] No matter people's strengths or vulnerabilities, no one should be treated as only a means to an end or reduced to merely a footnote in someone else's story.

Marion wrote that, "Even the highest virtues, when people raise them uncritically to an alleged holiness, are debased to the rank of fancies that are often more monstrous than shallow."[74] Glorifying or protecting "vulnerability" from nuanced critique transforms it into a monstrous catalyst for abuse. Ironically, Vanier was made *invulnerable* during his life to allegations of abuse due in part to his valorization of vulnerability. Vanier's apparent esteem for those who are vulnerable together with his reframing of sin as brokenness, combined with his physical presence, eloquence, and prestige, enhanced his reputation as a "living saint." This "holy" reputation acted as a camouflage, presenting a barrier to anyone who might challenge his actions or pose a counternarrative.[75]

Conclusion: Paradox and Potential

"The project of determining anyone's holiness must be abandoned . . . [the saint] remains for us formally invisible."[76] The verdict that Jean Vanier was no living saint is a foregone conclusion of this project. Thus, the question of sainthood is ultimately interesting only apart from this particular *reductio*

---

71. Stacy Clifford Simplican's writing on *complex dependency* has been helpful in this regard for me, and Cooreman-Guittin points to other resources in her chapter in this volume. See Clifford Simplican, "Care, Disability, and Violence."

72. Study Commission, *Control and Abuse*, 757.

73. Study Commission, *Control and Abuse*, 759.

74. Marion, "Invisibility of the Saint," 704.

75. Carol Penner observes, "I have observed that it is the magnificently gifted who get away with abuse for decades. . . . Warning signs go unheeded and victims are silenced. Charisma, intelligence and eloquence are powerful gifts for good, and, tragically, for evil" (Penner, "Report Names Jean Vanier," 12).

76. Marion, "Invisibility of the Saint," 705.

ad absurdum. If Jean Vanier is thought of as a paradox, it is only in contrast to public perception during his lifetime. We have too many experiences of "fallen men" to still be surprised by their abuses of power or view their downfall as paradoxical in an interesting way.

Moving forward, Jean Vanier's life and theology is most helpful for moving beyond Jean Vanier's life and theology. I have no doubt that the good in Vanier's work will be brought forward, in different times and from different voices from his own. My concern is that the pitfalls of his theology may be brought forward in the same way. Vanier left his fingerprint on the rise of contemporary disability theology. He elevated questions of brokenness and vulnerability in the context of disability and the human condition that demand further critique.

Vanier wrote in *Community and Growth*, "People with responsibility must always be concerned for the minorities in a community and those who have no voice, listening to them, and interpreting for them."[77] Indeed, Vanier did extensive interpreting—telling the stories of others, casting a vision for others, translating the story of Jesus for others.[78] Hindsight reveals how distorted these interpretations were in light of his private theology and lived example.

According to Marion, the paradox of holiness lies in its invisibility. Holiness can only be assessed by those who have *passed into it and do not come back from it*. We may speak of holiness, yet to ascribe it properly belongs to God alone and "our life hidden with Christ in God."[79] Holiness cannot be parsed by intelligent minds, discerned by erudite theologians, or simply claimed by those who pour enough effort into attaining it. We can only seek to live *before God* (*coram Deo*) "not to live 'divinely,' as God"—as Hans Ulrich stresses.[80] Christ carries God's holiness "all the way into the world, solely epitomizing the people presumed to be holy," yet remains invisible from the world's point of view—inaccessible to worldly devices.[81]

The invisibility of holiness comes as a gut-punch to those who want to bottle sanctity and sell it to the masses; those who parse the possibility of holiness by stated creed or denominational difference, and those who

---

77. Vanier, *Community and Growth*, 215.

78. Noting also Anne Master's critique of *imposed vocation* here. Masters, "Considerations for an Evolving Vision."

79. Marion, "Invisibility of the Saint," 710; Col 3:3.

80. Ulrich, "On Remaining in God's Story." Ulrich takes the communal/political implications of this direction further, suggesting that for L'Arche "everything depends on the distinction between this form of living in God's story and the dynamics of an intensified fulfillment of life."

81. Marion, "Invisibility of the Saint," 709.

claim spiritual encounters exempt from earthly accountability. It equally undermines the adoration of "saints" of caregiving or "angels" of the disabled experience. Yet, in the invisibility of holiness lies its potential. In holy hiddenness, every story may contain something of a divine encounter.

Laura MacGregor, in her research into the spiritual experience of Canadian caregivers, highlights the need for spiritual communities that hold room for paradoxical, confusing, and chaotic narratives—not only listening to multivalent voices but giving space to single voices that are paradoxical in themselves. In this research, caregivers "offered chaotic narratives of confusion, loneliness, isolation, loss, and pain, juxtaposed with stories of joy, love, and faith. Spiritually, parents lamented the unpredictability and perceived silence of God, yet continued to seek the solace and comfort of the Divine."[82] Similarly, the stories of people who have been abused may lack the narrative coherence expected by biased communities. It can take a long time for survivors to recognize the abuse, at which time details or timelines may be murky.[83] Survivors are often trying to make sense of their experience even as they share their stories. We need communities that not only amplify the voices of people with intellectual disabilities with varied communication styles but communities that make room for chaotic narrations of the caregiving experience and the diverse voices of abuse survivors. This would be a holy community, indeed.

Bibliography

L'Arche International. "Summary Report." February 22, 2020.
Bourdieu, Pierre. *Distinction: A Social Critique of the Judgement of Taste*. Translated by R. Nice. Cambridge: Harvard University Press, 1984.
———. "The Forms of Capital." In *Handbook of Theory and Research for the Sociology of Education*, edited by J. Richardson, 241–58. New York: Greenwood, 1986.
———. "Sport and Social Class." *Social Science Information* 17 (1978) 819–40.
Brown, Ian, and Jean Vanier. "After Morgentaler, Jean Vanier Kept His Order of Canada. Why?" *Globe and Mail*, November 29, 2008. https://www.theglobeandmail.com/news/national/after-morgentaler-jean-vanier-kept-his-order-of-canada-why/article20390793.
"The Caregiver: Jean Vanier." *Maclean's* 4 (2000) 33.
Clifford Simplican, Stacy. "Care, Disability, and Violence: Theorizing Complex Dependency in Eva Kittay and Judith Butler." *Hypatia* 30 (2014) 217–33.
Constant, Anne-Sophie. *Jean Vanier: Portrait of a Free Man*. Walden, NY: Plough, 2019.
Cooreman-Guittin, Talitha. "Who Wants to Be Vulnerable? On Vulnerability beyond Vanier." In *The Betrayal of Witness: Reflections on the Downfall of Jean Vanier*,

---

82. MacGregor, "Present Absence," 135.
83. Penner, "Report Names Jean Vanier," 12.

edited by Stanley Hauerwas and Hans S. Reinders, 56–70. Eugene, OR: Wipf & Stock, 2024.
Davis, Angela. "Progressive Struggles against Insidious Capitalist Individualism." In *Freedom Is a Constant Struggle: Ferguson, Palestine, and the Foundations of a Movement*, edited by Frank Barat, 1–12. Chicago: Haymarket, 2016.
Derrida, Jacques. *On Cosmopolitanism and Forgiveness*. London: Routledge, 2001.
Dulle, Colleen. "Jean Vanier, 'Living Saint' Who Ministered to People with Disabilities, Dies at 90." *America Magazine*, May 7 2019. https://www.americamagazine.org/faith/2019/05/07/jean-vanier-living-saint-who-ministered-people-disabilities-dies-90.
Farren, Paul. *Confession: Finding Freedom and Forgiveness*. Brewster, MA: Paraclete, 2014.
Florer-Bixler, Melissa. "Vulnerable at the Core: Jean Vanier (1928–2019)." *The Christian Century* 136 (2019) 12–13.
Greig, Jason R. "Sitting at the Table with a Sinner: Christian Witness and Truthfully Remembering Jean Vanier." In *The Betrayal of Witness: Reflections on the Downfall of Jean Vanier*, edited by Stanley Hauerwas and Hans S. Reinders, 1–17. Eugene, OR: Wipf & Stock, 2024.
Higgins, Michael W. "A Light Extinguished: Jean Vanier and the Betrayal of Trust." *Commonweal* 147 (April 2020) 14–15.
Lindqvist, Erik. "Height and Leadership." *Review of Economics and Statistics* 94 (2012) 1191–96.
MacGregor, Laura. "A Present Absence: The Spiritual Paradox of Parenting a Medically Complex Child." *The Canadian Journal of Theology, Mental Health and Disability* 1 (2021) 126–36.
Marion, Jean-Luc. "The Invisibility of the Saint." *Critical Inquiry* 35 (2009) 703–10.
Masters, Anne. "Considerations for an Evolving Vision of Identity and Witness." In *The Betrayal of Witness: Reflections on the Downfall of Jean Vanier*, edited by Stanley Hauerwas and Hans S. Reinders, 37–55. Eugene, OR: Wipf & Stock, 2024.
Matthews, Pia. "Putting Aside Charisma for Charism: A 'New Springtime' for L'Arche." In *The Betrayal of Witness: Reflections on the Downfall of Jean Vanier*, edited by Stanley Hauerwas and Hans S. Reinders, 71–88. Eugene, OR: Wipf & Stock, 2024.
McKearney, Patrick. "Disabling Virtue." In *The Betrayal of Witness: Reflections on the Downfall of Jean Vanier*, edited by Stanley Hauerwas and Hans S. Reinders, 89–103. Eugene, OR: Wipf & Stock, 2024.
Onyx, Fay. "Five Common Harmful Representations of Disability." *Mythcreants*, September 7, 2018. https://mythcreants.com/blog/five-common-harmful-representations-of-disability/.
Penner, Carol. "Report Names Jean Vanier as an Abuser." *Canadian Mennonite* (March 16, 2020) 12.
Study Commission Mandated by L'Arche International. *Control and Abuse Investigation on Thomas Philippe, Jean Vanier and L'Arche (1950–2019)*. Châteauneuf-sur-Charente, France: Frémur, 2023.
Stulp, Gert, et al. "Tall Claims? Sense and Nonsense about the Importance of Height of US Presidents." *The Leadership Quarterly* 24 (2013) 159–71.
Ulrich, Hans G. "On Remaining in God's Story as Passion." In *The Betrayal of Witness: Reflections on the Downfall of Jean Vanier*, edited by Stanley Hauerwas and Hans S. Reinders, 137–49. Eugene, OR: Wipf & Stock, 2024.

Vanier, Jean. "2015 Letter." *L'Arche International*, May 1, 2015.

———. "2016 Letter to the International Leadership Team." *L'Arche International*, October 17, 2016.

———. *Befriending the Stranger*. New York: Paulist, 2010.

———. *Community and Growth: Our Pilgrimage Together*. New York: Paulist, 1989.

———. "Seek Out the Weak and the Excluded." *U.S. Catholic*, May 18 2013. https://uscatholic.org/articles/201304/seek-out-the-weak-and-the-excluded/.

Willis, Janine, and Alexander Todorov. "First Impressions: Making Up Your Mind after a 100-Ms Exposure to a Face." *Psychological Science* 17 (2006) 592–98.

Chapter Three

Considerations for an Evolving Vision of Identity and Witness

ANNE MASTERS

How might L'Arche move from disorientation to reorientation with a new understanding of itself as witness in the world? Reflecting on the inquiry findings and L'Arche's resilience, Stephan Posner, leader of L'Arche International says, "Although the founding myth is collapsing, 'there's ground beneath the ground. There's a moment of imbalance, like a rug has been pulled from under my feet, but then I realize I'm standing on something deeper.'"[1] The collapsing myth that Posner refers to is the organization's founding story after the discovery of Vanier's sexual and spiritual abuse of at least six women assistants who worked and lived in L'Arche. Posner and Stacy Cates-Carney, L'Arche's vice-international leader promise to investigate its history so the organization can move forward with "greater justice, insight and freedom,"[2] and be faithful to its guiding principles.

The gift of hindsight offers an opportunity to reconsider its history in light of the abuse revelations. This chapter draws from three early reviews of L'Arche in the 1970s by Wolf Wolfensberger for context. They were published in collaboration with L'Arche Daybreak and the Canadian National Institute on Mental Retardation in Toronto (NIMR) where Wolfensberger

---

1. Posner and Hoyeau, "Stephen Posner, Standing Up," para. 7.
2. Posner and Cates-Carney, "Letter," February 22, 2020.

served as visiting scholar for two years. Allan Roeher, its director, wanted Wolfensberger to advance a comprehensive community-based service system predicated on the principle of normalization, which says persons with intellectual and/or developmental disabilities (PWIDD) should be able to participate in typical life events and activities in ordinary ways, rather than in segregated and isolated setting with restricted options.[3]

Vanier opposed the normalization principle, because he believed it imposed options based on material values without compassion.[4] However, Wolfensberger was convinced that the only way to achieve real appreciation of PWIDD and their access to a dignified life was through participation in socially valued ways within general society. This would lead to broader sustainable change for all, instead of only for those who lived in the homes.[5]

This chapter specifically focuses on the early period of L'Arche's development, with the hope of finding some hints of Vanier's thinking while he was still Vanier the man, before becoming Vanier the myth.[6] Wolfensberger's work in Canada and with Daybreak is particularly instructive as it was the first expansion of L'Arche outside of France and its early development provides some interesting counterpoints to Vanier's inclinations.

Wolfensberger's initial reviews were based on his first-hand experiences of L'Arche Daybreak and next with other homes in Canada. He did not visit Trosly until 1975, which influenced his updated review in 1978. This is an important point to remember, for a few reasons. It will be noted below some distinctions in approach between the Newroths and Vanier when they established L'Arche Daybreak and other homes in Canada and mentored other home founders in the US. The 2023 Study Commission report *Control and Abuse* notes Vanier's strategic networking contributed to L'Arche's expansion, noting in particular his collaborations with Wolfensberger, that others such as the Newroths also did.[7] Over time, Wolfensberger recognized differences between them that will be noted below.

Wolfensberger on "What Makes L'Arche Special?"

Wolfensberger was profoundly impacted and even humbled by many aspects of the L'Arche model that he observed at Daybreak.[8] His impressions

3. Wolfensberger, "Reflections on a Lifetime," 447; Nirje, "Basis and Logic," 65–68.
4. Wolfensberger, "Reflection on the Movement," 15.
5. Wolfensberger, "Reflection on the Movement," 15.
6. Whitney-Brown, *Sharing Life*, 14–33.
7. Study Commission, *Control and Abuse*, 363, 378.
8. Wolfensberger, "Reflection on the Movement," 10.

are worth noting as L'Arche considers what uniquely defines it. In fact, later while attending the International Federation Meeting in Shadow Lake in 1975, he suggested L'Arche define its culture.[9] Wolfensberger named five major observations that he believed had three implications for practice within residential settings, which all profoundly impacted him and his developing ideas. His five observations were:

1. *The absence of sentimentalized stereotypes about PWIDD.* Whether positively referenced as saints incapable of sinning, or negatively as animals, the result still marginalizes PWIDD from the larger community and all that includes.[10]

2. *The spirituality of core members.* Wolfensberger had not previously observed PWIDD as particularly spiritual, and now realized it was from lack of support, rather than inability. He observed the joy and comfort it provided, even to PWIDD who continued to struggle from the scars of their past.[11] This is something to remember going forward, as it questions Vanier's unqualified assumptions that PWIDD are innately "people of the heart."

3. *The nature of potential relationships between a "spiritualized person" with a disability and a person without a disability.* This flows from the two above. The person without a disability, spiritualized or not, could become less sophisticated and more open and introspective.

4. *The importance of joy and celebrations, within and extending to the broader community.* Wolfensberger had previously opposed recreation activities because they typically dominated programs at the expense of education, vocation, and residence services. They also tended to be age inappropriate, thus perpetuating the "age-old dehumanizing perceptions" of PWIDD as an "eternal child."[12]

5. *Less distinction between core members and assistants, attempting more reciprocal relationships.* This was reflected by shifting language from "we, us, staff, they, them, clients" to simply "we and us." Wolfensberger thought this increased the feeling of community, which is critical for a sense of security to overcome the history of discontinuity in people's

---

9. Wolfensberger, "Personal Journal Entry," from L'Arche International Federation Meeting, Shadow Lake, France, June 1975 (shared with author by Wolfensberger's daughter).

10. Wolfensberger, "Reflection on the Movement," 10–11.

11. Wolfensberger, "Reflection on the Movement," 11. Wofensberger listed this within his first observation, but it rally should be listed separately.

12. Wolfensberger, "Reflection on the Movement," 11.

lives and also help develop a new self-narrative.[13] It could also increase relatability between core members and assistants, which Wolfensberger thought could enhance the sense of vocation within assistants, that they were doing more than simply a job.[14]

These characteristics are not a discrete list, but interactive. Together they have the potential to transform a facility into a community. Wolfensberger did not think L'Arche could quantitatively impact residential needs, but he did believe it could be a major influence for the future as "a beacon of warmth and light felt around the world," one that others would benefit and draw from.[15]

From these observations, Wolfensberger envisioned three implications for future developments in residential options for PWIDD. Remember, his comments are based on conformity to the normalization principle:

1. Nurture the spiritual lives of PWIDD.
2. Foster creativity, enjoyment, and "innocent social merriment" occasions with a variety of individuals.
3. House architecture must enhance communal identity and life.

The only challenge these presented to the normalization principle would be a slightly larger home than typical to accommodate a larger common area with a bigger kitchen, dining room, and family room adjacent to each other. It was worthwhile because it fostered community and participation, supporting interaction between those who lived in the homes and their guests, as well as its participatory mealtime culture.[16]

This home design also facilitated L'Arche's engagement with the local public and Friends of L'Arche that Wolfensberger also praised. Steve and Anne Newroth, Daybreak's founding directors, introduced the Coffee House in September 1971, a weekly Friday night event of music and dancing. This provided opportunities for others to develop positive impressions of PWIDD, as well as fostering relationships between assistants, core members, and the community.[17] This observation may have influenced part of Wolfensberger's development of the normalization principle into social

---

13. Wolfensberger, "Some Implications, Part II," 38–40; Vanier, "Creation of Community," 21.
14. Wolfensberger, "Reflection on the Movement," 11.
15. Wolfensberger, "Twenty Possible Solutions," F12.
16. Wolfensberger, "Reflection on the Movement," 13–14; Vanier, "Creation of Community," 28–29.
17. Wolfensberger, "Reflection on the Movement," 11–12.

role valorization, which emphasizes the importance of developing positive impressions and experiences. He realized you cannot just bring people together and expect everything will be fine.[18]

More importantly, though, the events helped to change expectations about PWIDD, and it proved invaluable to counter a petition campaign against developing group homes in neighborhoods. When the petition reached Avoca Street, location of its home of the same name, it was opposed by its neighbors saying, "Those are our friends; we go there on Friday evenings for coffee and to sing."[19] No longer "those people," they had become friends and neighbors.

Regardless of Vanier's problems with the normalization principle at the time, Newroth actively accepted and incorporated it into development plans for L'Arche Daybreak and other homes he mentored in North America. The relationships and experiences Wolfensberger witnessed at Daybreak reflected the potential of the normalization principle that Wolfensberger envisioned. The Newroths followed a different path preparing for Daybreak than Vanier did in Trosly. Their post-Trosly preparation for opening Daybreak included working for three months in Camphill villages, a mostly insular farm-based community model that had impressed Vanier. However, Steve Newroth was also concerned to prepare more deeply, to increase his understanding of supporting development of PWIDD. He enrolled in a graduate program in psychology and special education in Canada as well.[20]

Wolfensberger's Concerns

Despite the strengths of L'Arche, Wolfensberger had three main concerns about L'Arche. They are:[21]

1. Stunting growth—potential for assistants to become dependent on being needed.
2. The potentially stifling implications of Vanier's "overpowering charismatic influence" that might stifle creativity and adaptability of future leaders.
3. Assistant burnout and support.

---

18. Wolfensberger, "Contribution to History," 54.
19. Whitney-Brown, *Sharing Life*, 66, 73.
20. Whitney-Brown, *Sharing Life*, 53.
21. Wolfensberger, "Reflection on the Movement," 10, 16.

The first two concerns were noted by Wolfensberger in his initial review of L'Arche in 1973. It was not until the following year after further association with Daybreak that the third issue became prominent. I will focus on the first and third concerns, as the second is addressed by others in this collection. However, it is worth noting the example of Newroth embracing the normalization principle above and his graduate work to support his work in L'Arche. It is an early example of a leader who greatly respected Vanier, but did not feel inhibited to reconsider his assumptions.

The following year the staff of Daybreak initiated and planned a conference in Aurora with NIMR, specifically to address its own concerns about assistant retention, as well as reflect on the model's integrity.[22] By this time Daybreak was one of twelve L'Arche homes in Canada.[23] The discussion of these concerns will draw predominantly from Wolf's initial review and comments made during the Aurora conference.

Needing to Be Needed

Anticipating a concern that would be voiced by many others, Wolfensberger wondered about assistants who may experience personal growth through their lived experiences with PWIDD and then develop an unhealthy dependency on these relationships.

> Where would their needs be met if the retarded [sic] could no longer meet them? This is a frightening thought, and we have to be aware of the fact that those who need the retarded [sic] too much may not be able to admit this danger into their own consciousness and may therefore tend to do less than they could in advancing retarded [sic] persons to more adaptive skills, to a higher social status in society, or to greater degrees of integration with the mainstream society.[24]

Such dependence by assistants would undermine the development of core members. This originates in sentimental attitudes about PWIDD, mindsets that typically see them as instruments of transformation that perpetuate sentimental stereotypes and narratives of innocence and eternal childhood, with consequently low expectations. Wolfensberger's insight that this may be unconscious is worth keeping in mind when considering Vanier's own tendency toward sentimental language about PWIDD.

---

22. Newroth, "Forward," iii–v.
23. Newroth, "Daybreak."
24. Wolfensberger, "Reflection on the Movement," 16.

Although Vanier admitted the limiting implications of others doing too much for PWIDD during the conference, he muddled his message when he says that they are "such good and wonderful assistants, wanting to help with such beauty and devotion."[25] In other words, their misdirected actions are sentimentalized and valorized by his descriptions. This is further reinforced when he adds, "Many of the assistants can come through their depression and their difficulties because of the eyes of the handicapped.... We must become conscious that they can be a source of healing," and "our hearts must be nourished by the handicapped."[26]

Vanier frequently emphasized the transformational impact of relationships with PWIDD, even confining them within this role.[27] Indeed, in a conference keynote for the US National Apostolate for the Mentally Retarded [sic] in 1972, he said that PWIDD are uniquely capable of communion because of their *dependent and uncritical acceptance* of others and their ideas. He said this aptitude for communion develops out of their woundedness that is born of low expectations and rejection with no sense of future autonomy.[28] So, rather than exploring ways to overcome this woundedness and nurturing development, he focuses on their simplicity and trust. Vanier clearly suggests that this uncritical acceptance is constitutive of communion.

Contrast this with Wolfensberger's understanding of Christian *communality*. It occurs within relationships, he says, and requires long-term proximity, familiarity, and trust.[29] But for Wolfensberger, it is a trust that *encourages* questioning, rather than stifling it. When speaking of his own first encounters with PWIDD, Vanier typically focused on their acceptance of him, in other words, how they made *him* feel. "The very first experience I had with handicapped [sic] people was ... the discovery of their great simplicity, easiness, and their acceptance of me," and the awakening of his heart and inner child during the first months at Trosly.[30] It is certainly a transformative experience when we are drawn out of ourselves and our own concerns to respond to the needs of another who is more objectively vulnerable than ourselves, and more significantly, into relationship.[31] Authentically engaged, this allows for *caritas*, which Pia Matthews explores

---

25. Vanier, "Creation of Community," 32.
26. Vanier, "Creation of Community," 32–33, 35.
27. Vanier, "Creation of Community," 32–33, 35; Vanier, *Community and Growth*, 262–63.
28. Vanier, "Living Our Faith," 3.
29. Wolfensberger, "Most Urgent Issues," 117–20.
30. Vanier, "Creation of Community," 7; Vanier, *Ark for the Poor*, 20.
31. Masters, "Who Do You Say That I Am?," 98, 121–23, 155–57.

in another chapter in this collection.[32] The problem comes when the focus remains on one's own experience and needs, without concern for the other person from their perspective. These perceptions were reinforced during Wolf's 1975 visit to the International Federation meeting at Shadow Lake and Trosly in 1975. He noticed a general lack of expectations of PWIDD, whether it be about hygiene, home contributions, or development.[33]

Assistant Support and Stress

Wolfensberger was deeply concerned about staff burnout as perhaps the single most important issue, not only in L'Arche but for all residential settings. If not solved, he felt sure it would have implications far into the future. Its impact was particularly disastrous for the residents who had experienced so much relationship discontinuity in their lives.[34]

Attracting staff was not the problem; the challenge was keeping them. He was frustrated that the reason given was usually vague, typically that they were going for further education, which he doubted was the real issue.[35] Wolfensberger believed the assistants were emotionally wiped out from the intense demands in relationships with PWIDD who were so wounded by their past experiences. Therefore, the central question was, "Why do people get wiped out?" Do assistants/staff need more personal space? Should living quarters be larger and more private rather than tiny and cramped? Or could the issue be related to insufficient proper training, the number of work hours, or maybe even staff shortage?[36] These were the questions he posed to the conference panel.

While Wolfensberger was very concerned with staff support, Vanier believed, "People who love their work ... can do it 24 hours a day," and said that people who burn out are not committed.[37] Yet, these statements seem overly simplistic and dismissive. Vanier seemed to prefer simpler strategies that did not require much organizational support. He said there are some simple things that can reduce apparent "big problems," such as "an old

---

32. Matthews, "Putting Aside Charisma."
33. Wolfensberger, personal journal entries dated June and September 1975. June entries were from observations while attending the International Federation Meeting at Shadow Lake. The September journal entries were about observations while visiting L'Arche in Trosly. Journal entries shared with author by Wolfensberger's daughter.
34. Wolfensberger, "Some Implications, Part I," 1–2.
35. Wolfensberger, "Some Implications, Part I," 3.
36. Wolfensberger, "Some Implications, Part I," 4–5.
37. Vanier, "Creation of Community," 13.

grandmother"; "go[ing] to bed with a hot chocolate"; or going for a walk.[38] He further minimized qualifications for assistants saying, "The great majority have no diplomas. They are just ordinary people. . . . Once you've gone through school then you really get complicated."[39] His emphasis for assistant development seemed to focus more on spiritual development provided by clergy, at least into the 1990s, with only some reference to lay people in this area and mentorship by more experienced assistants.[40]

The only formation Vanier discussed at the conference was bringing in vision-based speakers from outside L'Arche to help core members and assistants keep their own problems in perspective.[41] He said, "You know sometimes we just have an ingrown toenail and we think that we are dying of cancer, but it's not so; it's an ingrown toenail and we have to just try to put that ingrown toenail in the perspective of the whole body, that's all."[42] One might wonder what the staff at Daybreak was thinking as Vanier talked.

While recognizing the value of a slightly larger home to support communal activity, Wolfensberger was still very concerned about the potential to undermine its positive intentions if L'Arche continued with more largely populated homes and farms.[43] There were two reasons for this. The first is about imaging repercussions. The segregated and congregated settings suggested that PWIDD were better served separated from the larger community, reinforcing "they" are different from "us."[44] Another imaging concern were photos of adults with IDD portrayed in typically child-like ways, such as cuddling a teddy bear. Wolfensberger shared with colleagues that he could not understand why Vanier ignored its implications, as well as commented in writings,[45] because it reinforces the eternal child narrative Wolfensberger was pleased to *not see* at Daybreak, noted in the previous section.

The other impact was on home dynamics. Wolfensberger was very concerned that more people in a home increased complexity and demands on assistants, as well as potentially on core members, and he challenged

---

38. Vanier, "Creation of Community," 33–34.
39. Vanier, "Living Our Faith," 4.
40. Vanier, *Ark for the Poor*, 68–71.
41. Vanier, "Creation of Community," 14–15, 34.
42. Vanier, "Creation of Community," 35.
43. Wolfensberger, "Some Implications, Part I," 5.
44. Wolfensberger, "Twenty Possible Solutions," F10–12.
45. Telephone conversations with Wolfensberger's colleagues Susan Thomas and Raymond Lemay; Wolfensberger, "Twenty Possible Solutions," F11.

L'Arche to think very carefully about its commitment to this model.[46] But he praised Daybreak's apparent ability to adapt to future needs as it was developing in urban areas with proximity to employment opportunities.[47] Newroth had realized some of Daybreak's core members were stifled by the isolated farm setting.[48]

Despite Wolfensberger's concerns about larger homes, Vanier defensively countered that they engendered a larger spirit that could also preempt assistants' burnout.[49] Yet it was a prominent issue during the Shadow Lake meeting one year later, affirming Wolfensberger's concerns, and he sensed Vanier had tried to avoid it. He also wondered at the number of home founders no longer living in the homes.[50]

It is also worth noting that contrary to the community support for Avoca House, Vanier had confronted resistance to L'Arche's growing footprint in Trosly. He had not facilitated community engagement as the Newroths had.[51]

Exploring Wolfensberger's concerns about L'Arche is interesting from a historical perspective. But did others share them? Did they persist? This is what will be considered next.

Other Voices on Wolfensberger's Concerns

Wolfensberger was not the only person to raise these concerns about L'Arche. Dr. Franko, a psychiatrist who worked with L'Arche early in its history, also noticed the potential for assistants to become dependent on being needed by core members. Simply providing a place of sanctuary, Franko said, was only a first step toward helping dependent people. The second step required providing the freedom for each person to continue to grow and change even beyond needing the sheltered environment if they were able and so inclined. Without taking the second step, it would be manifesting the same dehumanizing mindset, he said which was "an imprisonment of another sort [as the Nazi camps and ovens for Jews]."[52] Further, he dismissed general platitudes, such as "being at L'Arche deepened their own respect for the human person

---

46. Wolfensberger, "Some Implications, Part I," 5.
47. Wolfensberger, "Reflection on the Movement," 15.
48. Newroth, "Daybreak," 4–7.
49. Vanier, "Creation of Community," 32.
50. Wolfensberger, personal journal entries dated June 1975.
51. Vanier, *Ark for the Poor*, 36.
52. Clarke, *Enough Room for Joy*, 98–100.

and enabled them to be more truly themselves,"[53] as meaningless. To be meaningful, this could only be spoken of in specific terms, of one assistant speaking of their relationship with a particular core member.[54]

While Wolfensberger never accused Vanier of this issue, though confused by his disregard as noted, others have.[55] And there are examples within L'Arche as well, such as Thérèse Vanier, Jean's sister. She was exasperated by his sentimental portrayals "on the joys of living with mentally handicapped [sic] people and their tremendous gifts of community . . . because he never spoke of how hard it could be at times."[56]

And what of the desires of the individual? Is their sense of vocation and how they want to live not important? Thelus George, a core member, expressed her grief over the number of assistants who leave. "Every year assistants come, and I get to know them, and we are friends, and then they leave. It hurts my heart. I get very sad." Vanier responds by saying, "Thelus, this is your vocation: to form them in love and send them out."[57] Whitney-Brown suggests that Vanier is calling George to expand her sense of herself, "forming people and then sending them out into the world to love."[58] However, the question still stands, what of George's interests, preferences, and own sense of vocation? Who was Vanier to decide for her? Could this be another example of him exerting his power over someone more precariously vulnerable? Is it not objectionable to claim a single homogeneous value or gift of a group of diverse individuals, unified by the general category of living with intellectual disability?

Similarly, in "A Holy Mess of a Story: Maternal Reflections on Caregiving, Chaos and Intellectual Disability," Laura MacGregor accuses Vanier of colonizing the stories of precariously vulnerable people for his own purposes. In the process, it similarly sentimentalizes mothers' experiences in the eyes of others, rather than fostering understanding and support.[59] It is important to consider this criticism seriously for what it implies about Vanier in light of current revelations, both for MacGregor and other parents and caregivers, but also the implications for PWIDD.

---

53. Clarke, *Enough Room for Joy*, 101.

54. Clarke, *Enough Room for Joy*, 101.

55. Burghardt, "Brokenness/Transformation," 2–10. Burghardt provides a good summary of diverse voices; Masters, "Who Do You Say That I Am?," 136–39.

56. Whitney-Brown, *Sharing Life*, 148.

57. Whitney-Brown, *Tender to the World*, 120.

58. Whitney-Brown, *Tender to the World*, 121.

59. MacGregor, "Holy Mess of a Story."

Vanier's sentimental narratives on the vulnerability of PWIDD that connect others without disabilities to their own vulnerability is deeply problematic because it becomes the uniting characteristic across all people. However, this does not differentiate between humanity's interdependent nature that we all share, and the increased vulnerability experienced by some people based on the social structures and attitudes that devalue and marginalize groups of people who lack social currency. This is precarity, an enhanced state of vulnerability beyond what is endemic to being human. It is experienced by devalued and marginalized groups of peoples.[60] Perpetuating this, as Franko pointed out, means not taking the second step to diminish the precarity of someone, which would otherwise provide the freedom to grow beyond one's own expectations of the other.

In *I Believe in You*, Luca Badetti cautions for the need to explore one's own marginalized self, one's own "shadow side" before accompanying people who have been marginalized. Doing so is part of developing self-awareness and becoming comfortable with oneself, which should mitigate against such unconscious instrumental use.[61]

Keith Dow points out one set of problems caused by Vanier's valorization of vulnerability elsewhere in this collection.[62] But there is another set of problems pertinent to this discussion when it is combined with the overarching sentimental narrative Vanier scripted about PWIDD as "people of the heart." Appreciating the precariousness of individuals that is brought on by subjective devaluation is lost in such instances. Without appreciating the role of precarity, protestations of humanity's shared vulnerability is merely a sentimental foil that attempts to claim connectedness with PWIDD and other marginalized peoples. Emphasizing commonality without also acknowledging distinctions only promotes a false sense of unity that obscures differences, typically leaving sources of precarity intact.[63] The Study Commission also noted Vanier's tendency to erase the individual distinctions of "the poor," thus sacralizing precariously vulnerable persons, thereby instrumentalizing them.[64] Similarly, the Commission wonders why Vanier never talks of the spirituality of PWIDD.[65] Though perhaps saving them from abuse, it is a strange omission for someone so focused on spiritual matters.

60. Keenan, "World at Risk," 132–49.
61. Badetti, *I Believe in You*, 102.
62. Dow, "Against Living Sainthood."
63. Dovidio et al., "Included but Invisible?," 11, 15–37.
64. Study Commission, *Control and Abuse*, 758–63.
65. Study Commission, *Control and Abuse*, 817.

While all humans are vulnerable, the fundamental value for people of faith is that every person is created in the image of God, *b'tselem Elohim*.[66] This is accepted across faith traditions and is an important distinction from a secular understanding of human dignity, which would be subject to human status attribution, based on judgements of perceived merit or capability.

Thérèse was also extremely concerned about support, or the lack of it, for assistants. She noted that as a doctor, she considered professional standards, training, and development for assistants very important, and she also wanted guidance when needed from disciplines such as psychiatry, psychology, and social work.[67] She recalled with animated frustration a significant leader of L'Arche in France who said stress did not exist at L'Arche![68] Another time, losing her temper, she said, "I saw absolutely no point in talking about the spirituality of L'Arche, or in deciding what it is, if there were no assistants around to live it. . . . We had to look at the needs of assistants in this regard because you can't split off spirituality from being well."[69] Thérèse insisted it be the theme for the Commission's 1995 meeting in Trosly, saying, "If we really wanted to have any assistants left to live the spirituality of L'Arche, we needed to do something about helping them stay on. . . . There were difficulties everywhere. People were getting much too tired and stressed and were giving up."[70] This clearly echoes Wolfensberger's concerns voiced twenty years earlier.

The discussion so far provides a brief presentation of early reviews of L'Arche by Wolfensberger, which were overwhelmingly positive. Yet, his concerns have been echoed by others in L'Arche and outside to differing degrees. This provides the framework for the real object of this project, to offer ideas L'Arche will hopefully find helpful as it considers its story going forward in light of its fuller awareness of its past.

Reclaiming Its Story—An Evolving Sense of Witness

As L'Arche reconsiders its identity in light of what it learns about its past, I hope it not only engages the shadows within its history and the attitudes that inform them, as Badetti discusses, but also considers new possibilities for an expanding sense of purpose with a renewed understanding of itself as witness in the world to keep up with its stated mission. This will certainly

66. Landsberg, "Jewish Voices," 7; Paul VI, *Gaudium et Spes*, 29.
67. Whitney-Brown, *Sharing Life*, 147.
68. Whitney-Brown, *Sharing Life*, 147.
69. Whitney-Brown, *Sharing Life*, 156.
70. Whitney-Brown, *Sharing Life*, 155–6.

require careful consideration. To be more concrete, part of L'Arche's mission is to "foster an environment in community that responds to the changing needs of our members, whilst being faithful to the core values of our founding story."[71] What does this really mean? Which founding story does L'Arche claim? That is, of course, part of the work L'Arche has before it.

There is one thread of L'Arche's history that is less known and particularly relevant for this discussion, because it includes two other men typically not spoken of even today. Jean-Louis Coïc, the invisible assistant, was an old friend from L'Eau Vive. Though he quickly realized this was not his calling, Coïc remained for a few months until two others came. And Dany, the invisible core member who did not demonstrate grateful dependence, only remained for one day.[72] He was deaf, couldn't speak and according to Vanier, was "a deeply disturbed man . . . living so much in his own world of pain and dreams."[73]

I am a bit concerned about the possibility of a circular loop without resolution in the question above about honoring its mission. To discover that something deeper Posner senses, I first suggest L'Arche consider its core value more closely that highlights mutuality in relationships between people with and without intellectual disability, trust in God, and "celebrates the unique value of every person and need for one another."[74] Where does the value come from? Does it come from the expressed need for each other? If yes, then core members could remain stuck within a cycle of dependency. Assessing needs can be quite subjective without a solid foundation. Though a faith-based organization, there is no basing human dignity on being created in the image of God in its Identity and Mission Statement, nor have I noticed it on any L'Arche websites. While considering its way forward, think about this carefully. Posner and Cates-Carney say near the end of their letter regarding the Commission report and considering what has been lost, "If there is something we have learned . . . it is the talent of people with disabilities have to shake up images and help us access a truer part of ourselves."[75] This comes very close to the reductive sentimental narratives discussed that ascribes "the talent" to a group of people categorized by experiencing disability.

The second is to ensure that Dany and Jean-Louis are present in its collective memory. Vanier's sentimental narratives about PWIDD and

---

71. L'Arche International, "Identity and Mission," para. 5.
72. Vanier, *Ark for the Poor*, 17–18; Whitney-Brown, *Sharing Life*, 25–28.
73. Vanier, *Ark for the Poor*, 17–18.
74. L'Arche International, "Identity and Mission."
75. Posner and Cates-Carney, "Letter," January 30, 2023.

assistants could be connected as part of one reductive narrative. In other words, his views about PWIDD and assistants may be reflections of each other, both through the lens of what Vanier wanted, without considering the other person truly from their own perspective.

The 2023 Study Commission report makes clear that the inspiration for L'Arche at least began to provide a "screen" for the reconstituted L'Eau Vive hidden below, literally as the water supporting the ark.[76] However, it also suggests Vanier had a coexistent authentic commitment to PWIDD.[77] Based on the numerous references to his duplicity in the report, I'm not sure how accurate that is, or if it simply wishful thinking. He demonstrated great adeptness at modulating his message for his audience. What began instrumentally to regather around Thomas Philippe came to serve another purpose, as I have already suggested, as Vanier experienced unquestioned acceptance and purpose in being needed, and was not concerned with the real needs of PWIDD.[78]

Despite inaccessibility to much of the past Newroth Daybreak archives due to the unresponsiveness of Saint Michael's University College to compare legitimacy practices of formal authority between Daybreak and Trosly, it would still be instructive to study the institutional establishment practices and ways of community engagement between the two. Whereas the Newroths actively engaged proactively with the growing understanding of evidence-based practices, Vanier's preference seemed more of a "homespun" approach that could possibly have been influenced by Philippe's "anti-intellectualism."[79]

Daybreak was influenced by Wolfensberger and the principle of normalization, and its successor, social role valorization (SRV) should be investigated. Both are concerned with supporting human flourishing and development; SRV emphasizes the importance of social roles, which are integral to identity, personal development, and social participation.[80] Its principles are geared toward a smaller systems approach that focuses on natural relationships, doing things in typical and ordinary ways. Wolfensberger regularly warned of service systems more concerned with their own vitality than the needs of the person it was intended to support, whose development might challenge their existence.[81] This is the systemic version of "needing to

---

76. Study Commission, *Control and Abuse*, 125, 154–55, 189, 828, 273–79, 198.
77. Study Commission, *Control and Abuse*, 828–29.
78. Vanier, "Living Our Faith," 3.
79. Study Commission, *Abuse and Control*, 239, 540, 584–85, 829.
80. Wolfensberger, "Brief Overview," 105–15.
81. Wolfensberger, "Reflections on a Lifetime," 448–54.

be needed." Recall Wolfensberger's reflections in his journal when visiting Trosly in 1975 in contrast to his experiences with Daybreak.

Strikingly, the Commission's report does refer to the collaboration of Vanier and Wolfensberger, though not for contrast. Rather, Vanier's engagement with "the greatest North American specialists of his time, particularly Wolf Wolfensberger" helped to broaden his and L'Arche's credibility, as does the successes of other L'Arche homes around the world, singularly naming the Newroths and Daybreak.[82] Here again it notes their work with Wolfensberger, but without awareness of the divergences discussed earlier. In 2001 Wolfensberger chastised L'Arche's congregated model, though he admitted it offered at least some form of engagement between persons with and without disabilities.[83]

Pope Francis seemingly affirms the principles of SRV (though not named) in *Fratelli Tutti* when he says, "Our concern should be not only to care for [PWD] but to ensure their 'active participation in the civil and ecclesial community' . . . that will gradually contribute to the formation of consciences capable of acknowledging each individual as a unique and unrepeatable person."[84] Francis notes the importance of witnessing the capabilities of PWD, because this can change people's awareness of their potentiality. As L'Arche reconsiders its identity as witness, it has an opportunity to facilitate a richer appreciation of PWIDD.

If it chooses to, L'Arche would be well-positioned to play a leading role in this ongoing process of social transformation. Not only to more effectively support core members to participate more fully in broader community life, but also to foster pathways of participation with community groups, including faith communities. L'Arche could help members of such groups appreciate PWIDD in themselves and feel comfortable welcoming them to be present, participate meaningfully as desired, and develop a true sense of belonging. This would require L'Arche to initiate collaboration with such groups at the local level, which I believe has already begun in some locations. There are also examples of L'Arche community members participating in the public forum to challenge systemic injustices against PWIDD.[85] Such practices are to be encouraged.

However, the role of witness, as a light in the distance that Wolfensberger suggested, is outdated. The role of witness is to be a light that is near

---

82. Study Commission, *Control and Abuse*, 364, 378.
83. Wolfensberger, "Response to the Responders," 150.
84. Francis, *Fratelli Tutti*, 98.
85. Badetti, *I Believe in You*, 109.

and warm.[86] It should be engaged with the larger community, as Francis calls for in *Fratelli Tutti,* modeling ways of accompanying PWIDD that is freeing rather than confining.[87] Such would demonstrate its readiness to expand its self-understanding from an example set apart, to one of true accompaniment in service of its purpose to nurture the ability of PWIDD to become capable of living in society and each valued in their uniqueness, as Newroth expressed many years ago.[88] It would be a reversal of the monastic hospitality Francis praises in *Fratelli Tutti.*[89] Rather than welcoming travelers within despite their intrusive presence, L'Arche would be moving out within the broader community to facilitate that deeper participation and appreciation. This would further promote the "growing end of human dignity" and its consequent responsibilities upon faith communities. L'Arche could be a valuable player in this. It only requires a willingness to open itself to unimagined possibilities facilitated by activities of the Spirit among God's people and in the world.[90]

Bibliography

L'Arche International. "Identity and Mission." n.d. https://www.larche.org/en/identity-and-mission.

Badetti, Luca. *I Believe in You.* Revised ed. Hyde Park, NY: New City, 2021.

Burghardt, Madeline. "Brokenness/Transformation: Reflections on Academic Critiques of L'Arche." *Disability Studies Quarterly* 36 (2016). https://dsq-sds.org/article/view/3734.

Clarke, Bill, SJ. *Enough Room for Joy.* Paperback ed. London: McClelland and Stewart, 1974.

Dovidio, John F., et al. "Included but Invisible? Subtle Bias, Common Identity, and the Darker Side of 'We.'" *Social Issues and Policy Review* 10 1 (2016) 6–46.

Dow, Keith. "Against Living Saints." In *The Betrayal of Witness: Reflections on the Downfall of Jean Vanier,* edited by Stanley Hauerwas and Hans S. Reinders, 18–36. Eugene, OR: Wipf & Stock, 2024.

Francis, Pope. *Fratelli Tutti.* Vatican, October 3, 2020. https://www.vatican.va/content/francesco/en/encyclicals/documents/papa-francesco_20201003_enciclica-fratelli-tutti.html.

John Paul, Pope, II. *Redemptoris Missio.* Vatican, December 7, 1990. https://www.vatican.va/content/john-paul-ii/en/encyclicals/documents/hf_jp-ii_enc_07121990_redemptoris-missio.html.

---

86. John Paul II, *Redemptoris Missio,* 24, 26–27, 42, 49.
87. Francis, *Fratelli Tutti,* paras. 64, 110, 274, 276, 279–80.
88. Newroth, "Daybreak," 3.
89. Francis, *Fratelli Tutti,* 90.
90. John Paul II, *Redemptoris Missio,* 21–30.

Keenan, James F. "The World at Risk: Vulnerability, Precarity, and Connectedness." *Theological Studies* 81 (2020) 132–49.

Landsberg, Lynne, Rabbi. "Jewish Voices on B'tselem Elohim." In *Guide to Jewish Values and Disability Rights*, edited by Rabbi Julia Watts Belser, 7. New York: Jewish Funders Network, 2016.

MacGregor, Laura. "A Holy Mess of a Story: Maternal Reflections on Caregiving, Chaos, and Intellectual Disability." *Journal of Disability & Religion* 1 (2021) 1–14.

Masters, Anne. "Who Do You Say That I Am? Overcoming the Marginalization of Persons with Intellectual and Developmental Disabilities in the US Catholic Church." PhD diss. Vrije Universiteit, 2020. https://research.vu.nl/en/publications/who-do-you-say-that-i-am-overcoming-the-marginalization-of-person.

Matthews, Pia. "Putting Aside Charisma for Charism: A 'New Springtime' for L'Arche." In *The Betrayal of Witness: Reflections on the Downfall of Jean Vanier*, edited by Stanley Hauerwas and Hans S. Reinders, 71–88. Eugene, OR: Wipf & Stock, 2024.

Newroth, Stephen. "Daybreak, Jean Vanier, and L'Arche." In *A Selective Overview of the Work of Jean Vanier and the Movement of L'Arche*, edited by Wolf Wolfensberger, 1–10. Toronto: Canada National Institute on Mental Retardation, 1973.

———. "Forward." In *Growing Together*, edited by Wolf Wolfensberger and Jean Vanier, 4. Richmond Hill, Ontario: Daybreak, 1974.

Nirje, Bengt. "The Basis and Logic of the Normalization Principle." *Australia and New Zealand Journal of Developmental Disabilities* 11 (1985) 65–68.

Paul, Pope, VI. *Gaudium et Spes*. Second Vatican Council. Vatican, 1965. https://www.vatican.va/archive/hist_councils/ii_vatican_council/documents/vat-ii_const_19651207_gaudium-et-spes_en.html.

Posner, Stephan, and Céline Hoyeau. "Stephan Posner, Standing Up When the Ground Slips from Under You." *La Croix International*, August 3, 2020. https://intranet.larche.org/web/guest/news/-/asset_publisher/mQsRZspJMdBy/content/when-the-ground-slips-from-under-you?.

Posner, Stephan, and Stacy Cates-Carney. "Letter-Federation International Leaders." Paris: L'Arche International, February 22, 2020. https://www.larcheusa.org/news_article/letter-of-stephan-posner-and-stacy-cates-carney-to-the-federation-of-larche/.

———. "Letter-Federation International Leaders." Paris: L'Arche International, January 2023. https://www.larche.org/wp-content/uploads/2023/01/Letter_Federation-International_Leaders-2023-01-30-EN.pdf.

Study Commission Mandated by L'Arche International. *Control and Abuse Investigation on Thomas Philippe, Jean Vanier and L'Arche (1950–2019)*. Châteauneuf-sur-Charente, France: Frémur, 2023.

Vanier, Jean. *An Ark for the Poor: The Story of L'Arche*. Toronto: Novalis, 1995.

———. *Community and Growth*. Revised ed. New York: Paulist, 1989.

———. "The Creation of Community—the Experience of L'Arche." In *Growing Together*, edited by Wolf Wolfensberger and Jean Vanier, 30. Richmond Hill, Ontario: Daybreak, 1974.

———. "Living Our Faith with the Retarded Person." Conference keynote address. *NAMR Quarterly Publication* 4 (1972) 2–5, 15.

Whitney-Brown, Carolyn. *Sharing Life: Stories of L'Arche Founders*. Mawah, NJ: Paulist, 2019.

———. *Tender to the World: Jean Vanier, L'Arche, and the United Church of Canada.* Montreal: McGill-Queen's University Press, 2019.

Wolfensberger, Wolf. "A Brief Overview of Social Role Valorization." *Mental Retardation* 38 (2000) 105–23.

———. "A Contribution to the History of Normalization, with Primary Emphasis on the Establishment of Normalization in North America between 1967–1975." In *A Quarter-Century of Normalization and Social Role Valorization: Evolution and Impact*, edited by Robert J Flynn and Raymond Lemay, 3–69. Ottawa: University of Ottowa Press, 1999.

———. "The Most Urgent Issues Facing Us as Christians Concerned with Handicapped Persons Today." *Journal of Religion, Disability & Health* 4 (2001) 91–102. Presentation at NAMR Annual Conference in Denver, August 10, 1983; condensed version in *NAMR Quarterly* 14 (1983) 4–9.

———. "A Reflection on the Movement of L'Arche." In *A Selective Overview of the Work of Jean Vanier and the Movement of L'Arche*, edited by Wolf Wolfensberger, 10–17. Toronto: Canada National Institute on Mental Retardation, 1973.

———. "Reflections on a Lifetime in Human Services and Mental Retardation." *Intellectual and Developmental Disabilities* 49 (2011) 441–55.

———. "Response to the Responders." *Journal of Religion, Disability & Health* 4 (2001) 149–57.

———. "Some Implications from the Aurora Conference Part I." In *Growing Together*, edited by Wolf Wolfensberger and Jean Vanier, 6. Richmond Hill, Ontario: Daybreak, 1974.

———. "Some Implications from the Aurora Conference Part II." In *Growing Together*, edited by Wolf Wolfensberger and Jean Vanier, 9. Richmond Hill, Ontario: Daybreak, 1974.

———. "Twenty Possible Solutions to the Relationship Discontinuity from the Aurora Conference." In *Residential Services: Community Housing Options for Handicapped People*, F6–F12. Toronto, Canada: National Institute on Mental Retardation, 1978. Reprint, Revised and improved summary of Aurora Conference first in *Growing Together*, 1974.

Chapter Four

Who Wants to Be Vulnerable?
On Vulnerability beyond Vanier

Talitha Cooreman-Guittin

When in 2020 the news was outed of the sexual and spiritual crimes perpetrated by Jean Vanier against women whose confidence he abused, it struck me as a bomb. The man who made me come to peace with my own vulnerability as a cornerstone of my humanity, who made me realize how precious friendships can be when they move beyond the barriers of disability prejudice, the man who inspired part of my doctoral research, suddenly proved to be no better than a sexual predator, or at least so it felt to me at the time. . . . All of a sudden it felt as if I couldn't rely upon Jean Vanier's writings anymore when I wanted to broach the subject of vulnerability. There is of course an ethical issue: can we look to Jean Vanier for moral guidance with regard to vulnerability, knowing he has sexually and spiritually abused women?

But there is more. There is an anthropological issue too: reading closer into Vanier's writings, his sometimes-angelic conception of vulnerability and intellectual disability appeared to me to be at odds with the lived experience of people who live in extreme states of vulnerability. The second issue seems of even bigger importance than the first one, and it is this second issue that will make up the bulk of my argument. Three years after "the fall," the time has come to bring forward a new understanding of vulnerability, more nuanced, nourished by the rich theological thinking of many researchers, and not based on the sole experience of one—fallible—human being.

In this contribution I will dwell on the common acceptance of vulnerability as an undesirable aspect of being human and confront it to its overtly positive consideration by authors like Brené Brown and Jean Vanier. I need to distinguish here between *existential* vulnerability as a universal aspect of createdness and *social* vulnerability, which often comes with existential vulnerability, but is the result of the rejection of persons who cannot defend themselves. Though the two are often, but not necessarily, related, I will focus here on existential vulnerability, which most people find complicated to come to terms with.

In recent work, the positive view of vulnerability has been staunchly criticized.[1] I will therefore suggest a more nuanced reading based on the notion of "existential porosity" coined by French ethicist Marie-Jo Thiel.[2] Building on my understanding of the parable of the talents I will argue that God-given vulnerability as an existential porosity entails a valuable dimension—but it also has its downsides. As I see it, Vanier, like the third servant, chose to not cooperate with God and in so doing, what he had was "taken from him." I will suggest we have to move beyond Vanier and take the notion of vulnerability to a more nuanced level, although still considering it as a possibly valuable dimension of what it means to be human.

"Cute Vulnerability?"

Vulnerability is most often understood as the state of being exposed to the possibility of being harmed. Hence it is not surprising that in ordinary conversations, vulnerability is not usually considered as a positive dimension of our humanness. Most of my interviewees associate it with disease, disability, and death.[3] As a friend and researcher at Université catholique de Louvain bluntly put it: "vulnerability stinks." Some of the persons with intellectual disabilities I interviewed also expressed the wish that they'd rather not be considered as vulnerable. Indeed, for most people, regardless of their abilities, vulnerability still appears as something that threatens our wellbeing, as

---

1. Notably by Maican, "Vulnerability and Solidarity"; Burghardt, "Brokenness/Transformation"; Masters, "Rethinking Charity"; Reinders and Gangemi, "Does L'Arche Need Another Saint?"

2. Thiel, *La Santé Augmentée* (translated quotations by the present author).

3. Fieldnotes of research conducted at the UCLouvain (Belgium) in 2019 on dementia and friendship (personal archives of the present author).

a sword of Damocles above the head of each and every one of us, as a state of being we want to avoid at all cost.

However, over the last fifteen years or so voices were raised against this pessimistic vision of vulnerability. Brené Brown is certainly among the most well-known advocates of vulnerability as the birthplace of creativity and joy.[4] Jean Vanier also counts as a fierce defender of vulnerability as more than tragedy. He repeatedly spoke out to affirm that becoming human entails discovering that we are vulnerable, and that the "mystery of vulnerability" invites us into relationships with one another. In his correspondence with Julia Kristeva[5] he explains that there is a profound joy to experience in the encounter with extremely vulnerable people, among whom he counts persons with profound intellectual disabilities. This encounter can unfold into a friendship in which these vulnerable individuals are no longer despised or ignored, but in which they become respected subjects with whom one can enter into joyful communion. Still, in a society that promotes autonomy, competition, and profitability, vulnerability does not enjoy a fine reputation. Therefore, friendships among and with vulnerable people disturb our vision of society, and many struggles still need to be fought before these kinds of friendships can be considered as ordinary and even desirable. These struggles are the price to pay to experience the joy of friendship. "Pleasure always springs from struggle," Vanier writes to his friend Julia, but for those who have had the privilege of living a true friendship with someone extremely vulnerable, they know the price is worth it.[6]

In my own research I have built on Jean Vanier's intuition of vulnerability as a positive dimension of our humanness, nourishing my understanding of who God is and what it means to be human before God for all people, with and without (recognized) disabilities. The vulnerability of people with disabilities becomes as such paradigmatic for our understanding of who we are as human beings. In the growing body of disability literature there is an important segment of work dedicated to the specific contribution of people with disabilities to our understanding of reality. Indeed, Brian Brock and Eva Feder Kittay are only two examples of researchers who testify on how their experience as parents of a child with a disability has shaped their worldview and enhanced their understanding of life.[7] This makes me wonder: if the vulnerability that comes with the disabilities of Adam and

4. Brown, *Daring Greatly*.
5. Kristeva and Vanier, *Leur regard perce nos ombres*.
6. Kristeva and Vanier, *Leur regard perce nos ombres*.
7. Among others: Kittay, *Learning from My Daughter*; Brock and Byassee, *Disability*; Matthews, *Pope John Paul II*; Romero, "Happiness of 'Those Who Lack'"; Young, *Arthur's Call*.

Sesha (the researchers' children) can be seen positively, as a source of good, how then can we relate it to the goodness of God? I believe the answer is love. Indeed, there cannot be love without vulnerability. You cannot love if you are not open, and thus exposed, to others. Hence, God who is almighty in love, must also be almighty in vulnerability. Let me get back to that later.

First, I would like to ponder this curious fact: from the very moment researchers started to try to give a more positive interpretation to vulnerability, I was struck by the fact that others outrightly started to reject it. In a recent congress on fragility in Quebec,[8] Canadian theologian Jean-Guy Nadeau openly rejected a vision of "cute vulnerability." According to Nadeau, the danger is that "emotional vulnerability" comes to overshadow other types of vulnerability and that vulnerability understood positively ends up taking up all the space. To talk about "positive vulnerability" to someone who is suffering from a major depression and who is on the verge of collapse, Nadeau argues, simply makes no sense. Like Nadeau, outspoken disability theologians like Petre Maican or Cristina Gangemi, who prefers *valu-ability* to *vulner-ability*, have also expressed their suspicion toward "positive vulnerability."[9]

Also, I am only too aware of the extremely difficult downsides of vulnerability, which I have never tried to hide. For example: in my interpretation of the Parable of the Talents,[10] I use the image of *heavy* bags to refer to the talents, which I suggest can be seen as God-given *vulner-abilities*. The fact that these vulnerable talents are heavy, and thus difficult to carry, illustrates the complicated aspects of vulnerability. When you are weak and lonely and depressed, you are extremely vulnerable, and just getting through the day may feel like carrying a ten-ton-bag up a hill . . . alone. The "heavy bag" dimension of vulnerability cannot be romanticized; there is nothing *cute* about it. However, vulnerability should not be limited to this dimension of heaviness, of brokenness. Leonard Cohen once sang that "there is a crack in everything, that's how the light gets in."[11] Indeed, without the porous cracks that characterize our being and make us vulnerable, human beings could neither be able to receive the light of love nor could they make their own love shine on others in relationships. Yet, entering into a relationship is never without some danger; it is always an opening to life and at the same time a potential exposure to threat and to hurt. Why did

8. "La fragilité—Dynamiques, postures et appels." Annual congress of the Société canadienne de théologie, May 24–25, 2021.

9. Maican, "Vulnerability and Solidarity"; Gangemi, "For The Wonder of Who I Am."

10. Cooreman-Guittin, "Growing in Humanity."

11. Cohen, "Anthem."

the creator see fit that it should be the very crack that exposes us to injury, that allows us to love? While this remains a mystery to me, I am convinced that it is not without reason. Of course, vulnerability can never be an excuse for harmful behavior. Still, if as theologians, we dismiss vulnerability as the mere openness that exposes us to manipulative and/or aggressive behavior, we are throwing the baby out with the bathwater. It is not the crack that is problematic; it is what we do with it. At least, that is what I think.

That cracks can be valuable is not a modern idea, it is in fact part of ancient wisdom. *Kintsugi*, for example, is an old Japanese art form that involves restoring broken pots and pottery with lacquer and gold powder. *Kintsugi* is built on the idea that by embracing flaws and imperfections, you can create an even stronger, more beautiful work of art. Without cracks, no *kintsugi*. The well-known tale of the Chinese water-bearer and the cracked pot[12] is just another example of how old stories value human vulnerability as an enrichment of our humanity.

Now, the tension between all these different appreciations of vulnerability obviously begs the question of a more complete description of the phenomenon. In the next section I dwell on the works of French theologian and medical doctor Marie-Jo Thiel to give a more nuanced understanding of vulnerability.

Vulnerability as Existential Porosity

In *La santé augmentée*, Marie-Jo Thiel develops her own definition of vulnerability, which she sees not only as a societal phenomenon—as a consequence of unequal economic systems—or as an inherent property of life in its capacity to be harmed, but also as an essential dimension of what it means to be human.[13] Articulating these last two characteristics, she writes: "Vulnerability refers to an existential situation where the subject knows that s/he is affected, touched and exposed in her/his very being."[14] She immediately adds that "through this constitutive porosity others reach out to me, men and women and the wholly Other, from whom I receive myself and to whom I can give myself."[15] There is indeed no relationship—no love—possible without this "existential porosity," this disquieting vulnerability, that frightens us so. And it is because it necessarily inscribes us in the

---

12. See "Cracked Pot."
13. Thiel, *La santé augmentée*.
14. Thiel, *La santé augmentée*, 242.
15. Thiel, *La santé augmentée*, 243.

inter-human relational game that we can consider it as an essential dimension, a cornerstone of our humanity.

Nevertheless, even if we perceive it as constitutive of our humanity, vulnerability remains difficult to accept. Does anyone really long to be vulnerable? Marie-Jo Thiel writes:

> Vulnerability is only accepted and acceptable insofar as there are one or more persons present around us, capable of recognition and closeness, of solicitude and empathy, encouraging a relational autonomy that does not take advantage of the other's weakness, but engages *with* him or her, a host who welcomes as much as he or she is welcomed, in a gracious accompaniment in which we share the same *pagnon*/bread, each one in a different way, and without obliging the other, on the contrary.[16]

I can only agree with Marie-Jo Thiel: it is undeniably crucial to have people around you who are capable of solicitude and closeness when you are in a situation of great vulnerability. Bringing people with different (vulner)abilities together is also the intuition at the core of L'Arche's philosophy.[17] However, I have realized, through informal conversations with colleagues and friends, that despite the presence of loved ones around us, the fear of becoming more and more vulnerable—like in old age—remains: fear of being sick, fear of being a burden, fear of losing one's dignity, fear of becoming dependent on others. Hence, vulnerability—and the dependence that so often goes hand in hand with it—doesn't become acceptable just because a presence is guaranteed for an extremely vulnerable person. For my friends, it seems as if dignity cannot be associated with dependence on the care of others. In our Western societies, where we brandish autonomy as a weapon to guarantee dignity, the fact of depending on others for the banal gestures of daily life is often felt as an attack on dignity, as an occasion for shame, as an acknowledgment of one's unwanted vulnerability.

Yet vulnerability, as an existential porosity, has been inscribed since the dawn of time in what it means to be human. In the opening pages of the Bible, the creation stories depict a dependent and vulnerable humanity, which is paradoxically fully in the image of God. This vulnerability and this dependence that we find so complicated to live with are also highlighted in a singularly empowering way by Jesus in the evening of his life, in the story of the feet washing in the gospel of John.[18] By this extraordinary gesture, Jesus shows that in order to *meet* God, it is human beings that we always must

---

16. Thiel, *La santé augmentée*, 251.
17. See the description on their website, "About L'Arche."
18. Cooreman-Guittin, "Looking at Dependence."

take care of. If we want to *love* God, it is human beings whom we always must love. The opposite is also true: we must always allow ourselves to be loved *by others*, because it is only through the love of others that God can reveal God's love for us.

But what a complicated task it is, to let oneself be loved by others! In homilies and in catechetical tools, it is generally emphasized how, in the account of the foot washing, Jesus enjoins us to put ourselves at the service of our neighbors. I remember the list of services to be rendered to our families that we received on Maundy Thursday in our Catholic primary school. We all wanted to follow the example of Jesus who calls us to be of service to others. However, the attitude of service is only part of the mission to which we are called in this story. And this might be the unexpected twist of this ancient story for our time: "Do you understand what I have done for you?" Jesus asks us. And we respond, "Yes, Lord, you invite us to be of service to others." That is fair enough, but it is only half the answer. We are too quick to forget that Jesus asks us to wash *one another's* feet—the adverbial reciprocity is beyond doubt. There is the service to be rendered and the service to be accepted. Rendering service can only be done by kneeling like Jesus before the other, in a posture of complete humility. Accepting the reciprocated foot washing means accepting one's vulnerability, one's existential porosity, and daring to be interdependent. Relationships of care and mutual aid thus become a holy place, for they reveal something of God's love for human beings.[19] This is obviously true for the sick, for the elderly, for the dependent, but it is true for each of us, whatever our state of health. We all need one another, we all need to learn to acknowledge our vulnerability, because this existential porosity enables us to love and be loved. It is a gift from God; it is part of what the Creator designed for human beings from the very beginning. Learning to accept this gift is a lifelong challenge.

Acknowledge and Accept Our Vulnerability

This is precisely where the problem lies: in our Western societies we idolize autonomy. It is very hard to acknowledge vulnerability for someone who does not know how to receive and does not know how to ask either. These postures are considered to be those of weak people, reserved for those who live on assistance. Let me just illustrate this with a very recognizable example: my friend and colleague Bethany, a renowned theologian of disability,

---

19. See Swinton, "Gentle Discipleship."

told me how, when she was ill last summer, she preferred to pay for food-delivery rather than to accept a meal from people of her community.[20]

This shows how even in Christian education there is an over-emphasis on giving and generosity as a source of charity, a source of good. The universal mechanism of exchange brought to light by Marcel Mauss—in the reciprocating of giving and receiving—seems to be self-evident.[21] The necessary initial step for creating social relationships is the act of giving; this obliges the receiver to accept the gift, for to refuse to receive is to reject the social bond; and reciprocating is obligatory, for not to reciprocate means to lose honor and status. What seems to have gone wrong, especially within the contemporary framework of care and relationships, is that in our Western societies people have forgotten how to accept a gift, especially when the recipient is under the impression that he or she will never be able to reciprocate. Or, as in Bethany's example, when we feel we don't have the right to disturb others because we have the financial means to pay for care, for service, for help.

In an interview on French catholic radio (RCF) following the publication of his book *Recevoir et rendre*, theologian-philosopher Pascal Ide brings to light an aspect often neglected in the dynamics of giving: namely that we need to receive *before* we can give.[22] Just as we need to breathe in first in order to breathe out, so we need to fill our reservoir before we can give. "It is when we forget that we need to receive first that we are at risk of burn-out," Ide explains.[23] Drawing from an image used by Saint Bernard, he shows that we are not *channels* who merely pass on gifts to others, but that we are above all *vessels*. Indeed, in order to be able to give or transmit what we have received, there is a moment when we must take the time to receive and to let ourselves be filled. Some time is required to appropriate what we have received. It is important to take the time to savor the gift received in one's heart; the gift in return will be all the more gushing and the link between giver and receiver all the deeper. Again, according to Pascal Ide, the process of Marcel Mauss's exchange dynamics cannot be limited to three movements: giving-receiving-reciprocating. We must add a fourth step to the process: a time for re-receiving or receiving-in-return. If we do not want to be accused of condescension or paternalistic assistance-providing, we should be aware that the action of giving requires putting oneself on the

---

20. My friend and colleague Bethany McKinney-Fox.

21. Mauss, *Gift*.

22. Ide, *Recevoir et rendre*. Hans Reinders developed this idea in *Receiving the Gift of Friendship*, 315–22.

23. In a radio interview, "Le Don, Cette Dynamique."

level of the one who receives: I put myself on this level when I accept to receive-in-return. Thus, we see that in giving, something goes out of me to the other—and that in receiving, I open myself to the gift of others while at the same time I become capable of giving back and/or giving further. All four steps require an openness, a porosity to the other, yes: vulnerability—this hollowness created by donation/reception allows the Spirit to circulate, enriching each participant through their mutual presence to one another.

For this four-step process to work throughout an entire life-span, it is important that our children learn from an early age to ask and receive well, that they become aware of the existential porosity that makes the dynamic of giving possible and that they learn to accept it. The evangelist Matthew must have been aware of this, for he insists heavily on the believer's duty to ask (Matt 7:7; Matt 10:8; Matt 21:22). There is a role in the education of children still to be filled, namely to teach them to ask, and to recognize their vulnerability, making it easier for them to accept dependency throughout their entire life. This is a small pedagogical and anthropological revolution, because it goes against our desire for autonomy, but I believe this is necessary and inevitable if we want to build the kingdom of God together. Additionally, vulnerability does not only challenge us in our anthropological perceptions, it also shakes up our representations of God.

God, Almighty in Vulnerability

If, as I believe, vulnerability is an essential and good aspect of our common humanity, in what way does it relate to God? Marie-Jo Thiel writes:

> Human beings receive the example of their God offering humanity the grace of God's vulnerability in God's Son Jesus, so that from now on all can live by the grace of the Spirit of the Father and of the Son in whom everything, including death, can be grace.[24]

Thiel is of course not the only theologian who reads vulnerability into the triune God through the incarnation of God's Son. Third-century author Origen already stated that God became flesh because God was moved by the suffering of humanity.[25] Much closer to us, François Varillon and Maurice Zundel have developed their theological reflections along similar lines, long before Jean Vanier wrote *Jésus vulnérable*.[26]

---

24. Thiel, *La santé augmentée*, 252.
25. Origen, *Exegetical Works on Ezekiel* 6, 195.
26. Vanier, *Jésus vulnérable*.

In Jesus Christ we can see how vulnerability is hinged at power in God: Christ accomplishes the saving power of God. This is also why the cross is the manifestation of salvation for the foolish and the weak and why the one who dies on the cross and rises again can be called the power of God in action.[27] According to another French theologian, Marc Vial, the vulnerability of God must be understood as referring to the Passion: "For all that, it is precisely this particular death . . . that constitutes what we could call the 'matrix' of the power of God: it is in this death, which is real, that the power of God has really unfolded."[28] I would like to take it even further: far from wanting to evacuate the omnipotence (saving in love) of God and wanting to replace it with divine vulnerability, it seems to me important to keep these two concepts together. Vulnerability is not just a modality of divine power, nor is it a simple aspect of God's being. God is vulnerability; God is power. God is all-powerful in the vulnerability that is in each of us, in the powerful as well as in the humble. It is from within this vulnerability that God acts *in us* and *through us* and puts us in a position to love, to receive, and to give. In this, vulnerability is empowering. It is the place from where God acts to make us grow in humanity, bringing us closer to God, ultimately uniting us to God's divinity.

Vulnerability is an integral part of God's divinity. It is also an integral part of our humanity. It is where our divinity and our humanity overlap. Let me try to illustrate this with my interpretation of the parable of the talents (Matt 25:14–30). In this parable the Master (God), gave heavy weights (*talanta* in Greek), bags filled with gold, to three of his servants. Now, imagine these bags were vulnerabilities: very complicated to live with, but also of unmeasurable worth. The first two servants use their *talanta* to grow in love, they invest in relationships—and when the Master returns they are invited to share in his joy. The third servant received only one bag; he is the least vulnerable of the servants, but he can't come to terms with his own vulnerability. He hides it away, in a hole under the ground and pretends to be invulnerable. When the Master returns, his verdict is merciless: "throw that worthless servant outside, into the darkness." The third servant did not enter God's plan for humanity, he refused the project of being-in-relation, of interdependence and by that, he put himself out of play. When human beings become insensitive to relationships, when they refuse their God-given vulnerability, they wither . . . and die.

The powerful, like the third servant in the parable of the talents, tend to hide their vulnerability, while for people in situations of extreme

---

27. 1 Cor 1:18.
28. Vial, "Croix du Christ."

vulnerability, it is not possible to claim invulnerability. Yet all these people have difficulty conceiving of their vulnerability as the place from within which God addresses them, as the place where God approaches them. Far from any attempt to bring the "divinization of the human" (*theosis*) closer to any kind of transhumanism, the understanding of a vulnerable God becomes an injunction to each human being to accede to his or her vulnerability. This vulnerability should not be seen as a failure to live up to an all-too-human idea of perfection, but as an original and unique path to the creative capacity that unites us to God. If God is vulnerable—and strong—this has an unsuspected effect: coming to terms with our own vulnerability becomes an indispensable step in *theosis*. For David Bentley Hart, divinization is not just a distant, unattainable horizon, nor is it a post-human chimera promised by transhumanists; rather, for the Orthodox theologian, it is the glory hidden deep within every human being, regardless of ability or vulnerability. It is "a glory... waiting to be revealed, a beauty and dignity and power of such magnificence and splendor that, could we see it now, it would move us either to worship or to terror."[29]

And What about Jean Vanier?

I started by making the point that it is not the crack that is problematic, it is what we do with it. Sometimes, vulnerabilities give rise to sinful, abusive, and even criminal behavior. The third servant in the parable certainly crossed that line. I wonder whether I should not consider Jean Vanier like this third servant; unable to come to terms with his own history of (moral) vulnerability, about which there is nothing *cute* to be said, he decided to hide it away, apparently moved to terror as to the consequences of facing it.

In an article on how vulnerability relates to sexual abuse, Marie-Jo Thiel defends the idea that the denial of one's vulnerability leads to abuse of power.[30] She wonders why ordained priests and religious people, who have accepted to become vulnerable in following Christ, offering their lives for and to love, become outright predators. She suggests that the denial of their own vulnerability is among the reasons these men become abusers. Maybe that is why Vanier never spoke about the downsides of vulnerability? Did God cry out to Jean Vanier from within this place of horror? We don't know, but I can only believe that God did. There have been explicit warnings from Jean Vanier's Catholic hierarchy about the illicit activities and harmful doctrine of Thomas Philippe, which Vanier chose to ignore. The rest is history.

29. Hart, "Anti-Theology of the Body."
30. Thiel, "La vulnérabilité."

Much of what Vanier wrote about vulnerability remains valid, though it needs to be completed with more nuanced interpretations of the concept, like I stated *supra*. This deals with the anthropological part of my contribution and I could have made the same argument if Jean Vanier had not "fallen." I do however think his testimony—the "exemplification" as Stanley Hauerwas called it—on the issue of vulnerability has lost its credibility for moral reasons too.[31] And I think I cannot sever the anthropology from the morality. In his correspondence with Julia Kristeva, Vanier wrote, "We humans are made for encounter, encounter as an end in itself. In a real encounter, we see each other's eyes, *we touch each other's bodies with reverence*, we hear the sound of each other's voices."[32] How can we continue to read this after Michèle-France Pesneau's harrowing description of how she was raped in Eric Quintin's documentary *Religieuses abusées, l'autre scandale de l'Église?*[33] For me, there is no way out. The fate of the third servant in the parable clearly shows that refusing to enter into God's plan for vulnerable creation, one will lose what was given. There is a huge caveat here: the parable's interpretation is charged with eschatological connotations (salvation or damnation) and I wouldn't want anyone to think I am speculating on Vanier's fate in the eschaton. I believe in a merciful God, and in Jesus Christ who died for our sins. This being said, I think that the parable was meant to give us guidance on this side of eternity. And so, in doing what he did, Vanier, like the third servant, chose to not confront his own history of vulnerable brokenness and in so doing, he went against God's wish for openness and honesty in respectful and loving relationships.

This, however, is not the end of the parable. The master of the parable claims back the bag of gold given to the third servant (Matt 25:28) and thus what this servant had is taken from him and given to the servant with the ten heavy bags—in my reading the most vulnerable of the servants. This is paramount: what Vanier had—i.e., his idea of valuable vulnerability—doesn't lose in value. On the contrary, it is so valuable that it is given to others. In her analysis of Vanier's writings, Gwennola Rimbault rightly stated that chaff does not spoil the good wheat.[34] It is upon those other than Vanier to separate the wheat from the chaff. It is upon them to care for what he had and go to work with it. This puts a huge responsibility on all the others, among whom I count persons with and without disabilities.

---

31. Hauerwas, "Why Jean Vanier Matters."
32. Kristeva and Vanier, *Leur regard perce nos ombres*, 26 (italics added).
33. Eric Quintin, dir. *Religieuses abusées*.
34. Study Commission, *Synthesis*, 121–23.

Others have indeed taken Jean Vanier's ideas and built upon them to write very powerful works. They have helped us gain a better understanding of vulnerability. It is to these works that I started looking for anthropological tools to reflect on the concept of vulnerability. When I talk about the importance of encounter, I prefer to cite Pia Matthews, who stated: "Encountering the other person is not simply a surface affair. . . . Encounter is not simply 'coming across' or meeting another. The gospels tell us that when Jesus encounters the men and women of his day, in that encounter is present a transforming power, yet a power that also respects the person's freedom. Encounter is always a path to conversion, communion and solidarity."[35] When I talk about vulnerability, I cite my colleague Laurent, who has a disabling disease but still considers himself to be an asset for his friends; I cite Thomas Reynolds and Marie-Jo Thiel, David Doat, or Agata Zielinski, and François Odinet.[36] These authors have taken the reflection on vulnerability to another level, fully acknowledging the downsides while not ignoring its valuable dimensions, they have shifted the focus away from the one-sided overtly positive view that Vanier wanted to confine it to and brought us to a more nuanced comprehension.

In conclusion, I think we have to move beyond Vanier when reflecting on vulnerability, for both anthropological and moral reasons. What he said on this issue only keeps its value if we enhance it with our own reflections and make his ideas bear fruit through our own works. We have the responsibility to use these ideas, and we can do so without referring to the life of Vanier. For my friends and colleagues who would prefer to dismiss the language of vulnerability all together, I would like to emphasize that to be vulnerable is to be valuable. Arguably, the concept of vulnerability is so negatively connoted in our Western societies that the language of existential porosity, in my opinion, offers a much better framework to work around this notion. All of us, like the most vulnerable servants in the parable of the talents, are now in charge of bringing together both the valuable and complicated dimensions of our existential porosity, thus glorifying our God, almighty in vulnerability. All together we have the charge to make it clear that the answer to the question in the title of this article (who wants to be vulnerable?) will be: *We!*

---

35. Matthews, "Life in Christ," presentation given by Pia Matthews in October 2017 during the congress organized by the Pontifical Council for New Evangelization: "Catechesis and Persons with Disabilities: A Necessary Engagement in the Daily Pastoral Life of the Church."

36. Reynolds, *Vulnerable Communion*; Thiel, *Souhaitable vulnérabilité?*; Doat, "La vulnérabilité"; Zielinski, "Reconnaissance de la vulnérabilité"; Odinet, *Les premiers ressuscités*.

Bibliography

"About L'Arche." L'Arche, n.d. https://www.larche.org/about-larche/.
Brock, Brian, and Jason Byassee. *Disability: Living into the Diversity of Christ's Body*. Grand Rapids, MI: Baker, 2021.
Brown, C. Brené. *Daring Greatly: How the Courage to Be Vulnerable Transforms the Way We Live, Love, Parent, and Lead*. New York: Gotham, 2012.
Burghardt, Madeline. "Brokenness/Transformation: Reflections on Academic Critiques of L'Arche." *Disability Studies Quarterly* 36 (2016). https://dsq-sds.org/article/view/3734.
Cohen, Leonard. "Anthem." Track 5 on *The Future*. Compact Disc, Columbia Records, 1992.
Cooreman-Guittin, Talitha. "Growing in Humanity: On Vulnerability, Capacitation, and Encounter in Religious Education: A Christian Practical Theological Approach." *Religious Education* 114 (2019) 143–54.
———. "Looking at Dependence: Vulnerability and Power in the Gospel of the Foot Washing." *Journal of Disability & Religion* 25 (2021) 4–14.
"The Cracked Pot." Moral Stories, n.d. https://www.moralstories.org/the-cracked-pot/.
Doat, David. "La vulnérabilité: Esquisse d'une reconstruction conceptuelle." *Revue de théologie et de philosophie* 148 (2016) 733–54.
"Le Don, Cette Dynamique Invisible qui Structure la Société." *RCF Radio*, November 23, 2023. https://www.rcf.fr/articles/bien-etre-et-psychologie/le-don-cette-dynamique-invisible-qui-structure-la-societe.
Gangemi, Cristina. "For the Wonder of Who I Am, I Praise You!" *Journal of Disability & Religion* 20 (2016) 352–60.
Hart, David Bentley. "The Anti-Theology of the Body." *The New Atlantis* 9 (2005) 65–73.
Hauerwas, Stanley. "Why Jean Vanier Matters: An Exemplary Exploration." In *Knowing, Being Known, and the Mystery of God: Essays in Honor of Professor Hans Reinders: Teacher, Friend, and Disciple*, edited by Bill Gaventa and Erik de Jongh, 229–40. Amsterdam: VU University Press, 2016.
Ide, Pascal. *Recevoir et rendre: Les dynamiques de réciprocité dans les organisations*. Paris: Nouvelle Cité, 2021.
Kittay, Eva Feder. *Learning from My Daughter: Valuing Disabled Minds and Caring that Matters*. New York: Oxford University Press, 2019.
Kristeva, Julia, and Jean Vanier. *Leur regard perce nos ombres*. Paris: Fayard, 2011.
Maican, Petre. "Vulnerability and Solidarity: An Improbable Connection." *Journal of Disability & Religion* 25 (2021) 55–67.
Masters, Anne. "Rethinking Charity." *Concilium* 5 (2020) 69–79.
Matthews, Pia. *Pope John Paul II and the Apparently "Non-Acting" Person*. Herefordshire, England: Gracewing, 2013.
Mauss, Marcel. *The Gift*. Mansfield Center, CT: Parlux, 2005.
Odinet, François. *Les premiers ressuscités: les pauvres, maîtres en résurrection*. Paris: Éditions Facultés jésuites de Paris, 2021.
Origen of Alexandria. *Exegetical Works on Ezekiel: The Fourteen Homilies and the Greek Fragments of the Homilies, Commentaries and Scholia: Text and Translation*. Ancient Texts in Translation 2. Edited by Roger Pearse. Ipswich: Chieftain, 2014.
Quintin, Eric, dir. *Religieuses abusées, l'autre scandale de l'Église?* Documentary, ARTE France, 2019.

Reinders, Hans S. *Receiving the Gift of Friendship: Profound Disability, Theological Anthropology, and Ethics*. Grand Rapids: Eerdmans, 2008.

Reinders, Hans S., and Cristina Gangemi. "Does L'Arche Need Another Saint?" In *Disciples and Friends: Investigations in Disability, Dementia, and Mental Health*, edited by Armand Léon van Ommen and Brian R. Brock, 117–38. Waco, TX: Baylor, 2022.

Reynolds, Thomas E. *Vulnerable Communion: A Theology of Disability and Hospitality*. Grand Rapids: Brazos, 2008.

Romero, Miguel. "The Happiness of 'Those Who Lack the Use of Reason.'" *The Thomist* 80 (2016) 49–96.

Study Commission Mandated by L'Arche International. *Synthesis of the Report Control and Abuse, an Investigation on Thomas Philippe, Jean Vanier, and L'Arche*. Châteauneuf-sur-Charente, France: Frémur, 2023.

Swinton, John. "Gentle Discipleship: Theological Reflections on Dementia." *ABC Religion and Ethics*, blog, July 10, 2016. https://www.abc.net.au/religion/gentle-discipleship-theological-reflections-on-dementia/10096784.

Thiel, Marie-Jo. *La santé augmentée, réaliste ou totalitaire?* Montrouge: Bayard, 2014.

———. *Souhaitable vulnérabilité?* Strasbourg: PUStrasbourg, 2016.

———. "La vulnérabilité, clé d'interprétation de la crise systémique des abus dans l'Église catholique." *Revue d'éthique et de théologie morale* (2023/HS), Éditions du Cerf, 45–58.

Vanier, Jean. *Jésus vulnérable*. Paris: Salvator, 2015.

Vial, Marc. "Croix Du Christ et Puissance de Dieu." In *La Sagesse et La Folie de Dieu*, edited by Hans-Christoph Askani and Christophe Chalamet, 157–73. Genève: Labor et Fides, 2017.

Young, Frances. *Arthur's Call: A Journey of Faith in the Face of Severe Learning Disability*. London: SPCK, 2014.

Zielinski, Agata. "Reconnaissance de la vulnérabilité: vers une éthique de la sollicitude." In *L'éthique de la dépendance face au corps vulnérable*, edited by Bernard N. Schumacher, 251–73. Toulouse: ERES, 2019.

Chapter Five

Putting Aside Charisma for Charism
A "New Springtime" for L'Arche

Pia Matthews

Introduction

L'Arche International and the survivors of sexual abuse perpetrated by Jean Vanier share a common goal: "to help L'Arche to reflect on the past, and to avoid any similar events in the future."[1] In coming forward, survivors had to overcome significant barriers, notably the "charismatic personality" of Vanier himself and his "predominant position" in L'Arche.[2] To reflect on the past in order to inform the future, this chapter explores the notion of charismatic personality, a danger faced by many new ecclesial movements such as L'Arche that emerged in the twentieth century as part of the "new springtime" of Christian activity,[3] and the chapter offers a contrasting theology of charism. Attention to the authentic lived witness of L'Arche as it confronts the pain of the past with transparency to strengthen its accompaniment and

---

1. L'Arche International, "Summary Report," para. 25; Study Commission, *Control and Abuse*, 20.
2. L'Arche International, "Summary Report."
3. John Paul II, *Homily, Eucharistic Celebration*, 2.

diligent oversight will hopefully identify renewal in the founding inspiration of L'Arche.

L'Arche: A New Movement of Charism

Charism as divine gift is part of the vocabulary of the New Testament. *Charism* also describes the Spirit-led emergence of monastic and religious orders, communities, and new lay movements. All of these emerge as ways of evangelization and living out the Gospel. The twentieth century saw a flourishing of new movements spurred on by the growth of Catholic Social Action, the promotion of an active lay apostolate incentivized by the Second Vatican Council's universal call to holiness, and the desire to engage with new social problems. The Catholic Church understood this flourishing as "the manifest action of the Holy Spirit" where God gives people "special gifts," charisms, for the service of others, and in communion with others and pastors.[4]

Notably, the Second Vatican Council warned of the temptation to domination. It reminded people gifted with this apostolate of the need for "a continuous exercise of faith, hope and charity"; constant conversion from ill will, deceit, and hypocrisy; and a holding to the virtues related to social behavior, to "honesty, sense of justice, sincerity, courtesy, moral courage."[5]

New ecclesial movements like L'Arche are an expression of a "new springtime" for Christianity in continuity with the outpouring of the Spirit at Pentecost.[6] Each movement has a unique charism, gifted to it by the Spirit, that is located in the inspiration of its founding event. Significantly, charisms are gifts to be shared, they are not given for the benefit of the person who receives them. Moreover, as Pope Francis explains, "it is always necessary to keep watch over the charism" so that it does not lead to distortions.[7]

Charisma and Charism

Jesus was no stranger to the activities of charismatics, people who claimed to be prophets, worked wonders, and cast out demons in his name. Indeed, Jesus spoke severely to those who said that they witnessed to the Lord but

---

4. Second Vatican Council, *Apostolicam Actuositatem*, 3, 27.
5. Second Vatican Council, *Apostolicam Actuositatem*, 8, 4.
6. John Paul II, *Homily, Eucharistic Celebration*, 2.
7. Francis, *Address to Members of the Neocatechumenal Way*, para. 3.

in fact were "evil doers," who did not do the Father's will.[8] Similarly, St. Paul observed that a person might have the faith to move mountains but if they did not have love then they were nothing.[9]

The idea that a person could work miracles, could move mountains, and yet not be Spirit-led seems perplexing. However, St. Thomas Aquinas explained that a sinner, in whom the Holy Spirit does not dwell, can work miracles for the benefit of others for "the wind blows where it pleases."[10] Miracles and the outworking of charisms are, after all, works of the power of God.[11] Nevertheless, Christianity asks for witness as a testimony of a life in accordance with the gospel because, unlike following a philosophical or social system, faith changes and challenges the person to new meanings. Faith commits the believer to a life in Christ.

There is a tension in the idea of charism as, on the one hand, a power for others, and on the other hand, power in itself, or power as dominion. St. Paul also met with many charismatics, in particular in Corinth, where the Christian community struggled with competition between leaders, and with spiritual elitism that was damaging the community. Writing to the Corinthians, St. Paul declared that there are many different gifts that are given by the Spirit. Yet, these charisms have one origin, the Spirit, and they serve a common purpose. Indeed, and showing that he did not see himself as a dominating leader, St. Paul urged the community to take responsibility rather than relying on him.[12] But whereas in the New Testament charism is a gift of the Spirit for the community, other secular interpretations locate charism in the personality of the person. Here *dunamis,* the dynamic power gifted by the Spirit as charism, gives way to the worldly power of charisma.

The secular world is no stranger to the power of charisma and the charismatic personality. However, to appreciate fully the power of the charismatic personality it is helpful to turn to political sociology. The German sociologist Max Weber (1864–1920) developed a comprehensive and influential analysis of charismatic leadership that effectively widened the scope of charisma beyond the New Testament understanding. Weber eliminated reference to authority and power located in the divine gift, placing authority and power in the individual. In contrast to the scriptural understanding that power is perfected in weakness precisely because it is God's power working

---

8. Matt 7:21–23.
9. 1 Cor 13:2.
10. Aquinas, *On 1 Corinthians*, 725.
11. Aquinas, *Summa Theologia* II.II.q.178a.2.
12. 1 Cor 14:20; Ehrensperger, *Paul and the Dynamics of Power*, 198–99.

through fragile human beings, under Weber's influence power as domination, power-over, became the most important element.[13]

However, as Martin Riesebrodt observed, today's popular understandings of charisma applied to celebrities and famous personalities does not fully reflect Weber's understanding.[14] This popular charisma is attractive and influential but also fickle and ephemeral. Nor does this popular account accurately reflect the power that confronted the survivors of Vanier's abuse. Weber's charismatic power was altogether more authoritative and domineering. Weber drew a distinction between three different sources of authority: authority related to custom or tradition, authority based in law, and authority derived from the personal charisma of a leader. Authority derived from personal charisma was relevant to L'Arche and Vanier. Although Weber did not definitively define charisma, a range of different interpretations have emerged. Among these interpretations Riesebrodt highlighted charisma as a "disruptive, potentially revolutionary force, . . . capable of transforming seemingly rigid social structures."[15] This sense of charisma chimes well with L'Arche's charisma as a force for change and a challenge to existing discriminatory and exclusive social structures.[16] Riesebrodt also highlighted charisma as not change but the "center" or "sacred" unalterable mystifying quality of power or authority. For many people, Vanier possessed that quasi-sacred power of authority. As one of the survivors recounted, "I realised that Jean Vanier was adored by hundreds of people, like a living saint."[17] As the Study Commission mandated by L'Arche International astutely observed, "the exercise of authority is one of the conditions for the possibility of relationships of influence and abusive acts" committed by founders.[18] This authoritative power surrounding Vanier became one of the major barriers to transparency and truth.

According to Riesebrodt, Weber relied on the German law professor Rudolf Sohm (1841–1917) to claim that all believers had a part in the one charisma to different degrees, but the highest charisma could be found in only a few. Notably, for Sohm but not for Weber, charisma was based on individual divine guidance, enabling Sohm to distance charisma from the structure and authority of institutions like the Catholic Church. Weber

---

13. 2 Cor 4:7; 12:9; Ehrensperger, *Paul and the Dynamics of Power*, 17.

14. Riesebrodt, "Charisma."

15. Riesebrodt, "Charisma," 2.

16. For an overview of the counter-cultural aspects of L'Arche, see Study Commission, *Control and Abuse*, 358–65.

17. L'Arche International, "Summary Report."

18. Study Commission, *Control and Abuse*, 39.

developed Sohm's notion of the prophet to create the idea of charismatic authority. For Weber, like prophets, charismatic leaders were needed in times of crisis. Charisma was personal, exceptional, and anti-traditional because it was an authority that did not emanate from legal or traditional authority.[19] Weber identified four features of this authority: first, voluntary recognition of the leader's charisma by his subjects; second, dissolution of certain existing normative standards, procedures, and organizational forms; third, formation of a community based on emotional attachment to the leader; fourth, proof and success in the eyes of followers for preserving belief in the leader's charisma. Weber's charisma became "a certain quality of an individual personality, by virtue of which he is set apart from ordinary men and treated as endowed with supernatural, superhuman, or at least specifically exceptional powers or qualities."[20] Weber's four features of personal charismatic authority played out clearly in Vanier's dealings with both L'Eau vive and L'Arche, with Vanier himself exercising a quasi-priestly function based on his instinctive "charismatic register."[21]

The dangers lurking in Weber's charismatic authority are self-evident. However, charisma also says something about the relationship of the charismatic leader to his disciples: charisma is about power, and the personal trust placed in the leader by his followers. As the Study Commission explained, Vanier's charismatic authority was based on emotional attachment and admiration for his abilities, "trust and belief" in his "prophetic role," and institutional legitimization.[22] Insidiously, Vanier exercised power in the form of "soft domination" in all spheres of the lives of his disciples: personal, spiritual, and professional.[23]

Charisma and the "Living Saint"

The notion of a "living saint" all too easily buys into this idea of charismatic power. The living saint seems able to do things that are unthinkable for ordinary or "normal" people. They seem to do no wrong. As the Study Commission pointed out, "for the victims, the reputation for sanctity prevents

19. Adair-Toteff, "Max Weber's Charismatic Prophets."

20. Weber, *On Charisma*, 48. The Study Commission characterizes the charismatic form of authority as having a "personal dimension, independence from institutions, and the demonstration of a singular charisma" (Study Commission, *Control and Abuse*, 353).

21. Study Commission, *Control and Abuse*, 144–46, noting that Vanier's ambitions to be ordained to the Catholic priesthood were consistently thwarted.

22. Study Commission, *Control and Abuse*, 444–64.

23. Study Commission, *Control and Abuse*, 495–97.

them from seeing the facts clearly. For the abusers it serves as a screen to hide their actions."[24] Moreover, "absolute confidence" and "blind trust" in the abuser was "reinforced" by "the apparent aura of sanctity" of Vanier in L'Arche, among Catholics and in "public and media space."[25]

St. Augustine dealt with a similar issue of individualised elevation in his remonstrations with Pelagius. According to St. Augustine, fallen human beings were not able to know or do any good thing: they were not able not to sin, *non posse non peccare*, without the aid of grace.[26] In contrast, in heaven, human beings were freer because human beings were not slaves to sin. Freed from the bondage of sin, the saints had free will, but they desired only the good and so they did not sin, *non posse peccare*. Through God's grace, sinning is impossible.[27] However, Pelagius claimed that human beings can be without sin and they can keep the commandments simply as a matter of choice.[28] Although Pelagius was deeply concerned about morality, he believed that salvation was worked out by human beings themselves. For Pope Francis, this "worship of the human will" and personal abilities leads to "self-centered and elitist complacency."[29] An aspect of this pelagian conviction lurked underneath the distorted abusive spirituality of Vanier and his mentor Father Thomas Philippe. This spirituality was shaped by rejection of the Catholic Church as an authoritative institution and by belief in an individualized revelation whereby theological argument was used to justify the choice of certain sexual practices reserved for "a small group of chosen ones."[30] The morality of acts depended not on reason but only on "private revelation."[31] As the Study Commission explained, Vanier, a self-proclaimed "professional" of spirituality, gave himself authority to convey the divine plan "as if he now were its custodian in charge of enlightening others."[32] "Groomed individuals" believed Vanier to be their "saviour," with "sanctity" and the "rightness" of deviant practices guaranteed by connection to Vanier's authority.[33]

---

24. Study Commission, *Control and Abuse*, 189.

25. Study Commission, *Control and Abuse*, 598–99.

26. Augustine, "Enchiridion," 30–32; Augustine, *Confessions*, 8.10; 10.31.

27. Augustine, "Enchiridion," 28.

28. Augustine, "Deeds of Pelagius," 16.

29. Francis, *Gaudete et Exsultate*, 57.

30. Study Commission, *Control and Abuse*, 261, 76–77, 265. See also Ulrich, "On Remaining."

31. Study Commission, *Control and Abuse*, 170–71.

32. Study Commission, *Control and Abuse*, 135.

33. Study Commission, *Control and Abuse*, 551, 576.

In contrast to an emotional and loyal commitment to a charismatic person acclaimed a "living saint," a plaster façade, with a "delusion of grandeur," Pope St. John Paul II spoke of the universal call to holiness.[34] This indicates that we cannot put individuals on pedestals or idolize them as living saints or saviors. People are capable of great evils and great goods, and much in between. Nevertheless, people are still called to holiness. As Pope St. John Paul II explained, the call to holiness is for everyone and according to the vocation of each person. Enabled by grace, holiness is the "high standard of ordinary Christian living," a standard for everyone and not only for a "few uncommon heroes."[35] For the Pope, "holiness, a message that convinces without the need of words, is the living reflection of the face of Christ."[36] Holiness is not just for the individual, rather it is for the whole community because each person is called to the perfection of love, thus helping others to grow in holiness.[37]

In terms of the process of canonization, the Catholic Church does not "make" a person a saint. Significantly, in early Christianity sainthood did not develop from the pagan practice of honoring ancestors or emperors or charismatic leaders. As St. Augustine explained in response to the Manichaean Faustus who claimed that only the perfect had sparks of the divine, every person can be a saint in heaven: worship or adoration, *latria*, is only given to God; humble reverence, *dulia*, is given to the saints in heaven notably in recognition of the gifts granted to them by God.[38]

Unsurprisingly, people who have been declared saints after their death include people with disabilities.[39] After all, heavenly eternal life is not about physical or mental perfection. God creates and rejoices in diversity. He calls us all, whatever our condition or situation, to grow in perfection, to cooperate with Him, and become what He wills us to be.[40] A life of holiness is a call to live a life of faith and allow grace to "take us by the hand."[41] As Pope St. John Paul II said, for people with disabilities, as for any other human being, it is not important that they do what others do but that they do what is truly good for them, increasingly making the most of their talents and

---

34. Study Commission, *Control and Abuse*, 97.
35. John Paul II, *Novo Millennio Ineunte*, 31.
36. John Paul II, *Novo Millennio Ineunte*, 7.
37. Second Vatican Council, *Lumen gentium*, 39.
38. Augustine, "Against Faustus," XX.21.
39. Matthews, *God's Wild Flowers*.
40. Second Vatican Council, *Lumen gentium*, 39–41.
41. ohn Paul II, *Novo Millennio Ineunte*, 19, 20.

responding faithfully to their own human and supernatural vocation.[42] We are encouraged to model ourselves on the saints, but they are help on the way; they are not due worship or praise. No one person holds everything together—only Christ.

Charism and Authentic Lived Witness

It is easy to see how charism can lose its New Testament sense and be reinterpreted into charisma and the domination of a powerful leader. It is also easy to see the charismatic attraction of the "living saint" who can do no wrong. This distortion has always been a temptation simply because we are, after all, fallen human beings. Regarding new movements, Cardinal Joseph Ratzinger, later Pope Benedict XVI, talked of the way in which the Spirit has "taken the floor," and he observed that "every irruption of the Holy Spirit always upsets human plans."[43] However, noting tendencies to "exclusivity" and "one-sidedness," or a zeal that might become fundamentalism, Ratzinger added that these new movements were not without their problems: "one could feel the power of the Spirit in them, but the Spirit works through human beings and does not simply free them from their human weaknesses."[44] By no means did Ratzinger have sexual abuse in mind, and although abuse is very far removed from simple human weakness, Ratzinger's point remains valid. Nevertheless, Ratzinger noted that the "event" of a new movement was always a "call" from God to a particular person or people. In contrast to Weber's superhuman charismatic leader, for Ratzinger this call could be accepted and lived only through an attitude of being "unceasingly shaped" and lived "charismatically" by the Spirit.[45] Ratzinger further outlined the essential characteristics of the new movements: "movements generally come from a charismatic leader and they take shape in concrete communities that live the whole gospel anew from this origin and recognize the Church without hesitation as the ground of their life, without which they could not exist."[46] Ratzinger noted that not all of these characteristics were applied in the same way in each movement, but the central theme for each member was "obedience in the following of Christ," being "struck and opened up by Christ in his inmost depth."[47] Moreover, this lived witness is not merely an

42. John Paul II, *On the Occasion*, 4.
43. Ratzinger, "Theological Locus," 481.
44. Ratzinger, "Theological Locus," 481.
45. Ratzinger, "Theological Locus," 482–83.
46. Ratzinger, "Theological Locus," 501.
47. Ratzinger, "Theological Locus," 501–2.

individual enterprise. Rather it is to "be builders of a better world, according to the '*ordo amoris*' (order of love) in which the beauty of human life is expressed."[48]

For some new movements it is problematic to identify the main characteristic of the movement with a founder who is gifted the particular charism. The brothers and Dominican priests Father Thomas and Father Marie-Dominique Philippe are cases in point. Thomas founded L'Eau vive, an international training center for young people, and he played an important role in the beginnings of L'Arche. Vanier, a member of L'Eau vive, was influenced by Thomas's own charismatic authority, and regarded himself as a "fervent disciple" of Thomas his spiritual father.[49] Before L'Arche was founded, Thomas was the subject of a canonical sanction for abusing nuns and suspended from public ministry, a suspension that he ignored.[50] Marie-Dominique was condemned by the Vatican for covering up this abuse. In 1975 Marie-Dominique founded the movement the Brothers of St. John. Only later in 2013 was it discovered that Marie-Dominique had also sexually abused women. Since this discovery the Brothers of St. John have condemned his abusive behavior and no longer recognize him as the inspiration for their movement.[51]

In 2014 new testimony revealed that Thomas had returned to his abusive behavior. L'Arche requested a canonical inquiry to investigate the allegations and the inquiry's report was published in 2015. Notably, L'Arche discerned a responsibility to continue this questioning to "shine a light" on the movement's past. L'Arche established an Independent Oversight Committee to evaluate the process and review the outcomes. L'Arche shared information about the process and provided a confidential e-mail address for anyone who wished to contact the inquiry team.[52]

Notably, the Catholic Church has recognized that good governance practices and oversight must extend to office holders themselves. This acknowledges that the office itself can give power to the holder. As the Study Commission observed, L'Arche's "permissive institutional framework" was

---

48. Benedict XVI, *Letter to Participants*.

49. Study Commission, *Control and Abuse*, 80–88.

50. For an explanation of delays in condemning Father Thomas, see the Study Commission, *Control and Abuse*, 105.

51. Heneghan, "Brothers of Saint John."

52. Letters from Stephan Posner and Stacy Cates-Carney June 2019, July 2019. It seems that a commitment to confidentiality for survivors as well as the high regard in which Vanier was held meant that the reality of abuse present since the foundation of L'Arche only became obvious after Vanier's death; Study Commission, *Control and Abuse*, 629.

"unable not only to control (and sanction if necessary) its founder, but also unable to do without him, the embodiment and 'man who made sense' of L'Arche."[53] The Dicastery for Laity, Family and Life, whose remit includes lay movements, noted that the absence of limits in terms of office "favours forms of appropriation of the charism, personalization, centralization and expressions of self-referentiality."[54] This unlimited term of office could lead not only to tensions in the community but also to "violations of personal dignity" and "real abuse." The Dicastery's General Decree *The Associations of the Faithful* has now limited the maximum length of each term of office in the central governing body of an association to five years. This limitation applies also to founders, however the limit may be dispensed where the association is still developing its charism.[55] While this attempt to limit power is part of good governance, the question of the power of the charismatic leader still remains an issue.

Charismatic gifts may originate in a founder, but they are shared and deepened.[56] Thus, the Brothers of St. John could acknowledge that Marie-Dominique Philippe was a part of the story of their movement but could also disown him as a founder. Similarly, L'Arche has distanced itself from Vanier. Significantly, the ceremony conferring the International Paul VI Award to Vanier and the members of L'Arche in 1997 demonstrated that L'Arche's founding was not the story of one charismatic man. This ceremony occurred before the revelations about Thomas or Vanier were made known and so it was not an exercise in damage limitation. Certainly, at the celebration Pope St. John Paul II remembered Thomas as the one who encouraged and inspired Vanier, because prior to 2014 that was the received history of L'Arche. However, Pope John Paul II's real insight was that the award was meant for all the people of L'Arche, notably for their "silent and generous service." He especially singled out Raphael Simi and Philippe Seux, the first two people with disabilities who he said were "the principal figures of L'Arche."[57] The founding event was the encounter with Raphael and Philippe who, along with core members and assistants, were the authentic witnesses to the charism of L'Arche. For Pope St. John Paul II, people with disabilities are "main actors" in the world. Through their witness all of us can see illness and disability in the light of Christ's death and resurrection. In this

---

53. Study Commission, *Control and Abuse*, 438–39.

54. Dicastery for Laity, Family and Life, "Associations of the Faithful," 9.

55. Dicastery for Laity, Family and Life, "Associations of the Faithful"; Francis, *Address to the Renewal*.

56. Congregation for the Doctrine of the Faith, *Iuvenescit Ecclesia*, 16.

57. John Paul II, *Address Conferring the International*, 2.

way disability is no longer an "exclusively negative event," rather it is an opportunity to release love.[58] In effect, Vanier's famous reputation rested on the selfless and silent work of members of L'Arche.[59]

Accompaniment and Oversight

Accompaniment and oversight must begin with recognizing the trauma and deep wound inflicted on the survivors of abuse. L'Arche has unreservedly condemned the actions of Vanier and Thomas. Notably, it has been actively open to the testimony of survivors, it has acknowledged the victims and the trauma they have endured, thanked them for their testimonies, and asked for their forgiveness.[60]

As a result of abuse and the covering up of abuse, the Catholic Church has had to reflect deeply and painfully on the dangerous power of personal charisma in contrast to the *dunamis* charism of the Spirit. Pope Francis asked new movements to take stock of their particular charisms; after all, "every charism is creative. It is not a statue in a museum."[61] Pope Francis also encouraged new movements to remain faithful to the original source and inspiration, the Spirit being the ultimate source, and to strive to rethink it as situations develop. He especially urged people to be aware of the dangers of self-absorption and "self-centeredness, which always leads to defending the institution to the detriment of individuals, and which can also lead to justifying or covering up forms of abuse."[62] Pope Francis noted "self-absorption prevents us from seeing mistakes and shortcomings; it hinders progress; it impedes an open review of institutional procedures and styles of governance." He urged that "instead, it is better to be courageous and to face problems with parrhesia and truth." He called for those responsible for governance "to foster and implement transparent consultation" making it clear that this should be at all levels based on the "logic of communion" whereby "all can place at the service of others their gifts and opinions in truth and with freedom."[63]

---

58. John Paul II, *World Day of the Sick I*, 5.

59. Study Commission, *Control and Abuse*, 179.

60. Posner and Cates-Carney, "Letter to International Leaders," February 2020; the Study Commission's approach was to be "respectful" to people's subjective experiences, *Control and Abuse*, 507.

61. Pope Francis, *Address to Participants in the General Assembly of the Focolare Movement*.

62. Pope Francis, *Address to Participants in the General Assembly*, para. 5.

63. Pope Francis, *Address to Participants in the General Assembly*, para. 8.

L'Arche has demonstrated courage by establishing an external independent inquiry, sharing relevant information, and seeking to be transparent. Additionally, L'Arche is undertaking a thorough and independent evaluation of its safeguarding procedures and policies; it is rolling out a new plan to support assistants to feel safe and heard; it has created a centralized whistleblowing procedure. It has also set up a safeguarding response team, partly made up of people outside L'Arche.[64]

L'Arche International's Study Commission has examined its history, culture, and anthropology, noting that the revelations of Vanier's abuse marked "a break" in L'Arche's history. The commission stated that there was now a "need to reread the past" to "move forward and deepen its particular mission and charism." The commission accepted that this rereading was to identify what was "problematic" as well as what remained "meaningful" for L'Arche. Significantly, the commission examined not just the behavior of Vanier and Thomas but also any institutional issues including governance, the exercise of authority, recruitment approaches, and the accompaniment of core members and assistants. Of pressing theological concern was the question of the spirituality of L'Arche in the light of the distorted abusive spirituality of Vanier and Thomas that had already been condemned by the Catholic Church.[65] Realistically, in answer to the question whether "ingredients for the development of controlling relationships" have disappeared in L'Arche, the Study Commission called for continued vigilance.[66]

Given the deep pain and shock in the wake of Vanier's abuse, L'Arche recognized that special accompaniment is needed for their members both with and without disabilities. "Spaces for dialogue and support" have been put in place to give people the opportunity to express their feelings, thoughts, and questions.[67] Undoubtedly, accompaniment will continue to be needed, especially when it comes to reframing the spirituality of L'Arche. For accompaniment, Pope Francis recommended taking up the "wise distinction" between the external and internal forum. The external forum concerns the "sphere of governance" and this is the place where organizational crises belong; the internal forum concerns the "sphere of conscience" and this is where individual spiritual crises should be dealt with prudently by those who do not hold positions of governance.[68] If the sphere of governance and the sphere of conscience are mixed then this raises the possibility of

---

64. L'Arche International, "L'Arche International Inquiry."
65. L'Arche International, "Summary Report."
66. Study Commission, *Control and Abuse*, 497.
67. Posner and Cates-Carney, "Letter to International Leaders," February 2020.
68. Francis, *Address to Participants in the General Assembly*, para. 6.

an abuse of power: what should be made in confidence risks being made public thus eroding trust and the possibility of disclosure; what should be made in public risks falling under concerns about confidentiality and may remain hidden.

Commenting on the crimes of sexual abuse in his *Motu Proprio*, personal decree, *Vos estis lux mundi*, Pope Francis stated that any abuse or cover up had to be reported to the appropriate church authorities, "save where to do so would be a breach of the sacramental seal."[69] Accusations of abuse officially reported to an ecclesiastical authority belong in the external forum. Thus, according to the "Management of Allegations and Concerns Policy," part of the National Safeguarding Policies for the Catholic Church in England and Wales, "all allegations of abuse made against those working in the name of the Church, regardless of whether the allegations or concerns relate to a person's behavior in relation to their role within the Church or another setting" must be reported to the statutory authorities.[70] However, in cases where an adult with capacity refuses to consent to the making of a referral about historic abuse, consideration is given to whether the person he or she accuses has access to children who may be at risk, and the name of the accused and details of the allegation will be referred to the statutory authorities, without disclosing the name of the victim. In the case of clerics, any imposed canonical penal sanctions such as dismissal from the clerical state belong in the external forum since these penalties concern public social relationships. However, Vanier was not a cleric. Moreover, it remains the case that the confession and forgiveness of sins belongs in the sacramental internal forum. The sacramental internal forum absolutely protects the penitent and the matter disclosed by an inviolable sacramental seal, even if the penitent has not been absolved. A priest-confessor can encourage and indeed urge the penitent to disclose abuse to the ecclesiastical and statutory authorities, but the confessor remains bound by the sacramental seal.[71] Nor can the confessor oblige penitents to turn themselves over to civil justice as a condition for absolution.[72] Defence of the sacramental seal and the sanctity of Confession are not any forms of "connivance" with sin. Instead, the sacramental seal and confession provide real opportunities for the person to be honest and open in ways that would be stifled should there be the possibility of lack of confidentiality, and to be converted and transformed

---

69. As reported to Independent Inquiry Child Sexual Abuse, IICSA, *Roman Catholic Investigation Report* C.2, 9–10.

70. Catholic Safeguarding Standards Agency, "National Safeguarding Policy."

71. Beal, Coriden, and Green, *New Commentary*, Canon 983, 1163–65.

72. Apostolic Penitentiary, *Note of the Apostolic Penitentiary*.

by God's love. At the same time, the very structure and validity of confession and reconciliation call for "sincere repentance" and a "firm intention to reform."[73] Notably, evidence presented to the IICSA (Independent Inquiry into Child Sexual Abuse) pointed out that in general abusers did not believe that they were doing anything wrong and so would not be likely to confess their behavior as a sin.[74] Indeed, the inquiry heard no evidence of a perpetrator confessing to being an abuser.[75]

Moving Forward to a Springtime

When people are suffering, feeling hurt and sorrow, it is difficult to feel that there is hope ahead. However, Pope Francis explained "every crisis is a call to new maturity; it is a time of the Spirit."[76] Certainly, and in spite of a deep sense of betrayal, L'Arche is showing resilience in trying to face difficulties with truth and hope, and in drawing opportunities from these difficulties. To help new movements facing difficulties, Pope Francis has drawn a distinction between charism exercised outside the new movement, and charism exercised within. Charism exercised outside a new movement can be a witness to love that overcomes all barriers and reaches every human condition and situation. Charism exercised within a new movement would benefit from a synodal approach.[77] Synodality is not a process like a convention, parliament, or senate where people "make deals and reach consensus." Rather, a synodal approach gives a "protected space in which the Church experiences the action of the Holy Spirit."[78] This protected space is not a space where safeguarding and due process are absent. It is a safe space where people can speak with honesty, *parrhesia* or apostolic zeal, and listen with humility.[79] Pope Francis promoted the synodal approach "so that all members, as depositaries of the same charism, may be co-responsible for and participants" in the life of the movement and its specific goals.[80]

The synodal approach has implications for movements that are overly dependent on one charismatic leader. As Pope Francis observed, there is a "great temptation" for leaders to think they are indispensable, the "ones in

73. Apostolic Penitentiary, *Note of the Apostolic Penitentiary*.
74. IICSA, *Roman Catholic Investigation Report* 1.4.24.
75. IICSA, *Roman Catholic Investigation Report* L.1.31.
76. Francis, *Address to Participants in the General Assembly*, para. 6.
77. Francis, *Address to Participants in the General Assembly*.
78. Francis, *Synod for the Family*, para. 5.
79. Francis, *Greeting to the Synod Fathers*.
80. Francis, *Address to Participants in the General Assembly*, para. 8.

command," "at the center." The temptation that makes the person go from "servant to master" and leads to "domination and vanity," also makes "'eternal' the position of those who consider themselves irreplaceable, a position that always has some form of power or dominance over others." In contrast, clearly "the only irreplaceable one in the Church is the Holy Spirit, and Jesus is the only Lord."[81]

Springtime in Lived Witness

For Pope Francis, faith is communicated through witness, witness not to "our own ideas" but to the gospel. Witness is "speaking with our whole lives: living consistently . . . living Christianity as an encounter with Jesus that brings me to others."[82] Pope Francis here echoed Pope St. John Paul II. In the Christian tradition the "single witness" to the gospel message is found in the witness of the Holy Spirit flowing from "the depth of the Trinitarian mystery of God" and the human witness of the apostles at Pentecost. This human witness is lived witness, and lived witness is crucial when it comes to proclaiming the gospel and by extension the unique value of each person. But as Pope St. John Paul II stated, "only the believer who lives what he professes with his lips has any hope of being heard." The witness of a life lived in an authentically Christian way has "convincing power, even if offered in silence."[83] For Pope St. John Paul II, people with disabilities are especially effective witnesses to the gospel: by bringing into question common apprehensions about the power of autonomy, appearances, function, speed, and efficiency, by highlighting the way that "inattentiveness sharpens suffering and loneliness," by demonstrating that "faith shown in love and generosity gives strength and meaning to life," people with disabilities can demonstrate that "love is the last word" and in this they are preparing the way for Christ.[84]

God can heal all wounds, including the deep wounds of abuse and the wound of a betrayal of witness. Grace from the cross "is capable of transforming suffering and even tragedy into a source of light and hope for humanity. In this passing from death to life lies the heart of Christianity and also of your charism."[85]

---

81. Francis, *Address to the Renewal*, para. 10.
82. Francis, *Address, Vigil of Pentecost*, para. 15.
83. John Paul II, *Homily, Vigil of Pentecost*, 4.
84. John Paul II, *Homily, Jubilee of the Disabled*, 5, 7.
85. Francis, *Address to Participants in the General Assembly*, para. 9.

Bibliography

Adair-Toteff, Christopher. "Max Weber's Charismatic Prophets." *History of the Human Sciences* 27 (2014) 3–20.

Apostolic Penitentiary. *Note of the Apostolic Penitentiary on the Importance of the Internal Forum and the Inviolability of the Sacramental Seal.* June 21, 2019.

Aquinas, Thomas. *On 1 Corinthians.* Translated by Fabian Larcher. https://isidore.co/aquinas/english/SS1Cor.htm.

———. *Summa Theologia.* Translated by Fathers of the English Dominican Province. Benziger Bros. ed., 1947. https://isidore.co/aquinas/summa/SS.html.

L'Arche International. "L'Arche International Inquiry into Historic Sexual Abuse by Jean Vanier." L'Arche, n.d. https://www.larche.org.uk/news/inquiry-statement.

———. "Summary Report." L'Arche, February 22, 2020.

Augustine. "Against Faustus." In *Nicene and Post Nicene Fathers*, First Series 4. Buffalo, NY: Christian Literature, 1887.

———. *Confessions.* New York: New York Press, 1997.

———. "Deeds of Pelagius." In *Answer to the Pelagians*, edited by Roland J. Teske and John E. Rotelle, 309–76. New York: New City, 1997.

———. "Enchiridion." In *On Christian Belief*, edited by Boniface Ramsey, 273–343. New York: New City, 2005.

Beal, John, James Coriden, and Thomas Green, eds. *New Commentary on the Code of Canon Law.* New York: Paulist, 2000.

Benedict XVI, Pope. *Letter to Participants of the 2nd World Meeting of Ecclesial Movements and New Communities.* Vatican, 2006. https://www.vatican.va/content/benedict-xvi/en/messages/pont-messages/2006/documents/hf_ben-xvi_mes_20060522_ecclesial-movements.html.

Congregation for the Doctrine of the Faith. *Iuvenescit Ecclesia.* Vatican, 2016. https://www.vatican.va/roman_curia/congregations/cfaith/documents/rc_con_cfaith_doc_20160516_iuvenescit-ecclesia_en.html.

Dicastery for Laity, Family and Life. "The Associations of the Faithful." Laity, Family and Life, n.d. http://www.laityfamilylife.va/content/dam/laityfamilylife/Pdf/decreto-mandati-governo/ENG%20NotaEsplicativa%2001.06.2021%20DEF.pdf.

Ehrensperger, Kathy. *Paul and the Dynamics of Power.* London: T&T Clark, 2007.

Francis, Pope. *Address to Members of the Neocatechumenal Way.* Vatican, March 18, 2016. https://www.vatican.va/content/francesco/en/speeches/2016/march/documents/papa-francesco_20160318_movimento-neocatecumenale.html.

———. *Address to Participants in the General Assembly of the Focolare Movement.* Vatican, February 6, 2021. https://www.vatican.va/content/francesco/en/speeches/2021/february/documents/papa-francesco_20210206_focolari.html.

———. *Address to the Participants in the Third World Congress of Ecclesial Movements and New Communities.* Vatican, November 22, 2014. https://www.vatican.va/content/francesco/en/speeches/2014/november/documents/papa-francesco_20141122_convegno-movimenti-ecclesiali.html.

———. *Address to the Renewal in the Holy Spirit Movement.* Vatican, July 3, 2015. https://www.vatican.va/content/francesco/en/speeches/2015/july/documents/papa-francesco_20150703_movimento-rinnovamento-spirito.html.

———. *Address, Vigil of Pentecost with Ecclesial Movements*. Vatican, May 18, 2013. https://www.vatican.va/content/francesco/en/speeches/2013/may/documents/papa-francesco_20130518_veglia-pentecoste.html.

———. *Gaudete et Exsultate*. Vatican, 2018. https://www.vatican.va/content/francesco/en/apost_exhortations/documents/papa-francesco_esortazione-ap_20180319_gaudete-et-exsultate.html.

———. *General Audience*. Vatican, November 6, 2013. https://www.vatican.va/content/francesco/en/audiences/2013/documents/papa-francesco_20131106_udienza-generale.html.

———. *General Audience*. Vatican, October 1, 2014. https://www.vatican.va/content/francesco/en/audiences/2014/documents/papa-francesco_20141001_udienza-generale.html.

———. *Greeting to the Synod Fathers During the First General Congregation of the Third Extraordinary General Assembly of the Synod of Bishops*. Vatican, October 6, 2014. https://www.vatican.va/content/francesco/en/speeches/2014/october/documents/papa-francesco_20141006_padri-sinodali.html.

———. *Synod for the Family, Introductory Remarks*. Vatican, October 5, 2015. https://www.vatican.va/content/francesco/en/speeches/2015/october/documents/papa-francesco_20151005_padri-sinodali.html.

Heneghan, Tom. "Brothers of Saint John Denounce Sexually Abusive Founder." *The Tablet*, November 11, 2019. https://www.thetablet.co.uk/news/12199/brothers-of-saint-john-denounce-sexually-abusive-founder-.

IICSA. *The Roman Catholic Investigation Report*. November 2020. https://www.iicsa.org.uk/key-documents/23357/view/catholic-church-investigation-report-4-december-2020.pdf.

John Paul II, Pope. *Address Conferring the International Paul VI Award on Mr Jean Vanier*. Vatican, June 19, 1997. https://www.clerus.org/bibliaclerusonline/EN/fzr.htm.

———. *Homily, Eucharistic Celebration*. Vatican, May 31, 1998. https://www.vatican.va/content/john-paul-ii/en/homilies/1998/documents/hf_jp-ii_hom_31051998.html.

———. *Homily, Jubilee of the Disabled*. Vatican, December 3, 2000. https://www.vatican.va/content/john-paul-ii/en/homilies/2000/documents/hf_jp-ii_hom_20001203_jubildisabled.html.

———. *Homily, Vigil of Pentecost*. Vatican, June 2000. https://www.vatican.va/content/john-paul-ii/en/homilies/2000/documents/hf_jp-ii_hom_20000610_pentecost-vigil.html.

———. *Message for the World Congress of Ecclesial Movements and New Communities*. Vatican, May 27, 1998. https://www.vatican.va/content/john-paul-ii/en/speeches/1998/may/documents/hf_jp-ii_spe_19980527_movimenti.html.

———. *Novo Millennio Ineunte*. Vatican, 2001. https://www.vatican.va/content/john-paul-ii/en/apost_letters/2001/documents/hf_jp-ii_apl_20010106_novo-millennio-ineunte.html.

———. *On the Occasion of the International Symposium on the Dignity and Rights of the Mentally Disabled Person*. Vatican, January 5, 2004. https://www.vatican.va/content/john-paul-ii/en/speeches/2004/january/documents/hf_jp-ii_spe_20040108_handicap-mentale.html.

———. *World Day of the Sick I*. Vatican, 1992. https://www.vatican.va/content/john-paul-ii/en/messages/sick/documents/hf_jp-ii_mes_21101992_world-day-of-the-sick-1993.html.

Matthews, Pia. *God's Wild Flowers: Saints with Disabilities*. Leominster: Gracewing, 2016.

Posner, Stephan, and Stacy Cates-Carney. "Letter to International Leaders." June 2019.

———. "Letter to International Leaders." July 2019.

———. "Letter to International Leaders." February 2020.

Ratzinger, Joseph. "Theological Locus of Ecclesial Movements." *Communio Catholic Review* 5 (1998) 480–504.

Riesebrodt, Martin. "Charisma in Max Weber's Sociology of Religion." *Religion* 29 (1999) 1–14.

Second Vatican Council. *Apostolicam Actuositatem*. Vatican, 1965. https://www.vatican.va/archive/hist_councils/ii_vatican_council/documents/vat-ii_decree_19651118_apostolicam-actuositatem_en.html.

———. *Lumen gentium*. Vatican, 1964. https://www.vatican.va/archive/hist_councils/ii_vatican_council/documents/vat-ii_const_19641121_lumen-gentium_en.html.

Study Commission. L'Arche International, 2021. https://intranet.larche.org/documents/10181/2994508/Study-commission_scientific-committee_AI_final_EN.pdf/95e55b3e-f431-4b79-810f-f74bc0fb3b31.

Study Commission Mandated by L'Arche International. *Control and Abuse Investigation on Thomas Philippe, Jean Vanier and L'Arche (1950–2019)*. Châteauneuf-sur-Charente, France: Frémur, 2023.

Ulrich, Hans G. "On Remaining in God's Story as Passion." In *The Betrayal of Witness: Reflections on the Downfall of Jean Vanier*, edited by Stanley Hauerwas and Hans S. Reinders, 137–49. Eugene, OR: Wipf & Stock, 2024.

Weber, Max. *On Charisma and Institution Building*. Chicago: University of Chicago Press, 1968.

Whitehead, Charles. "The Role of the Ecclesial Movements and the New Communities in the Life of the Church." In *New Religious Movements in the Catholic Church*, edited by Michael Hayes, 15–29. London: Burns & Oates, 2005.

Chapter Six

Disabling Virtue

Patrick McKearney

What is good about L'Arche? The 2023 Report from the Study Commission mandated by L'Arche International shows us that the story we have been telling about L'Arche is wrong in more ways the one.[1] How can we state that there is anything good about L'Arche now that we know that it was founded through deception, secrecy, and manipulation? How can we hold onto an image of L'Arche as embodying an ideal of warm, vulnerable, and egalitarian intimacy when we know that Vanier created and used this image to obscure a darker, more brutal reality? Should we even question, as the report does, whether that ideal, as it was articulated in Vanier's own theology, has something wrong at the heart of it that led directly to the abuse?

Such skeptical interrogation of our projections is important in this moment, in which people across L'Arche have unanimously condemned Vanier's actions. But that will not by itself resolve the question "what is good about L'Arche?" And that is because that question requires not just a clearer apprehension of the facts, but also a debate about what the good of L'Arche is. That is, it is about not just what L'Arche, in practice, has turned out to be, but also about what we think it should be. Underneath the unanimity brought about by this particular moment, there are substantial differences between ways of articulating what L'Arche is good for, or the ethical end that

---

1. Study Commission, *Control and Abuse*.

it works toward. There exist contrasting, even competing, ethical visions of L'Arche.

One such moral imagination is evident in the response to Vanier's actions, even within a document as seemingly so simply about "the facts" as the report itself. This dominant response continues a tradition of foregrounding a particular understanding of L'Arche as fundamentally about the compassionate virtues of the nondisabled members. But my own research on L'Arche has acquainted me with a quite different one.

I have worked in a particular L'Arche community in the UK—in varying capacities such as carer, committee member, advocate, and friend—but I am also a social anthropologist who has worked on L'Arche for about a decade. Within the L'Arche community I worked in, any foregrounding of the moral virtues of the nondisabled was typically rejected. New members of the community were, instead, trained into a different perspective on L'Arche, in which the people with intellectual disabilities are the main moral actors.

In this chapter, I surface the difference between these two moral imaginaries of L'Arche: one focused around nondisabled compassion, the other around the people with disabilities. I do so in order to present the latter to audiences not familiar with it and the challenge that it presents to the former narrative. My aim in confronting us with the difference between these competing visions is to press upon us a debate about the character and purpose of L'Arche that this moment affords and demands of us.

Nondisabled Virtue

Vanier's writing emphasized the importance of a particular type of humble, vulnerable, and open compassion. He often articulated this through a contrast between a "culture of power" and a "culture of relationships."[2] He called the nondisabled to give up their attempts at power and to learn, instead, virtues of gentleness, patience, and vulnerability. He articulated encountering people with intellectual disabilities as a particular challenge on this front. This is because they are normally interpreted primarily as people who do not have many things that the "outside world" values: strength, money, status, attractiveness. It is by letting go of valuing those things, and focusing on the value of relationships themselves, that nondisabled members of L'Arche learn to form kind, open, and intimate relationships.[3] L'Arche communities

---

2. Wakefield, "Jean Vanier's World," para. 14; Vanier, *Community and Growth*; Vanier, *From Brokenness to Community*.

3. Reimer, *Living L'Arche*.

thus should embody this kind of peaceful way of relating in order to rebut the competition and violence of a contemporary capitalist and consumerist society.[4]

Vanier's seeming embodiment of these virtues was valued across the religious, political, and social spectrum. It is striking, for instance, that he was lauded in the British press by commentators from the right and the left, religious and secular.[5] Within academic circles, also, Vanier and L'Arche received positive attention from the social sciences,[6] psychology,[7] and writers on disability.[8] Once again, the virtue of compassion was the linchpin in his and L'Arche's broad appeal. Kevin Reimer's secular psychological research, for example, takes exceptional compassion as the center of the movement Vanier founded. It investigates, from that premise, how this moral virtue is cultivated and sustained at such high levels by the nondisabled members of L'Arche such that they are able to care for the people with disabilities so well.

The discipline of theology, especially theological ethics, repeatedly took up L'Arche as an important and positive example of ethical and specifically Christian community.[9] This included a veneration of Vanier and his compassionate virtue that paid strikingly little heed to denominational boundaries. It is also surprising, given what we, thanks to the report's work, now know about just how far Vanier evaded Catholic Church discipline, that he was received with similar deference within the Catholic Church. As the report itself puts it:

> For decades, in the Catholic organizations close to L'Arche and in the media, Jean Vanier appeared as the living embodiment of the Gospel, the star layperson of the Catholic renewal under the pontificate of John-Paul II.[10]

A similar sentiment is echoed by British journalist Mary Wakefield:

> Jean Vanier is now 88 and, if you ask around in Catholic circles, it's whispered he's a saint. He still lives in Trosly-Breuil, but in his spare time he's a sort of secret superhero for peace—flying

---

4. Vanier, *Community and Growth*; Hauerwas, "Seeing Peace"; Hauerwas and Vanier, *Living Gently*.

5. Wakefield, "Jean Vanier's World."

6. Angrosino, "L'Arche"; Reinders, "Human Vulnerability"; McDonald and Keys, "L'Arche"; Reimer, *Living L'Arche*; Sumarah, "L'Arche"; Angrosino, "L'Arche."

7. Reimer, *Living L'Arche*.

8. McDonald and Keys, "L'Arche"; Burghardt, "Brokenness/Transformation."

9. E.g., Ford, *Christian Wisdom*; Downey, *Blessed Weakness*; Hauerwas, "Seeing Peace"; Young, *Encounter with Mystery*; Banner, *Ethics of Everyday Life*.

10. Study Commission, *Control and Abuse*, 13.

around the world to broker between powerful players. Justin Welby called on him this year to mediate between cross bishops, and it's said he made them all wash each other's feet. Though Vanier's life has been punctuated with great accomplishments and prestigious awards, it's that first invitation to Raphael and Philippe that seems most impressive.[11]

There have occasionally been people who interpreted Vanier as virtuous as a charitable and philanthropic figure. But anyone with even a passing acquaintance with Vanier's work and L'Arche's practice know that this emphasis on compassion was never about charity—but rather about a turn towards egalitarian intimacy and reciprocity. Vanier tells the story of the founding of L'Arche in just this way. He writes that he had initially felt like it was his religious duty to provide charity to the cognitively disabled people he invited to live with him, but he discovered that he was instead forming equal relationships with them.[12] The household he had formed with "benevolent" intentions was turning out to be a familial environment in which these individuals could really belong as worthwhile members of a community, rather than as recipients of a presumptuous grace.[13]

This way of telling the story implies that L'Arche calls the nondisabled toward not charity but rather this specific kind of compassionate descent: to give up their power, individuality, and status in order to form reciprocal relations with those with disabilities.[14] This is importantly different from a model of charity that maintains those hierarchical relations in the act of giving: *noblesse oblige* only being possible if the poor are poor and the rich are rich.[15] This reading of L'Arche rejects that kind of compassion, and lauds instead the genuine renunciation of one's higher position. The virtue here is letting go of what one had, not on giving from a place of strength.

But we should also note that this model works by treating the nondisabled as in a genuinely hierarchically superior position to begin with: they really do have something to give up. Indeed, Vanier narrated his own story, and found many who would join him in doing so, as characterized precisely by this compassionate descent from worldly strength to humble compassion. If egalitarian reciprocity is the end point of this story, Vanier's initial status is key to the descent and renunciation aspects of this trope. His own and others' narrations of him typically began with his noble background—son

---

11. Wakefield, "Jean Vanier's World," para. 7.
12. Vanier, *Ark for the Poor*.
13. Spink, *Miracle*; Vanier, *Ark for the Poor*.
14. Nouwen, *Selfless Way of Christ*.
15. Douglas, *Natural Symbols*.

of the governor-general of Canada, academically talented, etc.—precisely for the contrast it made to the life he went on to lead: a humble one among humble people.[16]

Not all of the authors cited above followed Vanier completely in this way of telling the story, and Vanier's own writing was importantly ambiguous. But there are many cited here, such as Reimer and Wakefield, who followed it closely—and many more within the media, academia, and the church who did the same. This way of narrating his life reads him as exemplary, not inasmuch as he retained his hierarchical status, but inasmuch as he compassionately gave it up in service of people more needy than him.[17]

Disabling Virtue

I conducted fifteen months of ethnographic research on a L'Arche community in the UK, including working and living as an assistant in one of the houses for over a year, conducting over sixty interviews, and visiting other L'Arche communities in the UK. While working in this community, it was not uncommon for us assistants to receive praise from members of the public or local churches when we were out and about supporting a person with intellectual disabilities. People regularly described us as "volunteers" rather than workers; coding our work as compassionate inasmuch as we were sacrificing something in order to give those with disabilities a fuller life. Even friends and family began to interpret me as special inasmuch as I was able to do this work. Though they did not interpret me as some kind of altruistic saint, and generally recognized how much I valued the relationships I was forming, they would still say "I could never do it" with a distinct hint of admiration.

Much to my initial surprise, experienced assistants in L'Arche did not accept these compliments. They rejected them and were very critical of the place they came from. As one long-standing carer called Peter once told me:

> You know a lot of people idealize L'Arche, and think the assistants are very good. But sometimes that's more a way to keep your distance from it than anything.

Another long-term worker called Elina similarly claimed that the idea that we need to give compassionately to people with intellectual disabilities came from "a fear about not wanting to get involved with people." As my time in L'Arche wore on, I came to discover that this was because assistants

---

16. Spink, *Miracle*; Wakefield, "Jean Vanier's World."
17. Spink, *Miracle*.

held an alternative interpretation of L'Arche that rejected compassion, even of the humble kind, as an ethical ideal for the nondisabled because they see it as distorting relationships with people with intellectual disabilities in two interconnected ways.

The first reason is that, as one carer put it, interpreting L'Arche as a practice of giving by the nondisabled assumes that people with intellectual disabilities are primarily passive, dependent recipients of the moral gifts of others—and thus needy and burdensome in and of themselves. People in the community describe that idea as not only inaccurate but also demeaning. That is, they regard practicing self-sacrifice as only deepening the marginalization of these individuals from social and ethical life—further preventing them from ever being related to as agents who could have something to contribute to the lives of others. As Hilary once told me:

> People with learning disabilities live with loss from the day they're born. Some have been deeply loved but there are losses all along that they cannot cover up. [As assistants] we come in and help them, and therefore they are always receiving. But they know that they are of value when they have something to give.

Compassion, in other words, is an ethic of donation that makes no real space for return, and so ignores the possibility that the recipient might, themselves, be an actor, agent, and giver.

The second problem that carers in L'Arche have with the frame of compassion is that it assumes the hierarchical difference that initially separates people with and without intellectual disabilities is real. As Vanessa put it:

> L'Arche was never about "us helping them," but about the ways in which we can transform and develop together. There may be differences in our intellectual disabilities, but no difference at all in our shared humanity.

And as Laura put it:

> Living with people very close in community, it's not like you just give, you receive as well.

Carers in L'Arche work consistently to undermine the idea that the nondisabled might have a higher place in a hierarchy, from which they must descend to help these poor disabled people. They do so by critiquing the idea that the nondisabled have anything to give and that the people with intellectual disabilities need anything.

In a series of training sessions run by more experienced carers and managers in L'Arche, us carers were encouraged to see ourselves not as highly capable and generous benefactors, but rather as people who also depend on intimate relationships with others for their own well-being. Hilary, for instance, led us in reflecting on a variety of documents that spelled out L'Arche's ethos. She urged us to think of our job not as a charitable or professional act of giving but, instead, as a way of entering into relationships with people. She did not say that we needed to cultivate virtues like compassion, patience, or generosity. The only way we could enter into relationships, she said, was by learning to become more dependent and vulnerable ourselves.

This was most clearly instantiated in a ritual where members of L'Arche—disabled and not—wash one another's feet on Maundy Thursday in the build up to Easter. Hilary described the symbolic importance of the event this way:

> You, as an assistant, wash their feet all the time. But for once, allow someone else to wash your feet. You become vulnerable before them. Deep within us all we feel good when we can help somebody else. Mutuality is much more about being able to say "I need you. I can't do it on my own. And you might need me as well."

Experienced assistants rarely articulate their time in L'Arche through reference to their own acts of will—and especially through reference to their own generosity. They, instead, typically reverse this equation, and describe a moral transformation in L'Arche that reversed their initial altruistic expectations. Kim described just such a shift to me in these terms:

> Being in L'Arche has really challenged me. Just being with people with disabilities. Now I realize I'm staying because it's good for me, not because it's good for those with learning disabilities or for the community. I get much more from them day-to-day than they do from me.

Long-term carers in L'Arche frequently narrate their own story in a way that effaces their own influence upon their lives, and foregrounds that of others. Elina wove this kind of self-effacing reversal into her narrative as well:

> Like everybody, you think you're coming to make a difference. But the reality is that it changes you more than it changes the people [with disabilities]. I wanted to save the world you know. But we don't ever have that much effect. We all want to see it; I'm just the same. We all have that arrogance that we want it to be about us.

As these practices work to undermine the idea that the nondisabled are strong and have something to give, they also challenge the idea that those with disabilities are weak and in need. When newcomers and visitors to L'Arche arrive in the community they are typically subjected to a barrage of stories that emphasize the surprising agency of these individuals.[18] Every evening in the large house where I conducted my research, all five residents with cognitive disabilities, along with the assistants scheduled to support them, would share a meal. During these dinner times, more experienced carers would often tell dramatic stories in which people with cognitive disabilities are the protagonists. During one such supper during my fieldwork, the assistants around the table were talking about Sarah, a resident with severe intellectual and physical impairments that would appear to render her unable to communicate verbally and to support herself with many daily tasks. At a certain point, a long-term assistant named Maria turned to her and said:

> Sarah, when I first arrived, for a while I didn't help you have a wash. And, when I first did it, I assumed that you didn't really know what was happening. I didn't know what I was doing, and at one point I had to think for ages about what to do next. And you just sat there very patiently and quietly. When I finally worked out what the right thing to do was, you looked at me dead in the eye—and then laughed at me!

At another meal, an experienced assistant called Priya narrated an incident involving another disabled resident.

> Ensy's communication is quite difficult for me to understand. He's definitely saying something; there's no doubt. One time we were on holiday, and he began to speak about something, but I just couldn't understand it. "Are you talking about this morning when we did this?" "No. No." I went through everything I could think. He was just saying "No" to everything I said. And then I said, "I am really sorry. I don't know what you're trying to tell me." He seemed very sad and looked at me. Suddenly—I don't know why—I said, "Is it because you saw that I was sad myself?" Just before we'd sat down something had happened and I'd been sad. And we'd gone through all the things I'd done that day. "Is it because you saw I was sad?" "Yes." God, that really moved me.

People with intellectual disabilities are also placed front and center in more practical ways at all of the dinner times, communal rituals, and

---

18. McKearney, "Ability to Judge"; McKearney, "Limits of Knowing"; McKearney, "Receiving the Gift."

celebrations in L'Arche. At dinner, for instance, more experienced carers would play with Louise until she spoke words I never thought she knew, dance with Dan until he felt inspired to perform one of his comedy routines, or remind Rachel of her tradition of initiating new assistants by not-so-subtly creeping up behind them and pouring a jug of water over their head. It is never the assistants who occupy this dramatic position, but always those with disabilities who are the subject of the attention. They are the people who do something funny in the middle of a solemn moment, or whose tales are told with a sense of wonder and excitement. The outcome of all of this is an atmosphere in which each person with intellectual disabilities becomes famous within the community, more so than any carer, for their distinctive characteristics, abilities, and achievements.

These practices are so widespread in the community they are impossible to miss when one first arrives. One can get almost nowhere in this L'Arche community with the assumption intact that people with disabilities are needy and passive recipients. The only way one can interact is by relating to them as particularly potent moral actors. As carers stay on in the community, they learn how to reproduce representations of particular people with disabilities as more capable than their assistants and learn how to challenge others who do not relate to these individuals in that way.

Compassion and Charisma

When people stay in the community for longer, they learn to talk about people with intellectual disabilities as possessing and transmitting "gifts."[19] This language was widespread in L'Arche, with more senior assistants often commenting casually on someone's humor, generosity, or assertiveness as a particular "gift." People with cognitive disabilities were regularly represented—such as in the stories I related above—as possessing particularly keen, and sometimes miraculous, emotional and relational abilities that could affect others in powerful ways. More generally, assistants frequently drew attention to the ways in which people with disabilities care for them, such as when these individuals ask after them, remember their preferences, or offer them affection. People with disabilities are also often praised for having extraordinary emotional perception. For instance, assistants often tell stories about times when they were sad and, while no-one else noticed, a person with disabilities reached out to them. An experienced assistant called Rayna once told me:

19. McKearney, "Receiving the Gift."

> You can't hide your personality from people with learning disabilities. You have to open yourself. They find your weaknesses and strengths very quickly, and that confronts you with your own disabilities and inabilities.

New carers learned, in this vein, how to speak about the idiosyncrasies of different individuals as blessings for those who interact with them. So, for instance, one carer described Rachel's enjoyment of looking at herself in the mirror as a gift because "it challenges those of us who don't like the way we look," while another talked about Ruth's attempts to get people's attention as a gift for openness and connection. What this amounts to is a reimagining of people with intellectual disabilities not as burdens and problems but as especially virtuous in one respect or another: Rachel was described, for instance, as amazingly emotionally intuitive to the point of perceiving vulnerabilities that cognitively able people were unable to recognize. Maden, for instance, told me that Rachel is:

> so clever also to see when you are in a good mood or not, when you're really sad. I mean sometimes when I have been so tired, or so sad, then she just comes up to me and gives me a hug. I have no clue how she can see that, but she does somehow.

This way of describing people with disabilities as gifted often draws attention to their difference from the nondisabled. It rarely implies that these individuals are reaching ethical standards that nondisabled people easily meet. Instead, it typically suggests that these individuals have gifts for things that nondisabled people are much worse at. The stories often imply that it is precisely because they cannot do the kind of intellectual work that others are so engaged in, that people with intellectual disabilities are so good at the face-to-face aspect of morality.

This model does not challenge the basic distinction between those with an intellectual disability and those without. It is not, for instance, an argument to abandon the category of intellectual disability. L'Arche's training does not work toward smoothing out differences between the carers and the cared for in order to claim that people with cognitive disabilities are *really*, underneath it all, typical cognitively able subjects. Instead, it systematically deepens the sense that people with cognitive disabilities are unusual. What this produces is a similar set of hierarchical differences, a compassionate movement from those higher up the hierarchy to those lower. But in this case the disabled are placed at the top of that hierarchy. It is they who embody the virtues of compassion, and they who generously impart their gifts to the needy (and even at times in these stories foolish) nondisabled.

This overturning transforms people with disabilities from recipients of compassion from the cognitively able into the people embodying this virtue and thus into the givers of this gift. The hierarchical reversal is also a transformation from passive to active. Each person with disabilities comes across as not simply a bundle of caring needs or as someone who has things done *to them*. Rather, the stories endow them with a public persona in which they are someone with a distinct story, a history of acts done *to others*.[20]

At times, this focus on their agency becomes elaborated in a way that departs even further from the compassionate framing of L'Arche's project—and even from the moral frame of "virtue" altogether. That is, people with intellectual disabilities are represented as powerful agents to be deferred to precisely for the ways in which they depart from all expectations: including those of what it means to be nice and kind. Common to all the stories—whether they praise preeminently moral virtues like generosity and empathy, or less obviously altruistic actions like laughing at others or admiring one's own reflection in the mirror—is the surprise and wonder that the revelation of this quality generates in those who witness it. When Maria describes her surprise at Sarah laughing at her quite unexpectedly, she depicts Sarah as someone who will interrupt you, who will disrupt and disturb any way that you have of evaluating her. All the stories make a similar point. Maden was not expecting that Rachel would pick up on her sadness; and Priya is astounded by Ensy's sensitivity. In this way, carers train to regard people with cognitive disabilities not simply as exemplifying a set of moral standards better than the nondisabled, but also as exceeding our attempts to comprehend them through any routinized moral framework.[21] The attitude cultivated is as much praise for how well they are doing, as it is wonder at who these unusual agents are. The nondisabled defer to them for their transgression of norms, for how unpredictable they are.

This representation disrupts the hierarchical movement of higher to lower by nondisabled to disabled, not exclusively by claiming that those with disabilities are more compassionate, but more broadly by demonstrating their charisma. Indeed, one could articulate even those stories that do center compassion as actually more fundamentally about this kind of subversion. For even those stories undermine the position from which the nondisabled try to establish judgments about moral virtue in the first place. The end result, across all of these practices and representations, is that the initial

---

20. McKearney, "L'Arche"; Arendt, *Human Condition*; McKearney, "Limits of Knowing."

21. Spink, *Miracle*, 1.

moral hierarchy between the disabled and the nondisabled (here centered around compassion) always gets overturned.[22]

Conclusion

It is quite right for us to tear down the image of Vanier as an exemplar of compassion. It is quite clear that this is not who he was. And it is quite clear, also, that the ways we bought into this image sustained the possibilities of the abuse he perpetuated. We owed his victims better, and we now owe them, at the very least, a clear-sighted attention to the damage he caused them. And we are now accountable to them, as well to all those who are affected by L'Arche, in how we pursue this moral project going forward.

Those who admired and praised Vanier as an exemplar of nondisabled compassionate descent take it as their responsibility now to reject Vanier precisely for his failure to live up to that ideal. His call for them to change their lives by giving up power was not something he himself ultimately did. But, not only that, he also sought a kind of non-conformist, charismatic, and erotic power that is particularly illicit in many of the social circles in which he was praised. He did work that was, from this perspective, salutary while secretly breaking many of the moral codes he professed—as well as those of the groups he appealed to.

But many within L'Arche never centered Vanier's compassion in the first place. The alternative narration of L'Arche that I have articulated here has always been skeptical of a focus on nondisabled virtue: *both* because it is about the nondisabled *and* because it is about virtue. There is no reason to suppose that this narrative's lack of interest in religious and moral conformity means it has no way to condemn Vanier's actions as manipulative and abusive. Its advocates in L'Arche are just as critical of Vanier's behavior as anyone else. But this alternative story focuses our attention going forward in a different direction: on people with intellectual disabilities as charismatic actors who disrupt existing moral schemas, touch the nondisabled in unexpected ways, and inaugurate a new kind of relationality beyond stable frames.

This narrative has never sat easily with those who center the routinization of nondisabled compassion. And in this moment I suspect it will sound, to their ears, downright dangerous to focus on these themes. The report, for instance, describes Vanier as having gone so wrong precisely because there was far too much charisma, liminality, and intimacy in his theology

---

22. McKearney, "Ability to Judge."

and practice.[23] The report judges his departures from theological orthodoxy as "corrupt,"[24] "twisted,"[25] "deluded,"[26] and "distorting"[27]—and links these charismatic and mystical departures from church teaching and discipline to the sexual abuse.[28] From this perspective, more emphasis on unorthodox interaction that goes beyond existing moral structures sounds very worrying indeed—and a risk to vulnerable people with disabilities.

But it is not at all clear to me that this is as obviously correct an answer to the question "where did Vanier go wrong?" as the report presents itself to be. It relies on a certain way of reading Vanier's theology, as well as a highly specific understanding of morality, of the relationship between authority and moral discipline, of the relationship between unorthodox thought and immoral practice, and of the moral agency of people with intellectual disabilities. And it demonstrates a curious lack of reflection on whether the ideals of nondisabled compassionate virtue and Catholic discipline might themselves have played a problematic role in this story—as if the main source of Vanier's wrongdoing was that he did not adhere to the moral codes of the culture and institutions he was part of. The alternative moral framing of L'Arche, which I have articulated in this chapter, raises questions about all of these assumptions as part of an explanation of Vanier's faults, and as a fitting moral response to communities that have distinctively recognized the agency of people with intellectual disabilities and their capacities for intimacy.

It also raises the question as to whether our answers to the query "where did Vanier go wrong?" has a significant bearing on the future of L'Arche at all. The alternative narrative might suggest, instead, that L'Arche has developed into something quite different from what Vanier intended, from what his own private practice involved, and from what anyone conforming or not conforming to the religious circles from which it sprung anticipated or desired. We might wonder, in line with this alternative story, whether its development into something so remarkable despite Vanier's evident secrecy, manipulation, and abuse was not due to the ways in which people with intellectual disabilities disrupted and overtook its story. Certainly, the unique development of L'Arche has been in part sustained by a

---

23. Study Commission, *Control and Abuse*.
24. Study Commission, *Control and Abuse*, 18.
25. Study Commission, *Control and Abuse*, 11.
26. Study Commission, *Control and Abuse*, 20.
27. Study Commission, *Control and Abuse*, 20.
28. Study Commission, *Control and Abuse*, e.g., 643, 762, 823.

narrative that decenters both the nondisabled and their virtues, and facilitates instead attention, recognition, and openness to the charisma of those with disabilities.

The dominant response to the revelations currently focuses our attention on the importance of nondisabled moral conformity and virtue—and on purifying L'Arche of the charismatic, the strange, and the disruptive. But this response proceeds from a set of assumptions that are not shared by many in L'Arche who instead see the project as good for quite different reasons. The alternative story I have articulated here has long nurtured L'Arche in its distinctive direction. What might it offer to L'Arche in this moment? How might decentering nondisabled virtue, more broadly, help L'Arche continue to develop in its own direction despite the now evident failings of its founder? What does it offer to thinking through the role of safety, touch, and intimacy in the communities—for disabled and nondisabled alike? How might attention to the charismatic, disruptive, and surprising agency of people with intellectual disabilities recenter their capacities and their needs in this story? It was always remiss to reduce L'Arche to the virtues of its founder. It would be even more so to limit it to his sins.

Bibliography

Angrosino, Michael V. "L'Arche: The Phenomenology of Christian Counterculturalism." *Qualitative Inquiry* 9.6 (January 12, 2003) 934–54.

Arendt, Hannah. *The Human Condition*. Chicago: University of Chicago Press, 1958.

Banner, Michael. *The Ethics of Everyday Life: Moral Theology, Social Anthropology, and the Imagination of the Human*. Oxford: Oxford University Press, 2014.

Burghardt, Madeline. "Brokenness/Transformation: Reflections on Academic Critiques of L'Arche." *Disability Studies Quarterly* 36.1 (2016).

Douglas, Mary. *Natural Symbols*. Middlesex, England: Penguin, 1973.

Downey, Michael. *A Blessed Weakness: The Spirit of Jean Vanier and L'Arche*. New York: Harper & Row, 1986.

Ford, David. *Christian Wisdom: Desiring God and Learning in Love*. Cambridge: Cambridge University Press, 2007.

Hauerwas, Stanley. "Seeing Peace: L'Arche as a Peace Movement." In *The Paradox of Disability: Responses to Jean Vanier and L'Arche Communities from Theology and the Sciences*, edited by Hans S. Reinders, 113–26. Grand Rapids: Eerdmans, 2010.

Hauerwas, Stanley, and Jean Vanier. *Living Gently in a Violent World: The Prophetic Witness of Weakness*. Downers Grove, IL: IVP, 2008.

McDonald, Katherine E., and Christopher B. Keys. "L'Arche: The Successes of Community, the Challenges of Empowerment in a Faith-Centered Setting." *Journal of Religion, Disability & Health* 9.4 (2006) 5–28.

McKearney, Patrick. "The Ability to Judge: Critique and Surprise in Theology, Anthropology, and L'Arche." *Ethnos* 86.3 (2021) 460–76. https://doi.org/10.1080/00141844.2019.1640261.

―――. "L'Arche, Learning Disability, and Domestic Citizenship: Dependent Political Belonging in a Contemporary British City." *City & Society* 29.2 (2017) 260–80. https://doi.org/10.1111/ciso.12126.

―――. "The Limits of Knowing Other Minds: Intellectual Disability and the Challenge of Opacity." *Social Analysis* 65.1 (2021) 1–22. https://doi.org/10.3167/sa.2020.650101.

―――. "Receiving the Gift of Cognitive Disability: Recognizing Agency in the Limits of the Rational Subject." *The Cambridge Journal of Anthropology* 36.1 (2018) 40–60.

Nouwen, Henri J. M. *The Selfless Way of Christ: Downward Mobility and the Spiritual Life.* New York: Orbis, 2007.

Reimer, Kevin. *Living L'Arche: Stories of Compassion, Love and Disability.* London: Continuum, 2009.

Reinders, Hans S. "Human Vulnerability: A Conversation at L'Arche." In *The Paradox of Disability: Responses to Jean Vanier and L'Arche Communities from Theology and the Sciences*, edited by Hans S. Reinders, 3–18. Grand Rapids: Eerdmans, 2010.

―――. *Receiving the Gift of Friendship: Profound Disability, Theological Anthropology, and Ethics.* Grand Rapids: Eerdmans, 2008.

Spink, Kathryn. *The Miracle, the Message, the Story: Jean Vanier and L'Arche.* Toronto: Novalis, 2006.

Study Commission Mandated by L'Arche International. *Control and Abuse Investigation on Thomas Philippe, Jean Vanier and L'Arche (1950–2019).* Châteauneuf-sur-Charente, France: Frémur, 2023.

―――. *Synthesis of the Report Control and Abuse, an Investigation on Thomas Philippe, Jean Vanier, and L'Arche.* Châteauneuf-sur-Charente, France: Frémur, 2023.

Sumarah, J. "L'Arche from a Participant Observer's Perspective: The Creation of Universal Community." *International Journal of Special Education* 3.2 (1988) 185–96.

Vanier, Jean. *An Ark for the Poor: The Story of L'Arche.* Toronto: Novalis, 1995.

―――. *Community and Growth.* New York: Paulist, 1989.

―――. *From Brokenness to Community.* New York: Paulist, 1992.

Wakefield, Mary. "Jean Vanier's World of Love and Kindness." *The Spectator*, July 1, 2017. https://www.spectator.co.uk/article/jean-vanier-s-world-of-love-and-kindness/.

Young, Frances, ed. *Encounter with Mystery: Reflections on L'Arche and Living with Disability.* London: Darton, Longman & Todd, 1997.

Chapter Seven

A Mixture of Light and Darkness
Accounting for My Vanier

HANS S. REINDERS

Our supposed listening is in fact a strange mixture of hearing and our own speaking, and, in accordance with the usual rule, it is most likely that our own speaking will be the really decisive event.[1]

Introduction

IT IS HARD TO imagine anyone who in some way has been attracted to the life and work of Jean Vanier—not to speak of the man himself—who would not be distressed by his horrific downfall. What to think about it? Even more important: *how* to think about it? Perhaps it is wise, perhaps it is a male thing, or perhaps it is just me, but let me try to stay away from all overwhelming feelings and start this essay with the recognition of a simple fact. There are, and always have been, two Vaniers. As "Jean Vanier" he has been a historical man; as "Vanier" he was, and still is, the representation of that historical man in our own thinking, which means that there have in fact been many more "Vaniers" than just two.

---

1. Karl Barth, *Church Dogmatics*, I, 2, 470.

The thing to acknowledge about the first Vanier is biographical. He is no longer; he *was*. We thought we knew the history of how Jean Vanier started L'Arche, what preceded that history, and how it developed over time. But we have also come to know he had a hidden history too—the history of his continuing practice of sexual abuse.

Next, the most important thing about the second Vanier is that he is textual. He is the figure that emerges from anyone's account of the historical Vanier construed out of what has been read or listened to. "Vanier" is a representation, and as such he still exists. My point is: we all have—or had—our own "Vanier."[2] For all readers and writers it is true that when they are thinking of Vanier, they are thinking in terms of their account of him. They are thinking of him, this is to say, through the lens of their "Vanier." In this essay I will try to account for my "Vanier." I feel obligated to do so, given the many applauding and admiring words I have written about him over the years.

To speak of "Vanier" as a representation is not to deny that such representation is rooted in historical facts. My "Vanier" is not just a figment of my imagination. It's not like we can make up our "Vanier" from scratch. There are historical facts guiding us in the way we construe our representation of the man. But which facts, what they mean, what weight they have, and why they are relevant—all that is another matter.

Furthermore, for the authors of the essays in the present volume, it is true that the history of his sexual misconduct has not been part of their "Vanier." At least it wasn't part of mine. The same I hold to be true for most of the readers of this volume. When it was brought to light, it was extremely painful, especially in the documentation published in January 2023.[3]

The distinction between Vanier and "Vanier" enables us to acknowledge that it has been painful in two different ways. It was painful first of all for the women who were the victims of his abusive behavior. They have been drawn into a secret history they didn't know existed, the history of Vanier being the most ardent disciple of Thomas Philippe.[4] What lead these women to bring their story to light was precisely the contradiction

---

2. The "we" in this sentence includes and refers to anyone who has been reading his books, and/or has been listening to him, and, eventually, has put his or her reflections on Vanier in writing.

3. Study Commission, *Control and Abuse*.

4. This holds true for the six women whose testimony occasioned the inquiry that led to the publication of "Summary Report" in February 2020. How Vanier's discipleship of Thomas Philippe—I use this word deliberately—developed over time is shown in the summary of report of Study Commission, *Synthesis*, 17 (*et passim*).

between their "Vanier" and what they suffered from the man.[5] The dominant representation of Jean Vanier as an example for the Roman Catholic Church was oblivious to what they knew about him. His public reputation as a "holy" man needed to be dethroned for their experience with Vanier to be recognized as real. It was a legitimate need. Over the years we have learned about sexual abuse that nothing is as devastating for its victims as having their experience denied.

When the publicly unknown part of Vanier's history came out, it was also painful in another way. For many of his admirers and friends, he had lied and betrayed his witness. Painful as the news about the hidden part of his life must have been, and still is, the difference between the two kinds of experience is important. In cases of sexual abuse we do not—and should not—raise the question of whether its victims are somehow responsible for what happened to them. They got in touch with Vanier for receiving spiritual guidance, but getting "in touch" took a form they did not premeditate. And in the cases we know of, they were appalled by what it turned out to be. In contrast, for others—scholars, colleagues, friends, admirers—it is appropriate to take responsibility for their representation of the man. There is no one responsible for my "Vanier" but me. As the above quote from Karl Barth indicates so eloquently, when I had my "Vanier" speaking to me, it was importantly my own voice that I was listening to. This is what "giving an account" entails, and that is not only true for me.

One more observation. Absent from this introduction are persons with intellectual disabilities who are living in L'Arche communities. What was Vanier to them? It is an important question, but I cannot pretend to know the answer. I can only offer a personal reflection. Visiting some of these communities over the past thirty years, located in various parts of the world, I was struck by the fact that Vanier appeared much less prominent than I had expected. Community leaders had heard of him, of course, they most likely had met him at a retreat, and read one or two of his books. But quite a number of assistants, not to speak of the members that I met on these occasions, had hardly any knowledge of the man.

While Vanier's reputation mainly served the interest of an external, public audience, he was no doubt an iconic figure for those who shared his concerns about persons with intellectual disabilities. Losing that iconic figure was, and still is, painful. However, it is important to recognize that the pain inflicted because of betrayed convictions, beliefs, ideas, even

---

5. These two aspects are reflected in the interchanging usage of "misconduct" and "abuse." For the women involved, "misconduct" would be too innocent a word; regarding others, "abuse" would be too strong. They were not abused, but certainly misled.

friendships—all of which are important things—is not equal to the pain of being abused.

Acknowledging this difference, my intention in this essay is to take responsibility for my own account of the man and his work. There are various ways to respond to what we have learned about the historical Vanier. Throwing stones at the man and his legacy, though debatable, is an option that we have seen used. For those who were more or less close to him, that is not an easy thing to do. At some point they will inevitably ask themselves, what did I miss, what did I do and not do? How did I respond that allowed me to be so terribly misled? Raising such questions, we are taking responsibility for *how* we construed our "Vanier." In the present case this requires asking why "Vanier" became an icon in my own project, and what I see as his key message.

Trying to find answers to these questions made me reflect on something I have never cared to think about before—Vanier's Catholicism. This assertion is loaded with potential misunderstandings, of course, so let me immediately add that what follows in no way considers Catholicism as such. The Roman Catholic Church in 1956 condemned the beliefs and practices that ultimately led Vanier in his sexual transgressions, which means the Catholicism he was committed to was declared heretical already before L'Arche got started. Had I paid attention to the question of what his version of the Catholic faith meant to him, I might not have taken him on his word as I have done over the years quite unreservedly.

Finally, it is important to note that I intend to review my construal of "Vanier" from what was known by me and most of my colleagues at the time. No doubt this takes on a quite different meaning in the light of the recently published report *Control and Abuse*.[6] However, I don't intend to engage in trying to understand why Vanier did what he did. Instead I take it to be my responsibility to reflect upon why I construed my "Vanier" in the way I did.

A Meeting in Amsterdam

As said, I have never paid much attention to Vanier's relation with the Roman Catholic Church and have not raised any question about it, mainly because I didn't see his Catholicism as crucial in his account of L'Arche. To illustrate this confession let me proceed with an anecdote from a meeting in Amsterdam about twenty-five years ago. It wasn't just a meeting, but a weekend retreat that I participated in, organized by Faith and Light,

---

6. Study Commission, *Control and Abuse*, 2023.

an organization that Vanier had cofounded. We were about sixty people, among whom were many with intellectual disabilities accompanied by family. The venue was a Catholic Church in the city.

Readers who have been to one of these retreats know from experience how powerful they can be. We had a wonderful time with stories and games and meals together. At the end of the first day there was a celebration with readings from Scripture and Jean preaching, followed by the sharing of bread and wine. To my Protestant mind it had everything of a celebration of the Gospel as Vanier had laid it out for us. In fact it had more spiritual presence and awareness than many of the services I had attended, both Catholic and Protestant. I was grateful for having been part of it.

The next morning, however, I was informed that afterwards Vanier together with a couple of nuns had gone to mass at another Catholic Church in the city. I found that quite puzzling. As if the celebration of the day before had been some kind of performance, something that was on the program. Apparently, instead of having participated in a beautiful experience of the Eucharist I had been part of a staged act. Now, of course, one must be a Protestant to take a sermon on the Gospel and the sharing of bread and wine for a full-blown Eucharist, considering that for true Catholics it cannot be the real thing unless it is celebrated by a Roman Catholic priest.

Should I have raised a question about it? Perhaps not immediately, but in view of what Vanier had preached there surely was reason to do so. Jesus's mission of sharing with the poor is *the key* to the Gospel, he said. Leaving aside the questionable language of identifying persons with intellectual disabilities as "the poor," it occurred to me this sharing was exactly what we had been doing that Saturday afternoon. Later in his work he named it "the sacrament of encounter" but on this day the sacramental meaning of our celebration was apparently lost on Vanier, as about two hours later he went to a regular mass.[7] I was reminded of this alienating experience when reading in the Study Commission's summary that there had always been a difference for Vanier between an inner circle and a broader public audience.[8]

---

7. For sharing with "the poor" as the "sacrament of encounter" see Vanier, *Signs of the Times*, 28. He wrote: "the sacrament of the altar, the Eucharist, is fulfilled in the 'sacrament of the poor'—which means an encounter with Jesus in the poor" (*Signs of the Times*, 50).

8. The summary speaks of "duplicity" (Study Commission, *Synthesis*, 15) and shows that the distinction between an inner circle and a larger public audience was at the heart of Vanier's mode of operation to continue his connections with Thomas Philippe with an eye on their shared practices.

Two Kinds of Moral Lives?

Looking back now, and rereading some of his work, I don't think one can conclude this duplicity from his writings, but there were surely signs pointing in that direction. In his book *An Ark for the Poor* from 1995 he describes the link of L'Arche with the Roman Catholic Church that he found embodied in the active presence of several priests.[9] Not only of his spiritual mentor Thomas Phillipe, but also of Fr. Desmazières, at that time a retired bishop from the Trosly area. He then continues with a list of priests that started a community, followed by a list of people coming out of L'Arche to be ordained as a priest.[10] Even though Vanier insists on L'Arche's vocation as "ecumenical" it seems that the presence of clergy is elevated above the presence of other people.[11]

There are other passages in his writings that, in hindsight, presented the occasion for similar questions. The following claim is central to his work, and regards the crucial meaning of forgiveness.

> I had to learn to accept myself without any illusions. I had to discover how to forgive *and* my own need for forgiveness. Little by little, the weak and the powerless helped me to accept my own poverty, become more fully human and grow in inner wholeness.[12]

The same emphasis on forgiveness as mutual acceptance appears again in *Community and Growth*.

> Community is the place of forgiveness. In spite of all the trust we may have in each other, there are always words that wound, self-promoting attitudes, situations where susceptibilities clash.

---

9. Vanier, *Ark for the Poor*, 72–79.

10. I pass by Vanier's struggle to be accepted for ordination as a priest, which his church blocked time and again until the application was finally dropped in 1977. See Antoine Mourges, "Almost Priest and Prophet," in Study Commission, *Control and Abuse*, 111–49.

11. He asserts that "L'Arche could not be defined as a Roman Catholic organization" (Vanier, *Ark for the Poor*, 78). He mentions as examples of its "ecumenical" vocation the communities of Daybreak in Canada (1969) founded by Anglicans, and Bangalore (1970) including Hindus (*Ark for the Poor*, 79). Its mission, as he saw it, was to deepen people's spiritual lives in their *own* tradition. What united the people in L'Arche was their response to "the poor" rather than their religious inspiration.

12. Vanier, *Heart of L'Arche*, 35. Leaving aside again the language of "the weak and the powerless," the connection between critical self-knowledge and forgiveness is what I had in mind when I characterized Vanier's view as "theological realism." (See Reinders "Being with the Disabled").

> That is why living together implies a cross, a consonant effort, an acceptance which is daily, and mutual forgiveness.[13]

This need for critical self-knowledge regarding how we relate to other people became the lens through which I read Vanier's work, but I failed to notice what followed on the very same page and moved in a quite different direction:

> For me it has been such a grace and gift over these years in community to verbalize my sins and to ask for forgiveness of a priest who listens and says, "I forgive you in the name of the Father, the Son, and the Holy Spirit."[14]

The question I should have raised is: why a priest? If the possibility of growth follows from the need to be forgiven by those whom one has harmed or hurt, as members of the same community, then confession to a priest cannot replace the significance of mutual forgiveness. If a space for communal growth can only be found by confessing the sin of using one's strength to manipulate others, and being forgiven by *these others*, then to seek forgiveness from a *priest* is a curious move indeed.[15]

A further example of the same ambiguity regards the question of celibacy.[16] Vanier seemed to see no difference in the needs of both single people and married couples within L'Arche in view of deepening their mutual relationships. Nonetheless he distinctly emphasized the importance of celibacy for understanding L'Arche's vocation: "If God has called L'Arche into existence, it is to reveal himself to the poor. This revelation involves the presence of single, committed, long-term assistants, assistants for whom L'Arche is truly a call, a vocation."[17]

Linking God's revelation to disabled persons with the presence of "single, committed, long-term assistants" suggests that in Vanier's eyes living in celibacy is a preferred distinction. But again, I have read such passages and not paid much attention to them. In the present case the question should have been whether the language of "revelation" was meant to say that the

---

13. Vanier, *Community and Growth*, 37.

14. Vanier, *Community and Growth*, 37. The Study Commission's Report shows it is more than likely that Vanier had a particular priest in mind here, namely his mentor Thomas Philippe.

15. Keith Dow's analysis of the lack of specificity of this kind of claim in Vanier's work is relevant here. Sin is taken seriously only in its concreteness of the one who is sinned against. (Dow, "Against Living Saints").

16. Vanier, *Ark for the Poor*, 102–3.

17. Vanier, *Ark for the Poor*, 103.

presence of priestly assistants would bring "the poor" closer to God. If that is what he meant, it is clear that his spiritual mentor taught him so.

As said, I never focused on Vanier's Catholicism *per se*. Particularly the findings of the recent Study Report show this omission was mistaken. The examples given above should have induced the question of whether Vanier was perhaps susceptible to the notion of a higher order of the priestly life.[18] The French historian Antoine Mourges showed that Thomas Philippe was definitely committed to this notion. Phillipe had no problem with calling upon his authority as a priest to override his victim's objection to his erotic-mystical practice of spiritual guidance.[19]

As early as 1956 he was convicted both by the Dominican Order and by the Holy Office of the Church for the heretical "mysticism" of his sacramental theology.[20] Particularly relevant in this connection: in his mystical theology the sacrament embodied by the priest (literally) transcended the limit of sin.[21] However, since I was not interested in Philippe's teachings, I did not see that I thereby failed to raise the question of whether Vanier shared this view.

The report *Control and Abuse* indicates that he did. In a most revealing passage Florian Michel discusses an unpublished, and partly handwritten, piece that at some point had been part of Vanier's doctoral thesis on Aristotle's ethics. It's on the very topic of "two moralities." The concept is unambiguously defended by Vanier. Michel summarizes his view as follows: "There is the 'common way' . . . it is the way of 'the Christian people' and 'laymen' that marks a life of piety and obedience to the Church; and there is the 'strait way' of those who renounce the world, among whom are the 'mystics' and the 'saints,' whom 'the Holy Spirit keeps for itself in quite a special way.'"[22] The latter phrase indicates a spiritual freedom beyond the limits of ecclesial teachings on the Christian life. Following his mentor Vanier endorsed that spiritual guidance may be opening up the space for a mystical experience of

---

18. For many years Vanier had been attempting to be received as a priest in the Roman Catholic Church without being willing to receive the necessary education as a seminarian, see Study Commission, *Synthesis*, 17.

19. Antoine Mourges, "Walking with Our History." Presentation at the "Traverser notre histoire" conférence, 2020.

20. Study Commission, *Synthesis*, 13, 15, 16, 21.

21. "The priest as power of the Mystical Body enters into the inner secrets of the heart. Strictly speaking, confession is limited to sin; but, given the very structure of this sacrament, it naturally tends to go beyond this limit" (Philippe, *Contemplative Life*, 83).

22. Michel, "Philosopher and Theologian," in Study Commission, *Control and Abuse*, 150–75, 174.

physical attachment, and when it does, it moves beyond the transgression of ordinary morality.

The only explanation for the failure to investigate these connections is that I took Vanier on his word that he had severed his ties with Philippe. As the Study Commission has shown this was clearly a lie. Vanier sought ways to stay in close contact with him, and make sure he could continue his secret practices of sexual abuse. That Vanier was no stranger to these practices is shown by the fact that he pressed his victims not to speak about their relationship because others wouldn't understand the depth of their shared "graces."[23] In fact Vanier *never* admitted his conduct was in fact abusive.[24]

All of this suggests that he too believed in the hierarchical order of two kinds of "moral" lives. The priestly life as distinct from, and superior to, the life of ordinary people, in that it could even go beyond the "ordinary" morality that was taught to "Christian people" by the Roman Catholic Church.

In view of this apparent appreciation of a hierarchical moral order, to the extent that my account is accurate, I can't help being reminded of the fact that Martin Luther was thrown out of the Catholic Church in the sixteenth century precisely because he was fighting against this alleged superiority of the priestly life, which he pointed at as the main source of a fraudulent and decadent priesthood.

More important in the present connection is the fact already referred to: the Holy Office of the Catholic Church rejected already in the 1950s the inspirational source from which Vanier had been tapping. As we now know, he never broke with his mentor, a man who, as Vanier would later tell Kathryn Spink, appeared to him as "a presence of God," echoing Philippe's own mystical theology.[25] The adherents' aspiration to being unified with God completely missed that within Catholic teaching any account of this unification is *only* possible on the basis of an analogy. The analogy of being, namely, of the divine and the human that does not only imply sameness but also an unbridgeable, ontological *difference*.[26]

23. Study Commission, *Synthesis*, 18.

24. L'Arche International, "Summary Report," 10–11.

25. Spink, *Miracle*, 39.

26. I think Hans Ulrich's insistence on the distinction between the "*pro me*" and "*extra nos*" is very insightful precisely at this point ("On Remaining in God's Story"). I disagree with Rimbaut's dismissal of looking at Vanier as a gnostic mainly because of her too narrow conception of Gnosticism. (Gwennola Rimbaut, "Jean Vanier: A New Spiritual Master?" in Study Commission, *Control and Abuse*, 733–52, 741). It is illuminating to look at Vanier's circle as gnostics because of their belief in a secret knowledge, for the reception of which ordinary humans are ill-prepared. Part of this knowledge is that the knower is initiated into it by a divine power, after which the knower and the known become identical. "To me he was God's presence." (Vanier on Thomas Philippe, Study Commission, *Control and Abuse*, 85).

Vanier's version of Roman Catholicism deviated significantly from the church's own teachings, then, and was previously condemned in the work of his mentor Thomas Philippe. In hindsight the reason for my omission to reflect on these views is obvious. Why I was attracted to Vanier's work didn't have a focus on the Roman Catholic Church to begin with.

"Vanier" against the Self-Image of the Age

The project of intellectual disability, theology, and ethics I was pursuing since the late 1980s was inspired by thinkers such as Macintyre and Hauerwas. The leading intuition was that if persons with intellectual disabilities suffer, they most likely suffer from other people's attitudes toward themselves. To spend time with these persons who will be conducive to their well-being, I believed, it is necessary to face tendencies in oneself that thwarted that goal. Most people's unreflective response to intellectual disability is one of superiority and condescension grounded in a false self-image.

This intuition I found strongly articulated in the philosophy of L'Arche as presented by my "Vanier." It aspired to resist the "dominant self-image of the age," to borrow a phrase from Macintyre.[27] The dominant image fed on the notion of self-determining individuals in control of their story. It reflects the ideal that contemporary society still tells people about themselves. They can choose who they want to be because they can choose the story they want to live in.[28]

The expression of this liberal conception of the self in the world of disability adopted the language of equal rights and equal citizenship, a language that spilled over to the world of intellectual disability.[29] The ensuing disability rights movement brought no doubt significant and salutary changes. At the same time, however, there was something misleading about the "new paradigm." It operated on the level of institutional change, but the attitudes of superiority and condescension on a personal level remained under the radar. Looking back my suspicion was that persons with intellectual disabilities would be welcome to the extent that in crucial respects they appear to be like "us." It troubled me that the disability rights movement did not see the risk of persons with intellectual disabilities ending up at the bottom of the pile, a risk I found confirmed in the emerging hierarchy of disability.[30]

27. Macintyre, *Against the Self-Images*.
28. See Hauerwas, *Communion of Character*, 149.
29. Charlton, *Nothing About Us*.
30. Reinders, *Receiving the Gift*, 26–27.

To find the key to a different approach I noticed the absence of friendship in many accounts of their lives. People with disabilities need friendship before they need citizenship, or so I argued. Insisting on friendship and belonging as "hyper-goods" of human existence, the argument revealed an important point. The gains of political action could alter the institutional conditions of having a life of one's own, but "being an equal citizen" could not as such fulfill its ultimate end. Friendship can provide that fulfillment.

Coming from this angle it is not difficult to see why L'Arche, and particularly Vanier's account of it, was an attractive voice. In fact, it seemed to turn the importance of "choice" on its head. Very few persons with intellectual disabilities experience the blessing of being chosen as a friend. What makes "being oneself" valuable, I contended, is that one is chosen by others to share stories and spend time with. While "choice" is important, it is "being chosen" that signals to people that they belong. This is what Vanier told his audience time and again to have discovered about the members of L'Arche:

> Their thirst for friendship, love, and communion leaves no one indifferent: either you harden your heart to their cry and reject them, or you open your heart and enter into a relationship built on trust, simple, tender gestures, and few words.[31]

If people with intellectual disabilities suffer, they most likely suffer from how "nondisabled" others think about themselves. Recognizing one's implicit, sometimes even hidden attitude of superiority toward disabled persons is everywhere in Vanier's work, which made him a crucial witness to my project. In a wider sense Vanier opposed the liberal self for its inability to see through its own hubris and for having no use for forgiveness and grace, which are the rewards for critical self-knowledge. Liberalism does not know how to make sense of his claim that "we are a mixture of light and darkness," or so I argued.[32]

The Second Calling

Asking myself what I ultimately considered to be crucial for my "Vanier" I am tempted to say that thoroughly doubting one's own moral motivations

---

31. Vanier, *Ark for the Poor*, 26.

32. Vanier, *Community and Growth*, 35. It's astonishing how deceitful these views were in the light of what Philippe and Vanier allowed themselves to do, as the Study Commission has shown. Appearances aside, their entire project of administering "special graces"—read: demanding sexual favors—was but a manifestation of hubris.

was the key to his faith. But it clearly wasn't. Standing before their God Christians know—or should know—that their mixed motivations make them susceptible to self-deception, which, if they don't see through it, makes them false witnesses. God judges the sinner's pretense, but forgives those who recognize their falsehood and ask for God's forgiveness. It is precisely the confession of being a mixture of light and darkness—as Vanier had it— that in prayer may help us counter the risk of self-deception. "Exterior walls are only the extension of our own inner walls," he wrote.[33]

Pursuing this as the heart of his Christian beliefs I found its ultimate confirmation in a story he told on various occasions. It regards what happened when he became responsible for the daily routine of a young man with hardly any possibility of communication. He was refusing to let Vanier wash and clothe him. Vanier could not handle this rejection. It made him so mad, he even felt an urge to use violence to make this boy comply.[34] In hindsight this episode made him realize he had been a bad Samaritan, a do-gooder who wasn't able to live up to his own philosophy.

Obviously I had found the key to the book I wrote about him, following a request made by Vanier himself. To his surprise the book turned out to be a novel. It's title was *The Second Calling*, which I got from his account of this episode in his life. It made him learn to see his own mixture of light and darkness the hard way. At least that was what I believed at the time.

The story of the novel is built around the main character of Ramón Jimenez Cardozo who has bought a house in a rural village close to Seville where he wants to share his life with a few people who have nowhere else to go. They have been rejected by their families mainly because their body or mind, or both, didn't do what they were expected to. After a few years of expansion and growth, all of which is part of the story, a community is shaped that includes misfits and outcasts, men and women, some with physical impairments, some with cognitive impairments, and also the people who are there to assist and work with them.

An important storyline is concerned with their finding out how to work with a girl by the name of Lucy Miles, "a fluttering bird" as one of her friends describes her. When the task falls on Ramón to take his turn, her chaotic and erratic ways bring him to the brink of a crisis. She won't comply, which frustrates Ramón to the point of becoming violent toward her. He is

---

33. Vanier, *Our Journey Home*, 28. Particularly in this book Vanier takes the position that anthropology is controlling social psychology and social theory.

34. Study Commission, *Synthesis*, 113, reads Vanier's account of his caring for this young man as a likely instance of sexually oriented conduct. Maybe it was, but if so, it appears to be a truth in hindsight. As far as I know there was no indication to see it in that light at the time when he told the story.

out of his wits because of Lucy's "unreason," and feels rejected. The girl does not want him, he believes, and he starts to hate her. Realizing that he does, he breaks down and has to admit that of all people he himself is the least capable of living his own vision. This is the dark hour of his second calling.

While this abstract omits all the horrific and wonderful details and events of the story, it suffices to understand how it illustrates Vanier's journey as I understood it.

> The second call comes later, when we accept that we cannot do big or heroic things for Jesus; it is a time of renunciation, humiliation, and humility. We feel useless; we are no longer appreciated. If the first passage is made at high noon, under a shining sun, the second call is often made at night. We feel alone and are afraid because we are in a world of confusion.[35]

To which we may add that the confusion is caused by the discovery of having been deceived by oneself. When after a decade Vanier bounced back from his interior walls, he arrived at his second calling. It was still a call to follow Jesus, but not without a healthy dose of unadorned, critical self-knowledge.

This, at least, is what I read in my "Vanier." It explains why I was attracted to his work. It confirmed my basic conviction that if persons with intellectual disability suffer, they most likely suffer from our attitudes toward them. It is a sad thing to acknowledge, after all we have learned about his past, that critical self-knowledge is not something one can ascribe to the man. At this point I can only conclude that my "Vanier," though not entirely a figment of my imagination, was the product of a selective reading of his work. It made him a cultural critic of liberalism's faith in the human person as a self-determining subject, and in doing so I missed the devotee of Thomas Philippe seeking to become a Roman Catholic priest for all the wrong reasons.

A Remaining Question

The historical truth about the man has been revealed in the Study Commission's Report *Control and Abuse* that was only recently published. As the above reflection is informed by that report it leaves me with several questions, of which I will address only one. This question I will finally try to state—not answer—as precisely as I can.

The "Vanier" whose work I appreciated is convinced that community life is hard in that it implies a cross, the cross of words that wound, of falling

---

35. Vanier, *Community and Growth*, 139.

short of one's expectations, of self-deception, and undeniably of mixed motives. But we now have read there was another version of the man too. The other "Vanier" is convinced that these shortcomings evaporate once one knows the secret of being unified with God that entails the fulfillment of body and mind. Put very simply, the question is how these two relate to one another.

One might be tempted to think that the second "Vanier" is in truth Thomas Phillipe, while the former is the "Vanier" who became renowned as the founder and leader of L'Arche. The recent report proves that this would be an act of wishful thinking. It shows that throughout his career Vanier seems to have had an insurmountable desire to follow Jesus, not only in a moral sense, but also in a metaphysical sense, understood as arriving at the intimate relationship with the divine in the mystical-erotic way he learned from Phillipe. Initiated in his master's sexual practices in *L'Eau Vive*, he developed his main insights a decade before L'Arche got started and did never abandon them. Mindboggling is the fact that after Philippe had been exiled, he not only went along with his sexually-oriented mysticism, but actually sought to continue his connection with his master and his sect-like group.

The Study Commission's conclusion at this point seems to be that both accounts of Vanier can only be explained, not reconciled, in terms of his duplicity.[36] The first "Vanier" was presented for a public audience. The image of a saintly hero brought fame, revenues, access to people in high places, all of which served as a useful cloak to distract attention from the secret sect in which the second "Vanier" was a key figure.[37] This group found the opportunity to pursue what they were after in a new environment that eventually would become L'Arche. This is quite shocking. The founding of L'Arche has always been a vital part in its storytelling.[38] It turns out that its founding story is far more than a myth. Some of the *intimi* from the inner circle of *L'Eau Vive* found a place to continue their ill-guided practices in order to welcome Thomas Philippe as soon as he would return from exile.[39]

It seems hard to escape the notion of a scam, a cloak, a veil, to mask what was really going on behind the myth of L'Arche's foundation, as created

---

36. Study Commission, *Synthesis*, 15.

37. A powerful testimony in this connection is presented by Mourges where he notes that the deceitful cooperation by Vanier with Thomas Philippe was already in place years before L'Arche got started (see above, note 19). Notwithstanding the fact of explicit orders of the Dominicans *and* of the Holy Office of the Church to not revive their cooperation after *L'Eau Vive* had been shut down, this is exactly what they secretly did.

38. Greig, "Disarmed Community," 62.

39. Study Commission, *Synthesis*, 62–63.

by its leadership. But there is a passage in *Synthesis* that may give us pause to think. The Commission hypothesizes that, in Jean Vanier's case, the importance of "the affective dimension," defined as a quest for mystical-loving communion, reveals something about his way of assimilating the beliefs and practices of Thomas Philippe. His remarks are therefore perhaps more attuned to a mystical-affective than mystical-sexual level, even if, as he recognized himself, the former led to the latter.[40]

The remaining question sharpens itself. Was L'Arche, and all that it stood for, mainly intended as a cloak behind which forbidden and condemned practices could be continued? A complete fraud to hide immoral intentions from the very start? Or was there in Vanier's case something like a "mystical-affective" objective to the effect that the difference between the first and second "Vanier" was not purely instrumental? Put differently: was Vanier truly committed to a communal life with persons with intellectual disabilities?

The Study Commission launches a hypothesis indicating a relevant difference between Vanier and his mentor. Recognizing that the question in no way excuses the abuse—Vanier himself acknowledging that "the one led to the other"—there is one observation indicating why it may be important to hypothesize this difference. The observation is this: if there is one thing that characterizes persons with intellectual disabilities, it must be that one cannot fool them with faked sympathy. They have a "sixth sense" for insincerity, so to speak. If one accepts this as true, would the members of L'Arche in Trosly-Breuil who met with Vanier almost on a daily basis not have sensed that the man was a fraud? Would they have accepted him when he was merely being "nice" to them, while in the meantime he was preying on very different schemes?

It is an important question that may help us to distinguish what was awfully wrong with Vanier from what was truly good about him. Perhaps the most poignant way to put it is this. If the publicly appealing "Vanier" was a scam because in truth he was primarily driven by sexual gratification, falsely mystified as divine unification, why would he have stopped short of abusing some of the intellectually disabled members of his community at Trosly-Breuil? Was it because there was a limit to what Philippe's morality for "mystics" and "saints" allowed him to do? Or was it, as the commission's hypothesis suggests, his commitment to persons with disabilities that held him back from crossing the line?

---

40. Study Commission, *Synthesis*, 75.

Bibliography

L'Arche International, "Summary Report." February 22, 2020.
Barth, Karl. *Church Dogmatics*. The Doctrine of the Word of God, I.2. Edited by George W. Bromiley and Thomas F. Torrance. New York, T&T Clark, 1956.
Charlton, James I. *Nothing About Us Without Us: Disability, Oppression, and Empowerment*. Oakland: University of California Press, 2000.
Dow, Keith. "Against Living Saints." In *The Betrayal of Witness: Reflections on the Downfall of Jean Vanier*, edited by Stanley Hauerwas and Hans S. Reinders, 18–36. Eugene, OR: Wipf & Stock, 2024.
Greig, Jason R. "The Disarmed Community: Reflecting on the Possibility of a Peace Ecclesiology in the Light of L'Arche." PhD diss., Vrije Universiteit Amsterdam, November 14, 2018.
Hauerwas, Stanley. *A Communion of Character: Towards a Constructive Christian Ethic*. Notre Dame: University of Notre Dame Press, 1981.
Macintyre, Alasdair. *Against the Self-Images of the Age: Essays on Ideology and Philosophy*. Notre Dame: University of Notre Dame Press, 1989.
Philippe, Thomas. *The Contemplative Life*. New Jersey: Dominican Nuns, 2009.
Reinders, Hans S. "Being with the Disabled: Jean Vanier's Theological Realism." In *Disability in the Christian Tradition*, edited by Brian Brock and John Swinton, 467–511. Grand Rapids: Eerdmans, 2012.
———. *Receiving the Gift of Friendship: Profound Disability, Theological Anthropology, and Ethics*. Grand Rapids: Eerdmans, 2008.
———. *The Second Calling: A Novel Inspired by the Life and Work of Jean Vanier*. London: Darton, Longman & Todd, 2015.
Spink, Kathryn. *The Miracle, the Message, the Story: Jean Vanier and L'Arche*. London: Darton, Longman and Todd, 2006.
Study Commission Mandated by L'Arche International. *Control and Abuse Investigation on Thomas Philippe, Jean Vanier and L'Arche (1950–2019)*. Châteauneuf-sur-Charente, France: Frémur, 2023.
———. *Synthesis of the Report Control and Abuse, an Investigation on Thomas Philippe, Jean Vanier, and L'Arche*. Châteauneuf-sur-Charente, France: Frémur, 2023.
Ulrich, Hans G. "On Remaining in God's Story as Passion." In *The Betrayal of Witness: Reflections on the Downfall of Jean Vanier*, edited by Stanley Hauerwas and Hans S. Reinders, 137–49. Eugene, OR: Wipf & Stock, 2024.
Vanier, Jean. *An Ark for the Poor: the Story of L'Arche*. Toronto: Novalis, 1995.
———. *Community and Growth*. Revised Edition. Mahwah, NJ: Paulist, 1989.
———. *The Heart of L'Arche. A Spirituality for Every Day*. Toronto: Novalis, 1995.
———. *Our Journey Home. Rediscovering a Common Humanity beyond Our Differences*. Maryknoll, NY: Orbis, 1997.
———. *Signs of the Times: Seven Paths of Hope for a Troubled World*. London: Darton, Longman and Todd, 2013.

Chapter Eight

Hidden in Plain View

BENJAMIN S. WALL

"HIDDEN IN PLAIN VIEW" is a way of naming the phenomenon of our individual and collective experiences of taking for granted our attunement to the world we inhabit, as if such awareness is a completely accurate representation of the world around us.[1] It is a way of making meaning of the many ways we fail to properly appreciate something or someone, which is often the result of overfamiliarity, or of assuming that something is true without questioning it. In short, a failure to pay attention to *how* we pay attention. It speaks to the paradox of how our focus—the consequence of all that we deem to be attention worthy—is often the result of what we effectively ignore. "Simply looking at something, for instance, does not guarantee, therefore, that you will in fact notice it."[2] Certainly, this was the case for many of us regarding the life, theology, and work of Jean Vanier.

This chapter is an attempt to signal the beginning of a re-evaluation and theological critique of Vanier's reading of Scripture, particularly Vanier's focus on passages where vulnerability and power are foregrounded in the biblical account. Throughout this chapter I will demonstrate that much of the theological background of Vanier's misconduct lies hidden in plain view in his exegesis. Central to this task is the conviction that it is only by

---

1. Zerubavel, *Hidden in Plain Sight*.
2. Zerubavel, *Hidden in Plain Sight*, 1.

attentive engagement with Vanier's hermeneutic that we can begin to make meaning of the complexities that lie before us.

Prophets, Power, and Possession

Vanier published more than thirty books spanning across half a century (1969–2019), which are linked together by ideas informed by his reading of Scripture and focused on the phenomenon of disability. Running in the foreground of this corpus are recurrent biblical passages Vanier re-presents to tell the story of L'Arche, which he told as a type of recapitulation of God's transformative purposes within the world. From the prophetic imagery of the Old Testament, to the characteristic spirit of the Beatitudes, as well as Paul's theology of weakness, Vanier drew heavily upon sacred tradition in his account of L'Arche. Yet, considering the contradiction with his actual practices that lies before us, it is precisely because so much of his thought was shaped by his reading of Scripture that a re-evaluation of Vanier's hermeneutic is necessary.

Throughout earlier works Vanier invokes the prophetic admonitions against the idolatry of the people of God in the Old Testament to warn against what he perceives as the disintegration of the self and society. Such social decline is the result of a cultural obsession with the self and its quest for power that in turn fosters fear of others leading to competitive modes of life and the marginalization of the poor. For Vanier, society is in need for a conversion of love. While there are many aspects regarding Vanier's pulse on society that demonstrate his ability to discern the signs of the time and cast a vision for what is required to break free from the chains of fear, megalomania, and narcissism, there are places within his exegesis and social critique that demand further consideration bearing in mind the revelations regarding his abuse of power.[3] The following analysis will focus on a sampling of places within Vanier's writings where his interpretation of Scripture and cultural exegesis presents difficulties, especially in the shadow of his transgressions.

In *Eruption to Hope* Vanier exposes what he perceives are the pressure points of modernity leading civilization into ruin. For Vanier, fear of the other has given rise to all sorts of moral and spiritual failures. Thus, Vanier pleads for those who are poor, lonely, and marginalized whereby he exhorts others to give of their substance by emphasizing that if we will share of our very being with love there is still time for an eruption to hope. For Vanier,

---

3. See also Reinders's "Mixture of Light and Darkness" on Vanier as a critic of contemporary culture.

the love that will give rise to an eruption of hope is embodied and requires the gift of presence and communion; one's person is integral to our being.[4] Throughout this work Vanier attempts to unmask prevailing forms of love that construct barriers within us and in turn engender barriers between us and others. Such forms of love are "not true love" but rather expressions of immaturity rooted in fear. For Vanier, love that does not involve sacrifice and gift of self to others is lacking and will inevitably manifest itself in "tensions, degenerating into jealousy or hatred, apathy or even despair."[5] On the contrary, love rooted in a total commitment and giving of self will beget a way of life marked by true liberation and peace.

Apart from the revelations regarding Vanier's abusive actions, his call to a love that is genuine on account of sacrifice and the gift of oneself is beyond doubt if not unreservedly biblical. Such love is embodied and perfectly fulfilled in and through the life of Jesus Christ, a way of life of love that all are invited into through his death, resurrection, and glorious ascension. Yet, Vanier's abuse of power problematizes the truthfulness of his claims regarding the message of love and self-givenness. "Gift" entails giving oneself willingly without being or feeling forced to do so.[6] Yet it was within the contexts of spiritual direction and accompaniment that Vanier used his position and power in coercive ways to exploit the presence and communion of vulnerable women. As such, Vanier's dehumanizing behavior casts a shadow over his use of the message of embodied love, presence, and communion, as well as over how this message is received. It goes without saying that Vanier's deplorable actions were not only rooted in and expressive of licentious vulgarity. It also resulted in his own degeneracy, and in turn the fear, pain, suffering, hatred, and despair of others—the very dangers from which he called us to flee.

Foregrounded throughout his writings is a recurring invocation of prophets of peace. Vanier writes, "Never before has the world been in such need of finding men and women to follow Jesus. We must find prophets of peace who will follow in his footsteps, and who walk gently but firmly between the two worlds, calling unceasingly to the rich to dispossess themselves and love, and calling forth to help those in suffering, misery, and poverty."[7] Society is in need of a type of conversion from a morality of egotistic pleasure to a morality of peace, justice, truth, and love, which

---

4. Vanier, *Eruption to Hope*, 16, 22.

5. Vanier, *Eruption to Hope*, 24.

6. For more on "gift" language in the context of L'Arche, see McKearney "Disabling Virtue."

7. Vanier, *Eruption to Hope*, preface.

Vanier contends will result in a more authentic receptivity of the other. For society to convert itself, we need people who possess great generosity to lead us in walking gently but firmly on the path of nonviolent resistance to the egoism and fear that rule the day. Such people, "must burn with new hearts and new spirit—hearts of flesh and spirits of fire as spoken by the prophet Ezekiel."[8] Following this logic Vanier invokes Isaiah 58 regarding the feast God established "to loose the bonds of wickedness, to undo the thongs of the yoke, to let the oppressed go free, and to break every yoke, to share bread with the hungry, to house the homeless and poor, to cover the naked, and to love."[9] Then, in call and response fashion Vanier offers a persuasive plea, "Listen to Yahweh speaking to us ... is this not our hope?"[10]

All throughout his exegesis Vanier diagnoses the spiritual crisis of his time, seeking to cultivate a longing for spiritual renewal through social and political action.[11] Like a megaphone, the prophetic imagery of Ezekiel and Isaiah functions to amplify the emphasis Vanier places on the need for "complete confidence in the action of the Spirit of God" regarding societal conversion and for prophets of peace to "proclaim without fear" God's message of love for the world.[12] Taking into account the continuity and immediacy of God's revelation in Scripture, Vanier's message of love and call for justice is straightforward. Yet, it is precisely Vanier's use of this very message of love and call for justice that has been cast into doubt in view of the man who compromised his own message through his own "death works"—actions opposed to the intelligibility of his message. Rather than walking firmly between the two worlds that his message envisions Vanier exchanged the *via media* for gnostic persuasion,[13] which he used to disregard intentionally the immanent reality of his transgressions; all of which he justified based on a false and unholy belief that their transgressions were nothing less than a complete confidence in the action of the Spirit of God.[14] What God calls evil Vanier pursued and named as good. As a result, he became the greatest danger he once warned against—the danger that the prophets of peace expose and admonish.

---

8. Vanier, *Eruption to Hope*, preface, 18. See Ezek 36:25–27; Isa 36:25–27.

9. Isa 58:11

10. Vanier, *Eruption to Hope*, 20.

11. Vanier, *Be Not Afraid*. Throughout this work the prophetic imagery of Isaiah, Ezekiel, Hosea, and Song of Songs fund Vanier's cultural exegesis (23–24, 48–49, 69, 110–11, 113–14, 116, 129–32).

12. Vanier, *Eruption to Hope*, 18–19.

13. See Ulrich, "On Remaining in God's Story."

14. L'Arche International, "Summary Report," 6.

Central to Vanier's cultural exegesis is a moral critique of power and its alluring appeal in society and relationships. Such critique features more prominently in *Finding Peace* wherein Vanier identifies sources of conflict and fear within and among individuals and communities that prevent us from finding peace. Among these sources is the seductive and controlling nature of power. Vanier writes,

> We can be seduced. . . . Those with power can use clever, psychological tricks and play upon our weaknesses and brokenness in order to attract us to their way of thinking. We can be manipulated into illusion. . . . How quickly we human beings fall into illusion. . . . We can all be seduced by false prophets who promise happiness. But when we submit to these illusions, very quickly we lose our true selves.[15]

This warning is paradigmatic of the general tone of Vanier's critique of power within many of his works; the tone of which appears in the form of an exhortation to beware of the alluring effects of power in relation to those that are powerful. It often carries an implicit rebuke of those he alludes to as "the powerful" who seek to control and enslave by feeding the ego of individuals, communities, and society as a whole.

While Vanier seems to have a good pulse on the moreish appetency of power's persuasion, particularly in relation to the extrinsic effects of power on individuals and groups, what is lacking in his critique of power is awareness of the self as the primary agent of power's infection. Vanier demonstrates repeatedly how power can corrupt but neglects naming how this reality exposes who people really are. It is as if Vanier sees the "we" he alludes to, and of which he is part, as only objects susceptible to power's seduction and persuasion. Within Vanier's critique, the "we" are always objects acted upon. We are the ones who are manipulated, controlled, and coaxed. For Vanier, "we" are never perceived as the powerful subjects whose preexistent moral qualities and tendencies might be aroused and exposed by our use of power's seduction and persuasion. Thus, what is ultimately absent from Vanier's critique is self-awareness that even he was or could be the subject of power who wields power over others and thus one to whom his message and that of the prophets cry out against. As his tragic story has revealed, he nor "we" are immune from being or becoming false prophets whose power seeks the possession of others.[16]

---

15. Vanier, *Finding Peace*, 53–54.

16. See for a similar critique of Vanier's way of addressing weakness, failure, and transgression in general terms, Dow, "Against Living Saints."

Back to the Well: Reconsidering John 4 after Vanier

Central to the foregoing analysis is the unreserved conviction that the overarching anatomy, posture, and orientation of Vanier's hermeneutic is inseparable from his life, which is to say that his work and theology cannot be treated independently from his reprehensible behavior; they go hand in hand, making each association intelligible. Because of the conviction that his person and writing are both apiece, his seductive rhetoric and condemnable actions should not lead us astray from exercising a hermeneutic of suspicion regarding his reading of Scripture. To this end, the following analysis will focus on Vanier's re-presentation of Jesus's encounter with the Samaritan woman in the Gospel of John.

Images of Love offers Vanier's description on the human condition in an age and time of much confusion.[17] As in many of his works, Vanier attempts to expose how economic, political, and social structures reflect our inner fears and how these fears influence our desire to escape pain, anguish, and vulnerability; his aim is to unmask the ethos of fear within society. To this end Vanier offers an alternative understanding of the role of pain and brokenness in ourselves and the world. "If we are to create a world where there can be healing, growth and wholeness" then we must learn the importance of accepting vulnerability and pain, not flee from it.[18] Vanier's logic for accepting pain and vulnerability is that these phenomena are about people. He writes:

> No one likes pain. We run from pain. But, of course, in running from pain, we run from people. Then we begin to feel guilty as the pain is internalized. We feel the need to justify ourselves and our flight from people in pain. This is the beginning of prejudice. We begin to despise certain people and certain groups of people in whom we see no value. This is totally opposed to God's vision.[19]

Here Vanier stresses how fleeing from vulnerability is endemic in the human condition and how such movement compounds our fears, hindering ourselves and others. Such flight is opposed to God's vision. But what is this vision of God to which Vanier alludes?

For Vanier, the vision of God is shaped by sacred tradition, particularly the way of Jesus in the gospels. Throughout his corpus Vanier frequently cites the gospels intending his audience will encounter the life of Jesus. A

---

17. Vanier, *Images of Love*, 9, 19–25.
18. Vanier, *Images of Love*, 26–33.
19. Vanier, *Images of Love*, 43.

primary example of this is in Vanier's re-presenting of Jesus's encounter with the woman of Samaria in John 4, a paradigm text around which many of Vanier's writings orbit, especially regarding his stories of transformation in L'Arche. Contextually, Vanier focuses his attention on the unexpected nature of the encounter between Jesus and the Samaritan woman and concludes that this woman had endured the burden of stigma on account of her promiscuous sexual history. He then re-presents what he perceives as the heart of John's gospel by accentuating the dynamics of personal and societal transformation past and present.

Such continuity is best expressed in Vanier's description of how the prevailing cross-cultural prejudice in John 4:9—regarding how Jews did not share things in common with Samaritans—remains present in our time, especially in relation to marginalized populations. Such disregard, Vanier concludes, is the result of fear. "The questions that each one of us has to ask are: Who is that person I despise? Who is that person I refuse to listen to? Who is that person that I am convinced can bring nothing to enrich my heart, or my intelligence, or my vision of the world, or my vision of humanity? Who is that person, or who is that cultural group or religious group?"[20] From here Vanier explains that the underlying reason why people prejudge is because we see in others what we do not want to look at in ourselves. "There is something dirty in myself and I do not want to see that."[21] Our unwillingness to accept what is true of ourselves holds us captive to fear, and in turn guides us in our disregard of others.[22]

Again, Vanier invokes John 4:9 to further illuminate his diagnosis. "Perhaps we reject the call to God because that would require us not to condemn others. Perhaps the Jewish people despise the Samaritans because the Samaritans remind them that there is an evil side to each of us."[23] Contextually, Vanier is referring to the call of Jesus to worship God in spirit and truth, which presumes a way of life that takes seriously Jesus's exhortation, "Do not judge." Jesus's way of life is antithetical to the vision of modernity, a vision that Vanier perceives as the cause of people being crushed. Such vision is rooted in what he calls "the gospel of Mary," the *Magnificat*, where Mary praises God for God's mighty works. Mary says that God takes down the powerful from their thrones, which Vanier translates, "all those who stand in judgement of others and He brings up the little. . . . This is the mystery of God. Then hopefully, as some go down and some come up, we are going to

---

20. Vanier, *Images of Love*, 44.
21. Vanier, *Images of Love*, 46.
22. Vanier, *Images of Love*, 46.
23. Vanier, *Images of Love*, 46.

have community because the hierarchy, where those at the top feel virtuous and those at the bottom feel condemned, is broken."[24]

At first glance Vanier's description of the vision of God, in relation to a world where at its core the weakest are indispensable, is uncomplicated. Those who are prone to disregard and rejection ought to be welcomed, celebrated, and loved. Without doubt this is the message of the gospel. To abide in Christ is to abide in love and welcome others. Such *habitus* is characteristic of the biblical vision of how the specificity of Christ's claim on oneself is made visible in our own lives through others.[25] The paradox of the other is that though they may be a source of pain reminding us of our own pain and inner fears, they can also be the way to liberation. God's vision for humanity is the way of liberation. Vanier is presumably correct in naming both fear as a fundamental cause of our disregard of others as well as how these others can put us on the path to inner freedom.[26] But the hermeneutical assumption that funds the logic of his interpretation is problematic; namely, his imaginative, prurient, and moralistic speculation of the Samaritan woman's character, which is wholly absent from the sacred text.[27]

Throughout his corpus Vanier imagines the Samaritan woman as one who is weak and broken, excluded and marginalized, and humiliated and despised.[28] Contrasting how Jesus speaks to the rich from the perspective of those who are poor, Vanier envisions the Samaritan woman as "one of the most wounded people in the whole gospel" not only on account of her "rejected race" but also because of the contempt she allegedly has brought upon herself.[29] "Freely he speaks to the despised Samaritan woman and asks her of water."[30] On account of the timing of her outing, Vanier insists that

---

24. Vanier, *Images of Love*, 45–48. See Matt 2:1–10; 7:1–6; Luke 1:46–55; 6:37; John 7–8.

25. Wall, *Welcome as a Way of Life*, 115.

26. Vanier, *Images of Love*, 45, 50.

27. See Gwennola Rimbaut, "Jean Vanier: A New Spiritual Master?" in Study Commission, *Control and Abuse*, 733–52, especially 736–39. Rimbaut highlights the imaginative nature of Vanier's hermeneutic that often yielded details that do not exist in the biblical narrative.

28. Vanier, *Befriending the Stranger*, 51–65, especially 51–52, 54, 57, 60; Vanier, *Broken Body*, 41; Vanier, *Drawn into the Mystery*, 89–100, esp. 89, 92; Vanier, *Images of Love*, 43–44; Vanier, *Jesus, the Gift*, 99, 111. See also Masters, "Considerations," wherein she highlights Vanier's tendency to narrate persons with disability in relation to their passivity; see also McKearney, "Disabling Virtue." Such tendency is present here with Vanier's re-presenting of John 4, a reading that overlooks the agency of the Samaritan woman.

29. Vanier, *Befriending the Stranger*, 51.

30. Vanier, *Broken Body*, 41.

this woman's very presence was disgraceful and scandalous to others, "making it difficult for her to meet others in public spaces as well as in places of worship."[31] Such rejection, Vanier imagines, must have led her to believe that she was rejected by God.

In other places Vanier imagines the Samaritan woman as a "woman full of guilt"[32] who was broken and had "broken relationships" resulting in "a broken self-image," and "deep feelings of guilt, of worthlessness, who feels that nobody could ever really love her."[33] Actually, it is on this account that Vanier believes the Samaritan woman represents the place of sorrow and shame within all of us. "This woman also lives within each one of us; she is the wounded, broken part of our being that we hide from others, and even from our own selves. She symbolizes the place of guilt in us."[34] Whether the result of her own self-reproach or the condemnation of others, such contempt, Vanier maintains, resulted in her own uncertainty. "The Samaritan woman was confused; she did not understand," writes Vanier.[35] What is interesting here is that Vanier's understanding of the Samaritan woman's uncertainty is based on her surprise by Jesus's words of promise.

More problematic than any of these portraitures is Vanier's more prurient speculation of the Samaritan woman's erotic personage where he imagines her a prostitute who had lived with many men. Vanier interprets her in need of God's penetrating love and as one who can reciprocally do something for her needy savior. Such interpretation is pure conjecture not to mention textually unwarranted.[36] In *The Broken Body* Vanier locates "his" despised Samaritan woman alongside the unnamed woman in Luke 7 who he imagines is "a victim of prostitution."[37] Such elaboration reveals Vanier's prurient tendency to turn women Jesus encounters into prostitutes as if the power of these stories is "here are some loose women who Jesus forgave of their promiscuous ways" rather than "a paradigm of discipleship . . . because she exhibits radical, profligate hospitality and love."[38]

Ill at ease with matters of sexual propriety, Vanier makes explicit his salacious presumption of the Samaritan woman in the latter development of this work by characterizing her not only as a woman among the oldest

31. Vanier, *Broken Body*, 52.
32. Vanier, *Befriending the Stranger*, 57.
33. Vanier, *Drawn into the Mystery*, 90–91, 96.
34. Vanier, *Befriending the Stranger*, 54, 57.
35. Vanier, *Befriending the Stranger*, 57, 60. See Vanier, *Drawn into the Mystery*, 97.
36. Vanier, *Broken Body*, 79.
37. Vanier, *Broken Body*, 41.
38. Clark-Soles, *Women in the Bible*. 197.

working profession but also of a specific breed, a "dirty" prostitute.[39] Vanier writes, "She belongs to what we call 'the fourth world': She had lived with five men and the man she was then living with was not her husband. She was . . . rejected by her own people. . . . Jesus looks at this woman, whom others scoff at and despise, the 'dirty prostitute.'"[40] Such smutty specificity signals a strengthening of Vanier's interpretive commitment that makes much of this woman's "sinfulness, her shady past, her dubious morals, her promiscuity, her aberrant sexual behavior."[41] All of this is completely absent from the text, however. From beginning to end Vanier's interpretation paints an eroticizing portrait of the Samaritan woman who functions as a model of sin on account of biblical voyeurism.[42]

Now, it is vital to note that Vanier is correct that this Samaritan woman is not like "most women." However, it is not on account of her sexual "history of broken relationships."[43] The text is clear on this. She is a model of faith and apostleship who bears witness to Jesus and as a result, her entire village comes to faith. In view of the glaring theme of light present in John's gospel, she exemplifies light as she "boldly, publicly appears in the brightest light of day to encounter the True Light, and as a result she is enlightened," and in turn lets her light shine.[44] She is self-aware and able to delineate cultural and gendered differences. Rather than being out of place she wastes no time calling attention to the fact that Jesus is the one out of place. "How is it that you, a Jew, ask a drink of me, a woman of Samaria?"[45] Uninhibited, she courageously and actively engages Jesus in deep theological inquiry. Equally so, she was capable of theological dialogue and knowledgeable about the Law and the Prophets. She recognized that Jesus was a prophet not because of his sixth sense concerning her marital history but because prophets are always exhorting the people of God to proper "worship in Spirit and in truth."[46]

39. Vanier, *Broken Body*, 79.

40. Vanier, *Broken Body*, 79. While Vanier's interpretation on why the woman was there at that time is common among male interpreters of the Bible, a good amount of work exists calling into question these readings, especially how they tend to downgrade and marginalize the Samaritan woman's status. In *The Gospel of John in Cultural and Rhetorical Perspective*, Neyrey addresses cultural stereotypes of woman in public and private spaces (143–71), which fund the type of interpretive moves Vanier and others make concerning the timing of the plot in John 4.

41. Gench, *Back to the Well*, 115–16.

42. Gench, *Back to the Well*, 123.

43. Vanier, *Drawn into the Mystery*, 90.

44. Clark-Soles, *Women in the Bible*, 210. Luke intentionally contrasts the Samaritan woman with Nicodemus, who comes to Jesus "by night" (John 3:2).

45. Clark-Soles, *Women in the Bible*, 210. See John 4:9.

46. Clark-Soles, *Women in the Bible*, 211. See John 4:24.

Actually, "Her question about worship opened the space for Jesus to explain his own identity and the new reality that he brought."[47] In apostolic fashion she demonstrates an eager enthusiasm for evangelism. "Leaving her water jar, the woman went back to the town and said to the people, 'Come, see a man who told me everything I ever did. Could this be the Messiah?'"[48] Far from being excluded, humiliated, and despised, she is trustworthy enough for her community to welcome her voice and its accompanying message as attention-worthy and desirable.[49] Perhaps they too were discerning enough to recognize the significance of her light of person and place among them. Perhaps we too can share in this light and begin to acknowledge that the Samaritan woman is a vessel of living water and that this woman is not like "most women."[50]

What about the "five men" in addition to the sixth man she was then living with who was not her husband either?[51] The Greek term for "husband," ἄνδρα, also can be translated as "man," which Vanier settles on in his exegesis without further reflection in preemptive ways. His commitment to "men" in contrast to "husbands" disallows him from discerning any possibility that the Samaritan woman was widowed five times and/or entangled in the custom of levirate marriage where the sixth male had abdicated his responsibility to marry her but remained willing to accommodate her; or that she was divorced over and over again not on account of her promiscuity but rather because of her barrenness, a recurring motif throughout the biblical story.[52] While the text does not tell us anything about why this Samaritan woman had five husbands, what is unquestionably clear here is that translation matters. The language of "husbands," unlike "men" permits alternative readings that refuse any validity to Vanier's elaborate and salacious imagination.

As a final note on Vanier's exegesis regarding the Samaritan woman, he is also correct when he insists that Jesus "does not judge or condemn her. He does not condescend or give her any moral lessons."[53] The glaring paradox

---

47. Reeder, *Samaritan Woman's Story*, 152.

48. John 4:28–30.

49. Clark-Soles, *Women in the Bible*, 211.

50. The main purpose of my account is not to moralize or reform the Samaritan woman from being a prostitute to being a saint but rather to problematize one clear interpretation of her that exclusively emphasizes her passivity and brokenness to highlight her agency and complexity, both of which are textually warranted.

51. John 4:39.

52. O'Day, *Word Disclosed*, 41–42; see Gench, *Back to the Well*, 116; Bridges, "John 4:5–42," 173–76.

53. Vanier, *Drawn into the Mystery*, 92.

here is that Vanier does, and more! By projecting an identity on her that is textually, transliterally, and speculatively unwarranted he instrumentalizes her as a "body in use" for Jesus's needs, thus simultaneously projecting onto Jesus an identity foreign to his character. Vanier imagines the Samaritan woman as a "bad woman," a "dirty prostitute" who had lived with many men who now finds herself in need of God's penetrating love, and who could do something for her needy savior.[54] Commenting on Jesus's request for water, Vanier writes, "he says, 'You can do something for me, I need your help.'"[55] In another place while exaggerating Jesus's fatigue Vanier writes, "He approaches her like a tired, thirsty beggar, asking her to do something for him,"[56] imagining her in need of some divine intrusion. Commenting on how the Samaritan woman is both a reality and symbol of guilt in all of us, Vanier writes, "If we do not let God penetrate into the shadow areas of our being, they risk governing our lives."[57] Such descriptions are parenthetically framed within a larger discourse of themes such as "meetings of love" and "touching our wounds"; themes that have been cast in the dark shadow of the revelations regarding Vanier's abuse of power in the confines of spiritual accompaniment behind closed doors "at dark." The unsettling nature of Vanier's universalizing appeal is that it presumes Jesus to be the one who can look at the woman, size her up as she walks toward him, make judgements about who and what she is, work out what good she can do for him and in turn he for her. Such posturing is characteristic of the way Vanier intrusively positioned himself toward and with the victims he abused. Such appeal and actions beg the question, "Why doesn't Vanier understand Jesus to be the one who receives from a stranger what he did not know he needed until it was so freely and unexpectedly offered, so that he stands beside this woman as one who is himself to encounter the mystery of grace?" Without such a turn-around in perspective both the Samaritan woman and Jesus remain prey to a type of hermeneutical instrumentalization whereby their purpose within the story is use for the other's generalized human needs; the risks becoming what Phyllis Trible called a text of terror, and not simply for women.[58]

54. Vanier, *Images of Love*, 44.
55. Vanier, *Broken Body*, 79.
56. Vanier, *Drawn into the Mystery*, 92.
57. Vanier, *Befriending the Stranger*, 53–4.
58. Trible, *Texts of Terror*.

Whose Story? Whose Transformation? Which Story?

Vanier's universalizing appeal about the Samaritan woman as a symbol of guilt in all of us not only proves problematic within his exegesis but also presents difficulty when it comes to his persistent retelling of stories of transformation in L'Arche, especially since the former directly illumines the latter and in turn reciprocally reifies his interpretive understandings. Peppered all throughout the larger body of his work are communal memories about how L'Arche is a place of transformation. One example of this is in Vanier's retelling of Eric, a severely autistic person who was born blind and deaf. At the age of four Eric had been placed in a psychiatric hospital. Eric's placement combined with his inability to walk or eat by himself gave rise to great inner anguish. Vanier writes, "I had never met anyone so filled with anguish and a desire to die."[59] But it was life in L'Arche that gave life to Eric as "he discovered he was loved and thus he was someone."[60] The more he discovered he was loved the more he discovered his true self and "became more peaceful and learned to eat by himself and gradually to walk."[61] Gradually, Eric experienced genuine transformation. On this account, Vanier imagines Eric's transformation as a type of witness to his understanding of how L'Arche is a type of entry point into participating in God's story. Put another way, the story of Eric is a story of transformation that reciprocally reveals the woman at the well in John 4; a possible reason why Eric's story, like that of the Samaritan woman's, functions canonically throughout Vanier's works, and often in close association with the other.[62] Like the story of the Samaritan woman, Eric's transformation illustrates an encounter Vanier insists is so central to the heart of L'Arche. In retelling Eric's story Vanier focuses on vital aspects of Eric's growing sense of his true self in community and how encounter therein led to Eric's transformation from his false self toward becoming more human in community. For Vanier, Eric's story of transformation witnesses to the gospel as a reciprocal re-presenting of Scripture in L'Arche, thus portraying L'Arche as a type of modern translation of the gospel (in personalist tone) that radically challenges prevailing cultural assumptions of those regarded least.

Like the Samaritan woman, Eric is fragile, broken, humiliated, and despised. Personifying himself as a redemptive figure in his retelling, Vanier

---

59. Vanier, "Towards Transformational Reading," 238.

60. Vanier, "Towards Transformational Reading," 238.

61. Vanier, "Towards Transformational Reading," 238.

62. Vanier, *From Brokenness to Community*, 13, 25; Vanier, *Scandal of Service*, 35–46; Vanier, "Towards Transformational Reading," 237–38; Vanier, *Becoming Human*, 10–12; Vanier, *Heart of L'Arche*, 38–42.

welcomes Eric who is also excluded and marginalized.[63] Like Jesus who told the Samaritan woman "everything she ever did" Vanier speaks as if he knows the depth of Eric's anguish and negative self-image. Like the Samaritan woman, "Eric was not like most men." Throughout his retelling Vanier, as representative of L'Arche, approaches Eric in a way that results in Eric's discovery that he is loved revealing his true self, the revelation of which is visibly expressed in Eric being at peace and in good health. Like the Samaritan woman Eric is now able to walk and share in the common life within his community without shame. Whether it's the story of Eric, Claudia, or others that Vanier tells, he always places emphasis on their transformation in terms of a transition from rejection, anguish/fear, and exclusion to welcome, self-discovery, and love. Such emphasis indubitably seems to reify some of Vanier's hermeneutical commitments that we have already explored in the foregoing analysis of his reading of John 4.

Another significant concern of Vanier's retelling is that it relies solely on his own interpretive authority/power and judgments. Eric's story, and that of others, are always and exclusively secondhand, disallowing Eric and others to own their stories. What power does Eric possess over his own representation? Like many of the stories he tells, no space is given for Eric to voice the transformation Vanier claims occurred and expects us to believe. Just like the Samaritan woman in Vanier's exegesis, Eric instrumentally functions as a heuristic trope within the larger body of Vanier's work. Because of Eric's deafness and blindness, Vanier could project upon him all the emotive qualities he desired, turning him into a symbol of transformation. This is not to deny the possibility or reality of the lived experience of transformation in Eric's life or that of others whom Vanier writes/tells. Rather, it is to flag up the possible discursive dangers of interpretive authority/power at play in subject construction (Eric's desolation) and object formation (Eric's transfiguration) in storytelling, especially considering the elaborate, imaginative, and moralistic nature of Vanier's interpretive tendencies. Since the story of Eric is a story of transformation that reciprocally reveals the woman at the well in John 4 and vice versa, such tendencies are causes for concern about the reliability of representation within Vanier's storytelling as much as the authenticity between Vanier and those subject to his "othering."[64] As such, the following questions come to the fore. Who's story is being told,

---

63. Another problematic feature of Vanier's retelling of John 4 is that he repeatedly speaks as if Jesus is the one who welcomes the Samaritan woman when the text is clear that Jesus is the uninvited guest to whom the Samaritan woman shows radical hospitality.

64. "Othering" relates to the process (political/social) whereby an individual or group uses negative or unwarranted attributes to define and/or subordinate others.

Eric's or Vanier's? What prevents Eric's story, and consequently Eric himself, from becoming prey to the power of the storyteller and thus Vanier's possession? What prevents us from being more critically suspicious of Vanier's project as a whole, especially since Vanier distanced himself from the very process of transformation he so willingly declares on behalf of others? Such distancing I believe is the ultimate cause of the unsettling paradox that is his life and work and begs the question of whether his storytelling of L'Arche as an invitation into God's story has any merit at all or if it is nothing more than a decoy he used to inveigle others to participate in his story.

Final Thoughts

Central to the foregoing account is the conviction that much of the trouble Vanier got into lies "hidden in plain view" in his biography and exegesis. From the contours that form the background of his life, work, and theological vision to the hermeneutical commitments that gave definite shape to his exegesis (scriptural/cultural), much if not all that I have highlighted above has been in full view from the beginning. Still, much more remains hidden in plain view that deserves further investigation and reevaluation. How are we to make meaning of the story-form logic of entering into God's story in light of Vanier's attempt to live divinely as God versus living humanly before God who enters into the story of our lives?[65] To what extent did Vanier's self-identification with the weak and in turn his practice of separating the weak and powerful into two separate groups result in his lack of self-awareness and theological understanding that all of humanity can be weak or powerful? To what degree did authority and power have a depriving effect on Vanier's ability to hear the third call, the call of God in and through his victims, the ecclesial and public condemnation of Père Thomas's actions, and L'Arche's invitation for Vanier to come forward prior to his passing? In what ways do Vanier's hermeneutical commitments to a form of liberation theology and to a particular set of anthropological beliefs make possible his conviction that he knows what God's love means? Central to theologies of liberation is the notion of the "sacrament of the other." Considering Vanier's seductive rhetoric, a total reevaluation of his understanding of sacrament and liberation is needed. Vanier insisted to victims that his body was not his body but that of Jesus. Like a sacramental chalice that holds the body and blood of Jesus Christ, Vanier saw himself as a vessel replete with the divine. As such, he set out to coopt others into celebrating this unholy communion ("this is not two, but we are one") through acts of love (sexual abuse), which

65. See Ulrich, "On Remaining in God's Story."

he blessed on the basis of his "mystical and spiritual" justifications. These and many more questions lay the foundation for the need for further theological engagement and reevaluation vis-à-vis the relationship between text and life regarding Vanier. My hope is that others will join in this exercise of reevaluation as we seek to remain faithful to the witness of Scripture and sacred tradition in view of the complexities that lie before us concerning Vanier.

Bibliography

L'Arche International. "Summary Report." February 22, 2020.

Bridges, Linda McKinnish. "John 4:5–42." *Interpretation: A Journal of Bible and Theology* 48.2 (1994) 173–76.

Clark-Soles, Jamie. *Women in the Bible: Interpretation: Resources for the Use of Scripture in the Church*. Louisville, KY: Westminster John Knox, 2020.

Dow, Keith. "Against Living Saints." In *The Betrayal of Witness: Reflections on the Downfall of Jean Vanier*, edited by Stanley Hauerwas and Hans S. Reinders, 18–36. Eugene, OR: Wipf & Stock, 2024.

Gench, Frances Taylor. *Back to the Well: Women's Encounters with Jesus in the Gospels*. Louisville, KY: Westminster John Knox, 2004.

Masters, Anne. "Considerations for an Evolving Vision of Identity and Witness." In *The Betrayal of Witness: Reflections on the Downfall of Jean Vanier*, edited by Stanley Hauerwas and Hans S. Reinders, 37–55. Eugene, OR: Wipf & Stock, 2024.

McKearney, Patrick. "Disabling Virtue." In *The Betrayal of Witness: Reflections on the Downfall of Jean Vanier*, edited by Stanley Hauerwas and Hans S. Reinders, 89–103. Eugene, OR: Wipf & Stock, 2024.

Neyrey, Jerome H. *The Gospel of John in Cultural and Rhetorical Perspective*. Grand Rapids, MI: Eerdmans, 2009.

O'Day, Gail. *The Word Disclosed: Preaching the Gospel of John*. St. Louis, MO: Chalice, 2002.

Reeder, Caryn A. *The Samaritan Woman's Story: Reconsidering John 4 After #ChurchToo*. Downers Grove, IL: InterVarsity, 2022.

Reinders, Hans S. "A Mixture of Light and Darkness: Accounting for My Vanier." In *The Betrayal of Witness: Reflections on the Downfall of Jean Vanier*, edited by Stanley Hauerwas and Hans S. Reinders, 104–19. Eugene, OR: Wipf & Stock, 2024.

Study Commission Mandated by L'Arche International. *Control and Abuse Investigation on Thomas Philippe, Jean Vanier and L'Arche (1950–2019)*. Châteauneuf-sur-Charente, France: Frémur, 2023.

Trible, Phyllis. *Texts of Terror: Literary-Feminist Readings of Biblical Narratives*. 40th anniversary ed. Minneapolis, MN: Fortress, 2022.

Ulrich, Hans G. "On Remaining in God's Story as Passion." In *The Betrayal of Witness: Reflections on the Downfall of Jean Vanier*, edited by Stanley Hauerwas and Hans S. Reinders, 137–49. Eugene, OR: Wipf & Stock, 2024.

Vanier, Jean. *Becoming Human*. London: Darton, Longman, & Todd, 2010.

———. *Befriending the Stranger*. London: Darton, Longman, & Todd, 2005.

———. *Be Not Afraid*. New York: Paulist, 1975.

———. *The Broken Body*. London: Darton, Longman, & Todd, 2009.
———. *Community and Growth*. London: Darton, Longman, & Todd, 2007.
———. *Drawn into the Mystery of Jesus through the Gospel of John*. New York: Paulist, 2004.
———. *Eruption to Hope*. Toronto: Griffin House, 1971.
———. *Finding Peace*. New York: Continuum, 2003.
———. *From Brokenness to Community*. New York: Paulist, 1992.
———. *The Heart of L'Arche*. Toronto: Novalis, 2012.
———. *Images of Love, Words of Hope*. Hantsport, Nova Scotia: Lancelot, 1991.
———. *Jesus, The Gift of Love*. New York: Crossroad, 2011.
———. *Scandal of Service*. London: Darton, Longman, & Todd, 1997.
———. "Towards Transformational Reading of Scripture." In *Canon and Biblical Interpretation*, edited by Craig Bartholomew, Scott Hahn, and Robin Parry, 237–41. Grand Rapids, MI: Zondervan, 2006.
Wall, Benjamin. *Welcome as a Way of Life: A Practical Theology of Jean Vanier*. Eugene, OR: Cascade, 2016.
Zerubavel, Eviatar. *Hidden in Plain Sight: The Social Structure of Irrelevance*. London: Oxford University Press, 2015.

Chapter Nine

On Remaining in God's Story as Passion

Hans G. Ulrich

THE STORY OF JEAN Vanier, the story of L'Arche, and the stories of all those who come along with its movement are testimony of a people who follow a particular, unique passion. The same holds for the unfolding theology that supports and accompanies it. It is in this passion that those who trust God are attentive to God's action, that they meet and come together in witnessing God's active presence.[1] What Jean Vanier unfolds in his writings genuinely reflects how this passion is lived in L'Arche and, conversely, I have read his theology as the communication of this form of life articulated as a witness of a receiving community. I will therefore understand the witness of L'Arche as the endeavor of living in God's story.[2]

---

1. "Passion" is a crucial term in this chapter, but one that resists a neat definition. It refers to a committed but also ardent pursuit of a cause by which one is not only driven but also captivated. In the present case, that cause is being drawn into the story of God's revelation in Jesus Christ as acting presence. "Passion" thus denotes a commitment one finds oneself inescapably drawn into, and, in that sense, it contains an element of passivity. It expresses a sense of being overcome. All of these different aspects of the term are at stake here, which makes it fitting to gesture at the extraordinary witness of L'Arche. The reader is invited to hear the term "passion" throughout this essay in its multifaceted richness.

2. In view of the Study Commission's report *Control and Abuse* I should emphasize that the witness of L'Arche—as distinct from the witness of Vanier—is my main point of reference.

Because of this witness Vanier's theological unfolding and grasping of it moves independent of, and counter to, the dominant grammars of contemporary moral culture. L'Arche embodies the counter-cultural grammar of that story. The dominant grammars prescribe seemingly evidential markers of what truly matters in human lives. In other words, they signal that if people will follow them they will find fulfillment. Dominant in our present culture is the grammar of individual achievement, driven by the power and ability to do one's own thing. This is not the grammar of witnessing life in God's passion that speaks to us in Jesus Christ. Here it applies what Jesus says in Mark 8:

> Whosoever will come after me, let him deny himself, and take up his cross, and follow me. For whosoever will save his life shall lose it; but whosoever shall lose his life for my sake and the gospel's, the same shall save it. (Mark 8:34–35)

Accordingly, Vanier's writings follow the logic of what it is to receive oneself in communication with others. He describes this theologically as the story of a passion that tells how people live together and become aware of what sustains and shapes their communal life. Whichever people were involved in L'Arche, for whatever reason, the question they faced was which passion they found themselves in—in which story of trust, of vocation, of transformation. It is crucial that the story of this passion remains determinant. It is a passion that reveals God's action in the experience of encounter and community.[3]

Vanier's account runs counter to the dynamics in which many of our contemporaries pursue something of their own will, as well as to the dynamics of whatever it is that "drives" them. The grammar of a passion that make people recognize and be aware of God's action and activity is guiding the theological grammar that shapes and supports the communities of L'Arche. This is the reason why living together with persons with a cognitive impairment appears as the paradigm for human life as such. Abstracted from this passion, every human life is subject to a fundamental loss of reality, the reality namely of living in the purview of God's action. This is the full reality of all that appears in the form of living together in communication with one another as people with whom God pursues and continues his story.

---

3. Obviously the way Vanier answered this question in his life is scrutinized by the Study Commission mandated by L'Arche International. It's findings suggest that that—at best—he was led by another kind of passion that was definitely not following God's action.

Hans Reinders has brought this into view anew as God's "providence."[4] The theological account of providence does not explain how God is the author of what we humans experience as determining our lives. Instead, it accounts for how all that is happening to us is saved into what God has provided in God's passion. Everything depends on whether people are attentive and are a witness to the story of what God pursues with the people who are his creatures. This then is the dignity that every human being has, the dignity of being chosen by God, the dignity of being allowed to live trustfully in God's passion. This is not the dignity of the human being *per se* that we are to preserve as a moral "value" operating as a guiding principle of our actions, for example regarding the protection of human life. Instead, it is the dignity of being chosen by God, which no human being can concede, or even deny to another.

This is not to be misunderstood as downplaying or even ignoring the different conditions of life between human beings. These conditions can be so serious that some persons cannot but experience themselves as "disabled." It is crucial to note that these differences are saved into the story of God's providence. In that story there is no dividing people into the "strong" and the "weak," the "normal" and the "abnormal," which implies it does not support the logic of exclusion and inclusion. Such practices of comparison, demarcation, and classification may determine the position of individual people in society. However, being attentive to God's purpose with each of his creatures implies a paradigm shift. It implies learning the grammar of a passion that is God's story in which people trust God and come and live together, in recognition of the different conditions of their lives.

The passion of L'Arche is recognized as theologically truthful because it leads out of the fixation on what people can achieve by themselves and for themselves. That is to say, while people certainly have different support needs, there is no one without any such needs. In other words, it leads out of the individual concern for achieving one's goals in life and into the witness of a common passion that is shared with differing others. All activities and achievements receive a new purpose, however different people might be. It reveals another form of life as reflected in Jesus's words that those who struggle for a "fulfilled" life will lose it, and those who follow this passion will win the life determined by God's initiative and action.

The paradigm of human life thus revealed in the communities of L'Arche can only be recognized theologically. This is the reason why Jean Vanier's theological witness is so universal and fundamental.[5] It goes be-

---

4. Reinders, *Disability, Providence, and Ethics*.
5. Admittedly this description follows the hypothesis stated in the Study

yond any ethical instruction on how to live with persons with a disability. To put it thetically, in his endeavor to describe L'Arche, Vanier's writings unfold a theological genealogy of the reality of God's work in human life that is fulfilled by God' gifts. God's gifts are not states of achievement, like the state of success, or of accomplishments, or even of happiness. The reality of God's gift appears as the transformation of human life. In this reality human beings find themselves initiated in God's story by God's action and activity.

In this respect it is distinct from the dynamic of a humanism that follows the logic of realizing humane ideals. Here I am not merely speaking of the realization of a contrasting and competing worldview. Instead, the fulfillment of God's story with his creatures is the fulfillment of God's passion. In this sense it was said above that abstracted from this passion, every human life is subject to a fundamental loss of reality, the reality namely of living with one another as people with whom God continues God's story. It is in this special sense that we should speak of the "fullness of life," the only fullness of human life that is given in God's action and activity.

Two Types of Theology

However, it is precisely here that we can detect a serious flaw in Vanier's theological reflections. He has not fully grasped the reality of a human life fulfilled *in God's activity*. In Vanier's account of witness a necessary distinction is missing—the distinction between a witness of the passion according to which God's activity fulfills the life of each and every human being, versus a search for fulfillment that is driven by its own dynamic even though it may proceed in reference to that passion. While this distinction is being ignored, Vanier's witness displaces the passion as *God's* activity, so that the only thing that matters for human beings is to find each other and come to fulfill their story together according to their own spirit.

In contrast, the passion in which human beings are initiated by God's activity follows no other dynamic than that which God has provided. Here all is about the fulfillment of God's will, as it says in the Lord's Prayer, "Thy will be done, on earth as it is in heaven."

When one reads Vanier, it is apparent on first sight that remaining attentive to God's action is replaced by whatever the dynamics of living

---

Commission summary that Vanier's writings appear to be driven by a "quest for mystical-loving communion" more than by the "mystical-sexual" drive that it ascribes to Thomas Philippe (Study Commission, *Synthesis*, 75). This is not to excuse Vanier's participation in Philippe's practices, but it is to emphasize the recognition of what he describes as living in L'Arche as exemplification of communal life.

together requires. There is a deeper reason behind this, which is to be traced here, because, as we have seen, it has a profound impact on the witness of L'Arche.

To indicate the background of this critical heuristic we can refer to a well-known problem in the history of theology that has arisen again and again, and that can be pointedly expressed by referring to Martin Luther's account. At stake is Martin Luther's critique of a misunderstood "*pro me*" of which we have been reminded by Hans-Joachim Iwand.[6] God's saving action is done "for me" but it is also done "to me." The misunderstood "*pro me*" concerns the loss of this other aspect, the always given "*extra nos*" of what God works and gives, which is necessarily part of the "*pro me.*" Without this distinction human beings' permanent position before God—"*coram Deo*"— is lost, which also means the loss of being permanently posited before one another.

The problem, then, is the loss of a fundamental distinction that all too easily disappears in a theology that does not follow the biblically given grammar of God's passion as it appeared in every step in Jesus Christ. In the context of Vanier's theology this means we have to be particularly attentive to the pneumatological dimension of this problem because of the "*extra nos*" of the Holy Spirit. The Spirit works its gifts, received as "*charismata*," but they do not become a possession, but are only given, and received, *in actu*.[7]

Thus, we are encountering the distinction between a theology of an accomplished and intensified human life and a theology that describes and reflects on how people find themselves initiated in the story of God's passion. In the one people seek and find fulfillment in each other on their own account, in the other they are attentive to finding themselves in that story and receiving the life that God has given them.

It is worthwhile to note in this connection that the second kind of community is a "*communio sanctorum*," that is, a community of people who acknowledge God's action and activity to be working, because the "*sancti*," the saints, are the people who allow God to act on them, they are the people of this passion. They are not captivated by the question of how they arrive at a state of fulfillment in the human sense.[8] Instead, they seek their fulfillment in the story of Jesus. They live a passion that keeps God's action and activity present, God's address, God's forgiveness, God's promise, God's consolation,

6. Iwand, "Wider den Mißbrauch des '*pro me*,'" 225–30. (Against the Abuse of the "*pro me*").

7. Brock, *Wondrously Wounded*. See also Pia Matthews' argument to emphasize this point by replacing "charism" for "charisma" (Matthews, "Putting Aside Charisma").

8. See Dow, "Against Living Saints."

and God's merciful intervention. Everything is about people coming together in this reality as their common story, the story that became apparent in Jesus Christ. They are living in the hope that God's story will continue with each of them such that it does not end in nothingness. This constitutes the community of those who, like Jesus, live accordingly in God's will.

It is a community that remains in encounter with God's action and activity. It does not dissolve into an undefined, somehow enriched "reality."[9] It is a community of people living together as those in whom God acts. This allows them to be free from seeking the satisfaction of their desires, including the desire for love and living together in unity.

This is an all-important difference following from the critique of a lacking appreciation of the "*extra nos*," the fact that we remain permanently posited before God and, therefore, also before one another. It allows people to remain free from taking over the other person or becoming captive to the forces and dynamics of their togetherness.

Thus, the task remains to distinguish between two types of theology. A theology that reflects living together in God's passion in which God works and acts, versus a theology that aims at a conception of a fulfilled humane life, the life of "becoming human," as Vanier has it. Recognizing this distinction is pivotal to the witness of L'Arche because without it the fact that everything and everyone lives from God's action gets lost and mixed up. The story in which people live in the face of God and in the face of one another is replaced by a story that turns on the elevation of the human heart in a craving for unity. The communities of L'Arche are special because in them the "fullness" of God's story is realized in witnessing what is received from God.

This is not to say that Jean Vanier was not attentive to God's story, but it is to say that whoever follows a theology of that other passion—the passion for unity—exposes himself to the danger and the temptation that the distinction of the "*pro me*" and "*extra nos*" dissolves, as the history of theology shows. The danger is to see God's action and activity realized in an intensified form of human life that is perceived as a transformation. The risk is that this new form of life will gain its own dynamic and thus forgets about the passion of God's story.

Vanier, in his account of an intensified human life, was able to speak vividly about the movement of L'Arche as a transformation that resulted

---

9. The Study Commission writes: "Being 'free,' he—Vanier sc.—now only has one vocation: mystic union. All the things rejected are more or less the expression of the Church as an institution: its relevance is thus reduced and somehow separated from the mystic Church, whose invisible reality prevails" (Study Commission, *Control and Abuse*, 261).

from the growth in the dynamics of communal life.[10] In contrast, a reference to the New Testament and the struggle, especially in Paul, for the building up of the Christian communities may be helpful. Paul spoke of certain *indispensable structures* of the Christian community, without which no building up, no structured house of a community ("*oikodome*"), no "body of Christ" could emerge.[11] There is a whole series of references in the New Testament to these constitutive structures, and thus of the grammar of the definite action by God to form a new creation, as distinct from an indefinite "spiritualized" intensification of human life. A case in point is Paul's description of love (1 Cor 13–14), where he aims to grasp love itself not as an amorphous state of unified togetherness, but as the definite medium in which living together over time finds its possibility. Thus, he states that "love" does not seek its own (1 Cor 13:5). Love is not the desired state and fulfillment of human life but is the demanding vehicle of human coexistence.

This is how Martin Buber understood love in his treatise on "I and Thou," which has also been compared with Vanier's descriptions.[12] However, particularly in Vanier's description of love in which he means to follow Paul, there is that vagueness in which ultimately the possibility of an encounter is lost. On the one hand, we read in Jean Vanier's *Life's Great Questions* that "to grow in love is to grow towards an encounter with the other, face to face."[13] God, it is recognized, remains seeking the encounter in his love for us human beings and our love for him. On the other hand, we read about a growth in love that does not recognize the remaining "face to face" but instead is focused on a "mysterious unity."

> Growth begins when I can say: "There is a brokenness within me. With some people I can be open, at ease and welcoming. But with others I can become closed off and mean. I find myself unable to trust them, and there is something that makes me want to turn away." . . . There is a struggle even in the reality of my own body. Perhaps I know that you are precious, but I am unable to look at you and see that; I am unable to imbue the touch of my hand with respect for you as a human person. Somewhere I am not confident in my own humanity. I need you.

---

10. Vanier, *Community and Growth*. In this connection the Study Commission's observation is relevant where it notices Vanier's preference for the mystic church: "All the things rejected are more or less the expression of the Church as an institution: its relevance is thus reduced and somehow separated from the mystic Church" (Study Commission, *Control and Abuse*, 261).

11. See especially Brock, *Wondrously Wounded*.

12. Wall, *Welcome as a Way of Life*, 66.

13. Vanier, *Life's Great Questions*, 82.

In some mysterious way, we are united in one human family. But the uncertainty of it all raises anguish. It is when we dare to accept this anguish that we can begin to love.[14]

A Gnostic Grammar

Such passages are a reminder of what appears in the New Testament, especially in Paul, as the guiding problem of a truthful Christian life. It is the problem that has emerged in the history of theology as the ever-present danger of *gnosis*. *Gnosis* is the process of becoming new, of healing and redemption, aiming at the fulfillment of human life, either in a transformative perfection or in an ecstatic elevation in a perfect other reality. However this is described and grasped, in this gnostic dynamic the grammar of God's re-creation is dissolved. Within that grammar God remains present in his work and action encountering human beings and does not disappear in any dynamic of life fulfillment, nor in any other form of perfectly actualized selfhood, or other intensification dynamics. God's story does not end in the fulfillment of human life or in its elevation in an otherworldly reality. Instead, God's story bespeaks God's will to live eternally in communion with each and every human being.

This living together in the encounter with God begins here, in this *eon*, in the form of human life that remains attentive to God's action and activity. It raises the further question of how this form of human life can be connected with a kind of mysticism, the unity in God's mystery, and how the necessary distinctions are to be made here as well. In any case, properly understood, living in God's passion entails what is to be heard from God, in what is to be experienced from God's merciful forgiveness, as well as in what God's Spirit works, all of which is bound to God's Word. This is how God's story with Jesus Christ has become present. Human beings are saved into this story as God's creatures.

The problem of *gnosis* has always been to dismiss the creaturely form of life and neglect the structures that make it possible in order to be elevated into the spiritual life. There have been ever new manifestations in history up to the present, for example through the *gnosis* of a humanism that translates God's story into a history of human transformation and avoids the very reality that is present in the passion of God's activity and action.[15]

---

14. Vanier, *Life's Great Questions*, 68.

15. See Reinders' support for recognizing a gnostic tendency in Vanier's thinking. (Reinders, "Mixture of Light and Darkness.").

The return of this problem throughout history warrants our attention when other than theological voices point to the same phenomenon and point to the universal program of intensification in which human life is drifting, regardless of how rich or poor it is. People of our time are permanently in intensifying transformation—this is how Tristan Garcia describes this program that appears as a paradigm of humane life.[16] Garcia analyzes this as a paradoxical state of a life that is constantly aiming at an intensifying transformation, but at the same time is trapped in this very state and therefore—paradoxically—remains captive to it. It is a transformation that can no longer be measured by anything, no longer by certain steps of progress. It has no objectives or ideals outside itself, but can only be measured by its own dynamic, which is designed to intensify. Only the promise of a perfection in which all intensification comes to rest can counter it. But this promise, which Garcia recognizes in religious promises of salvation that will be fulfilled in an indefinite future, implies the end of the dynamic of intensification. It is thus an escape from the actual reality of this dynamic.

Garcia seeks a solution for this lack of balance between the desire for intensification and the continuity in human life that is present in the form of discursive thinking. Discursive thinking is just as much an indispensable part of human life as the striving for intensification. According to Garcia, both must be preserved in human life as a truly vital life. Whatever this philosophical attempt may mean for capturing the phenomenon of intensification, it remains a signal that this very phenomenon is observed as omnipresent in its own dynamic. In any case, it can be perceived as a warning that human life, in its own vitality, all too easily can lose itself in that dynamic. The question of how to repair this imbalance is one thing. The other, however, is that in this philosophical recommendation human life appears to be thrown back on itself, and is best preserved itself in balance, which implies, by all means, that the dynamic of intensification remains intact.

Noticeable, however, is that this philosophical analysis conspicuously lacks the perception of any other grammar that describes another form of human life than the therapy of a life balance and the preservation of "aliveness." That other grammar is about people, however balanced, not being absorbed in this or that life dynamic, but becoming aware of what is happening to them in a truly new, different life, and in communal living together. Earlier we saw how in Mark 8:34–35 Jesus speaks directly of this other life: "Whoever wants to gain his life will lose it; whoever loses his life for my sake will gain it." This other life is not determined by the balanced dynamics of intensifying life, but by people encountering each other on a

---

16. Garcia, *Letting Be*.

common journey as promised in the story that God is pursuing with them according to his providence. In every moment of life, everything depends on remaining in this encounter—like the prayer of Psalm 130: "I wait for the *Lord*, my soul does wait, and in his word do I hope. My soul waits for the *Lord* more than they that watch for the morning: I say, more than they that watch for the morning" (Ps 130:5–6).

Here we are not looking for something lasting that can be grasped in thought—as in Garcia's philosophical contemplation—and that then stands in balance for each person in the intensification of life. Instead, the worshipper of Psalm 130 seeks an encounter with the Word that applies to him, in which he knows he is addressed, through which it is confirmed that God continues his story with him for all eternity. In this way, the everlasting can only be recognized eschatologically.

"Life in encounter"—this is how Martin Buber characterized the life of "I and Thou." This is the form of life that has its paradigmatic place in prayer. This form of life is paradigmatic for living together in L'Arche. It is about this always present vis-à-vis, in which people meet each other regardless of what they have in common or what makes them different. They encounter each other in God's story with each and every one that is saved into the story of God's creation.

Friendship

In this connection we may also think anew about "friendship." What friendship can mean also corresponds to this encounter in a special way, if it is not in turn subject to other grammars. Friendship is the form of such an encounter. This is how Hans Reinders has impressively described it.[17] Friendship is the form in which it paradigmatically appears how people come together irrespective of what they have in common other than they become each other's friends. This is the passion of receiving friendship, which involves one "choosing" the other as a friend and thus granting them both the gift of friendship. Significantly, friendship appears as a figure for that trustful passion because it does not consist in what one has to offer to the other, not in mutual enrichment and intensification. It is always a matter of friends with their own story coming together in a common story, and each of their own histories bearing witness to something of this common story. Each bear witness to something of what has happened to people, what has determined their own story and thus something of how a life in encounter, a life in such passion, remains.

17. Reinders, *Receiving the Gift of Friendship*.

L'Arche as a lasting witness cannot be understood in any other way than as a place where this form of life and living together has been significantly lived. However, the threat to this form of life is immediate, given precisely with this form, because it is based on a passion, which means on a trustful letting happen of what is given to us in human coexistence. It is therefore crucial that this gift of communal life in L'Arche—like the gift of friendship—will prove to be resistant to losing its unique form and not follow other dynamics. Here, everything depends on the distinction between this form of living in God's story and the dynamics of an intensified fulfillment of life.

To be aware of this does not mean to recognize and acknowledge that the reality of L'Arche is just so endangered or vulnerable that one has to reckon with it going astray. On the contrary, it is to be noticed all the more clearly that the people in L'Arche bear witness to a different reality, a reality that precisely resists such dynamics and grammars. When this witness fails, it is not simply a confirmation of being led astray, the confirmation of that given danger, a sign of ambivalence, or a paradox. Instead, it is catastrophic.

It is at this point that succumbing to abusive sexual behavior by Jean Vanier and Thomas Phillipe becomes apparent in its most painful and disastrous manifestation, as an attempt to life in unity with God. Succumbing to their desire is catastrophic in that it makes all the more evident the challenge that has entered in this world with the witness of God's truthful passion. The challenge is to live humanly before God, not to live "divinely" as God.

The mistake by Vanier in the form of a perverted "mystical-erotic" practice is not only a deviation from the witness of L'Arche that is to be condemned, it also destroys its core message. Its witness consists in contradicting forms of human life that preclude full participation in the passion of God's story. The very mission of L'Arche is to guard against them. It is therefore all the more bitter that the "mystical" stance before God—that could have a very different meaning in L'Arche—has itself been perverted into the desire of a complete and fulfilled human life, thereby annihilating that guard, as the report of the Study Commission has shown.[18]

When the people involved fall prey to the desire for an intensified, fulfilled human life, they have not just succumbed to a threat, they have in fact crossed a line. Their transgression is catastrophic inasmuch as this line is not clearly demarcated, or even willfully denied.

The witness of God's passion marks the rift between on the one hand this world with all its potential for "ulterior" transformation, however destroyable by its own dynamic, and on the other hand the new life that

---

18. Study Commission, *Control and Abuse*.

remains in God's story, in which God's action remains present, his forgiveness, his consolation, his merciful intervention, and his promise that he wants to live together with his people for eternity. This other reality has appeared in this world in the story of Jesus Christ. God has opened up this real story to all his people. To follow this story with one's own story is called discipleship (come after Jesus). The "cross" that everyone should take upon themselves is the cross of the Passion that was spoken of here.

> Whosoever will come after me, let him deny himself, and take up his cross, and follow me. For whosoever will save his life shall lose it; but whosoever shall lose his life for my sake and the gospel's, the same shall save it. (Mark 8:34–35)

Stanley Hauerwas's description of "Christian friendship," quoted by Reinders, points precisely to this unique context.[19]

> Christians must not only see friends as gifts to one another, they must see their friendship itself as a gift. They can do this precisely because they understand themselves to be actors within a story authored not by them but by God. As Christians our friendship is not made constant by an act of our own will, individual or corporate, or even by our own virtue, but rather because we and others find ourselves through participation in a common activity that makes us faithful both to ourselves and the other. That activity is not, as it seems to be in Aristotle, mutual enjoyment as an end in itself, but rather it is the activity of a task we have been given. That task is nothing less than to participate in a new way of life made possible by the life of the man Jesus.[20]

Reinders adds: "That task . . . is an invitation to be truthful to the story of the triune God, who has drawn us into the communion of Father, Son, and Spirit. In other words, it is an invitation to remain faithful to the gifts of communion we have received through divine action."[21]

This is the enduring witness of L'Arche, which is recognized theologically in this way, in no other descriptions of social or interpersonal dramas. Such would run counter to the permanent "task" and the challenge that remains unmistakably given with L'Arche, the challenge of such a *vita passiva*.

---

19. Reinders, *Receiving the Gift of Friendship*, 366–67.
20. Hauerwas and Pinches, *Christians Among the Virtues*, 49.
21. Reinders, *Receiving the Gift of Friendship*, 367.

Bibliography

Brock, Brian. *Wondrously Wounded: Theology, Disability, and the Body of Christ*. Studies in Religion, Theology, and Disability. Waco: Baylor University Press, 2019.

Dow, Keith. "Against Living Saints." In *The Betrayal of Witness: Reflections on the Downfall of Jean Vanier*, edited by Stanley Hauerwas and Hans S. Reinders, 18–36. Eugene, OR: Wipf & Stock, 2024.

Garcia, Tristan. *Letting Be*. Volume I, *The Life Intense: A Modern Obsession*. Translated by Abigail Ray Alexander, Christopher Ray Alexander, and Jon Cogburn. Edinburgh: Edinburgh University Press, 2018.

Hauerwas, Stanley, and Charles Pinches. *Christians Among the Virtues: Theological Conversations with Ancient and Modern Ethics*. Notre Dame: The University of Notre Dame Press, 1997.

Iwand, Hans-Joachim. "Wider den Mißbrauch des pro me als methodisches Princip in der Theologie." In *Briefe, Vorträge, Predigtmeditationen*, edited by Peter-Paul Sänger, 225–30. Berlin: Evangelische Verlagsanstalt, 1979.

Matthews, Pia. "Putting Aside Charisma for Charism: A 'New Springtime' for L'Arche." In *The Betrayal of Witness: Reflections on the Downfall of Jean Vanier*, edited by Stanley Hauerwas and Hans S. Reinders, 71–88. Eugene, OR: Wipf & Stock, 2024.

Reinders, Hans S. *Disability, Providence, and Ethics: Bridging Gaps, Transforming Lives*. Studies in Religion, Theology, and Disability. Waco: Baylor University Press, 2014.

———. "A Mixture of Light and Darkness: Accounting for My Vanier." In *The Betrayal of Witness: Reflections on the Downfall of Jean Vanier*, edited by Stanley Hauerwas and Hans S. Reinders, 104–19. Eugene, OR: Wipf & Stock, 2024.

———. *Receiving the Gift of Friendship: Profound Disability, Theological Anthropology, and Ethics*. Grand Rapids, MI: Eerdmans, 2008.

Study Commission Mandated by L'Arche International. *Control and Abuse Investigation on Thomas Philippe, Jean Vanier and L'Arche (1950–2019)*. Châteauneuf-sur-Charente, France: Frémur, 2023.

———. *Synthesis of the Report Control and Abuse, an Investigation on Thomas Philippe, Jean Vanier, and L'Arche*. Châteauneuf-sur-Charente, France: Frémur, 2023.

Vanier, Jean. *Community and Growth*. Revised ed. Mahwah NJ: Paulist, 1989.

———. *Life's Great Questions*. Cincinnati: Franciscan Media, 2015.

Wall, Benjamin S. *Welcome as a Way of Life: A Practical Theology of Jean Vanier*. Eugene, OR: Wipf and Stock, 2016.

Chapter Ten

Jean Vanier
A Paradox for Cancel Culture

MEDI ANN VOLPE

THE #METOO MOVEMENT RAISED awareness of the prevalence of sexual assault and gave women hope that they would be believed. One side effect of the movement is the cultural trend of cancelling anyone found guilty (whether in a court of law or in the court of public opinion) of sexual misconduct, which reduces the individuals involved to perpetrators and victims. Cancellation is a blunt and clumsy response to a real and serious problem. As a Christian response to wrongdoing, it is inappropriate. In this essay I suggest that a simple "cancellation" of Jean Vanier, despite his corrupt and abusive sexual behavior, will not do, not for me as a person or a theologian, not for the people he influenced, and not for the organizations he founded and cofounded (L'Arche and Faith and Light). We who have learned from Vanier cannot simply write him out of our history.[1] Nor can L'Arche pretend Jean Vanier did not begin its story in 1964.[2] I am not attempting here to say how

    1. Karen Guth has addressed similar questions with regard to the late John Howard Yoder, using the framework of restorative justice. See Guth, "Doing Justice."

    2. The independent study commission began work in autumn 2020 to address a "need to reread the past" to help L'Arche "to move forward and deepen its particular mission and charism." Now that the report has been released (Study Commission, *Control and Abuse*), L'Arche faces the difficult task of renewing its self-understanding in its light, as the organization comes to terms with Jean's misconduct and adapts its origin story. Those of us who previously bore Jean's intellectual legacy will also need to come

that history should be rewritten. Those who hold the organization's memory and tell its story must find a way to tell the story transparently and faithfully in light of the findings of the independent Study Commission's report released in January 2023. My intention here is to open a space within which that story can be told *hopefully*—with hope for L'Arche, hope for healing for the women Jean abused, and hope for Jean himself to be reconciled to God through the cross of Christ. I offer a framework within which we might begin to think theologically about Jean's grievous misconduct.[3] Although we may never come to terms with what Jean has done, I believe that such a framework may also help to disentangle the marred legacy of Jean Vanier from the ongoing witness of L'Arche.

Jean Vanier: A Character in an Ongoing Story

I first met Jean Vanier in the early 1990s—not in person, though, and that is crucial for what I have to say. I found Vanier in the pages of *The Return of the Prodigal Son*, where he remained an anonymous exemplar for many years. In the book's final chapter, Henri Nouwen described a person whose hope and peace I desperately wanted to find:

> I have a friend who is so deeply connected with God that he can see joy where I expect only sadness. He travels much and meets countless people. When he returns home, I always expect him to tell me about the difficult economic situation of the countries he visited, about the great injustices he heard about, and the pain he has seen. But even though he is very aware of the great upheaval of the world, he seldom speaks of it. When he shares his experiences, he tells about the hidden joys he has discovered. He tells about a man, a woman, or a child who brought him hope and peace. He tells about little groups of people who are faithful to each other in the midst of all the turmoil. He tells about the small wonders of God. At times I realize that I am disappointed because I want to hear "newspaper news," exciting and exhilarating stories that can be talked about among friends. But he never responds to my need for sensationalism. He keeps saying "I saw something very small and very beautiful, something that gave me much joy."[4]

---

to terms with the way in which his writings and his life shaped us before the release of the L'Arche International's initial "Summary Report" in 2020.

3. I say "misconduct" rather that abuse, because I include Jean's denial of knowing anything about Pere Thomas Philippe's systematic abuse of women.

4. Nouwen, *Return of the Prodigal Son*, 115.

Nouwen is describing the joy that the return of the prodigal son brings to the father, which he compares to the joy of the Good Shepherd on finding just one lost sheep. The man he calls his friend was a joyful, peaceful man, a man who was content, a man who did not need to impress anyone, a man who had hope. This anonymous friend cast Nouwen's own cynicism into sharp relief. I wanted to know who this person was. I wanted that kind of contentment and peace, but I had not yet heard of L'Arche, or of Jean Vanier.

I might never have discovered who this anonymous figure was, had I not borne a child with Down Syndrome in 2001. Everything began to change as I came to terms—very slowly and reluctantly, I must admit—with my new reality: things were not going to go according to my plans. Family life did not unfold as I had hoped. I needed to make sense of what was happening; I sought teachers and guides. In 2011, I found the person I had been looking for since 1990-something. My husband gave me the collection of Vanier's letters, and I devoured it.[5] About halfway through the volume, it dawned on me: this was Nouwen's friend. I was especially struck by the frequency with which he closed his letters by asking for prayers that he would remain faithful: "Pray for me that I am faithful to the call of Jesus, that my heart becomes gentle and humble like the heart of Jesus."[6]

When I first met Jean, a few years after I read the letters, I asked him whether Nouwen had been speaking about him. He didn't seem interested in talking about it. Understandable, I suppose. He said "I don't know" in the least convincing way imaginable, and I went away sure that I'd found the character who had impressed me so much all those years before. On my last visit to La Ferme, I was asked to give the vote of thanks at the final lunch. I was delighted, of course, and told a version of the story I have just related. During the meal, I sat next to Jean, who did not deny the connection I had made. That was the last time I saw Jean before he died. In May 2019, I watched the funeral, and I grieved; I thought that a great light had gone from the world. Nine months later, the devastating news came to light, and the earth shook under my naïve feet.

I tell the story to provide background: I was introduced to Jean anonymously by Nouwen, identified him in the letters, and encountered him in person at La Ferme. Only after I had read his letters and met Jean did I begin to read his work more widely and think about his contribution to theology. The Study Commission's report, which confirms in detail Jean's misconduct, forces us to think carefully about his legacy, both his intellectual legacy for

---

5. Vanier, *Our Life Together*.
6. Vanier, *Our Life Together*, 380; also 335, 353, 413, 420, 429, 468.

those of use shaped by his writing and his legacy as the founder of L'Arche International and cofounder of Faith and Light.

My first step in building a theological framework within which to consider Jean's legacy is to call God to account: where was God when Jean's spirituality was being warped? Where was God when Jean was taking advantage of those women? There are questions of theodicy that cannot be answered but nonetheless need to be raised to give space for thinking theologically. Second, in light of those questions, I break apart the either/or that tends to frame our responses to sexual misconduct. The move to cancel perpetrators implies that there are only two kinds of human beings: those few who commit such vile acts, and the rest of us, whose peccadillos hardly bear mentioning. Of course that's not true, and I use a handful of fictional characters to explore the ways we tell the stories of redeemed and irredeemable villains. Finally, I draw attention to two theological principles that ought to frame our reflection: a theological anthropology that insists that the wholeness of each human being lies in her belonging to God, and an eschatology in which each one of us will be made new.

Revelations of a Spirituality Gone Wrong

The publication of L'Arche International's "Summary Report" in 2020 caused grief and anger and led some to cut Jean out of their stories. SPCK's decision to withdraw Jean's books from sale is one example of this response.[7] Such a response raises the question to what extent the issues around Jean Vanier's misconduct mirror the Hollywood sex abuse crisis. A cancellation response copied from Hollywood is inappropriate for Christians, because such a response rejects those who commit crimes that are considered unforgivable. For Christians, there is—as loathe as we might be to admit it—no such thing. I will return to the theme of forgiveness and grace below.

The ongoing good that L'Arche does in the world prompted others to condemn Jean and defend L'Arche. For example, an editorial in *Christian Century* describes the findings of the report, illustrated by testimony from one of the women whom Vanier abused.[8] The editors observed that L'Arche's values of vulnerability and mutuality "can be twisted" and that "accompaniment relationships can be fraught with power." The editorial is entitled "L'Arche after Vanier," and that is the direction of the piece: "L'Arche International's leaders," it says, "know that their work has never been about Vanier." It is only an editorial (but one with a vast readership), so I shouldn't expect

---

7. Richardson, "A Statement Regarding Jean Vanier."
8. "Editorial," *Christian Century*, March 25, 2020.

a nuanced approach to the problem of disentangling the institution and its values from the founder who shaped and nurtured it. The same could be said of the much longer attempt to do the same thing, *Weeds among Wheat*.[9] Fr. Dennis Billy sets out the spirituality and values of L'Arche without mentioning Vanier at all. Publications like these seem to solve the problem of Vanier's misconduct by distancing the organization from him. But is this the way forward—"cancelling" Vanier and keeping L'Arche? Tempting, but I think it is insufficient, because it fails to acknowledge the possibility of complicity among Jean's colleagues and friends. Nor does it help L'Arche to tell its origin story faithfully.

The acknowledgment that Jean's misconduct presents us with a paradox hits much closer to the mark. John Bernard Church laments that the story of Jean's deceit "makes no sense, and leaves one lost and bewildered. This is not a man we can just write off as rotten to the core. The pieces don't fit neatly together and the paradox is extreme."[10] As I will contend, the difficulty in fitting the pieces together should remain just that: a difficulty.

While it is tempting to suggest that Jean's apparent goodness was all a sham, and that we were simply deceived, the good that L'Arche has done compels us to reckon with the fact that Jean Vanier was the person through whom God began this work. How could a good God allow his apparently faithful servant to go so wrong? As I have suggested, there are no answers to such questions. Any justification of the harm Jean did is impossible. We cannot excuse or overlook his misconduct because L'Arche is and has been a force for good in the world. Jean Vanier appeared to live a faithful life and yet caused irreversible harm to the women he mistreated. How can we make sense of the narrative of Jean's life? I turn now to look at the complexity of reading fragmented lives.

Telling the Story of a Fragmented Self

I begin with *Middlemarch*, in which George Eliot offers characters whose mistakes in judgement shape the narrative, as in the case of her main character, Dorothea Brooke. While there is no comparison between the errors in romantic discernment of a fictional, nineteenth-century character and the sexual predation of a man who was described as "a living saint,"[11] Eliot's

---

9. Billy, *Weeds among Wheat*.
10. Church, "To Whom Shall We Go?"
11. Dulle, "Jean Vanier." The author cites Fr. James Martin, though he only affirmed the application of the phrase "living saint" to Vanier and was not the original source of the appellation.

observation about the way history reports our forebears to us is a helpful starting place. Near the end of the book, she reflects that those in Middlemarch "who had not seen anything of Dorothea usually observed that she could not have been 'a nice woman,' else she would not have married either the one or the other [of her husbands]." A younger generation familiar only with the "tradition concerning [Dorothea's second marriage]" failed to appreciate the character of the girl, who was only nineteen at the time of her first marriage, and was widowed and remarried within a couple of years. Eliot muses:

> Certainly those determining acts of her life were not ideally beautiful. They were the mixed result of young and noble impulse struggling amidst the conditions of an imperfect social state, in which great feelings will often take the aspect of error, and great faith the aspect of illusion. For there is no creature whose inward being is so strong that it is not greatly determined by what lies outside it.[12]

Who was Dorothea? A young woman who married scandalously, twice? Or a person whose "spiritual grandeur" unfolded in the circumstances of an imperfect life? Although Eliot portrays Dorothea as a potential saint whose circumstances make great deeds impossible, Eliot does not justify Dorothea's choices. The mistakes remain *mistakes*. It is not the case that, in retrospect, Dorothea was really right to marry Edward Casaubon and Will Ladislaw. No: Dorothea's "great feelings" never found a suitable river-bed in which to flow; instead, the fullness of her spirit "spent itself in channels which had no great name on the earth."[13] Her romantic misadventures may have spoiled her early promise, but her two dodgy marriages did not cancel out that promise. Instead, the good effect of her being in the world trickled out in "unhistorical acts" whose beneficiaries were "those around her" rather than the wider world.

In a sense, all of *Middlemarch* is Dorothea's backstory, which begins with the comparison to young Teresa of Ávila and unfolds page by page to the denouement we have just seen. *Middlemarch* is full of characters like Dorothea, whose lives do not proceed according to their grand plans. Eliot's portrayal of Dorothea manages to incorporate her mistakes into the story that leads to the "happy ending," without excusing, justifying, or whitewashing them. Those mistakes will never count as "ideally beautiful"; yet making mistakes does not prevent hers from being a life "faithfully lived." Dorothea's story teaches us to interpret them and trains the eyes of our hearts to read

---

12. Eliot, *Middlemarch*, 924.
13. Eliot, *Middlemarch*, 924.

others' lives with patience and compassion. I suspect the next character I propose to consider will test the limits of our patience and compassion: Darth Vader.

Eliot's portrayal of Dorothea suggests that there is more to every character than either "not a nice woman" or a saint, but this requires testing, I think, with respect to a character whose wrongdoing far exceeds Dorothea's. Let us consider another happy ending: that of *Return of the Jedi*. Anakin Skywalker appears alongside Yoda and Obi-wan Kenobi as a force ghost. Luke is pleased to have succeeded in reawakening the goodness in his father; his hope is fulfilled and his persistence is rewarded. Darth Vader was not, it turns out, "only a master of evil"—which was Obi-wan's assessment in *A New Hope*, the first Star Wars film. We might have squirmed a bit in 1983, however, if we'd known the extent of Anakin/Vader's cruelty. Nor is it as simple as "Anakin good–Vader bad." In *Attack of the Clones*, Anakin avenges his mother's death by slaughtering the entire tribe of the people who enslaved her. "Not just the men," he tells Padmé, "but the women and the children." Chilling. In the next installment, *Revenge of the Sith*, Anakin kills all the masters and padawans he can in an attempt to wipe out the Jedi order. Anakin Skywalker's heinous crimes began well before he put on the black mask and became Darth Vader.

The happy ending of *The Return of the Jedi* is a happy ending to Luke's story, and to Anakin Skywalker's. We see through Luke's eyes—Luke, who was determined to uncover some goodness in a character that was regarded as "only . . . evil" and depicted unreservedly as a super villain in the first and second Star Wars films. The edition of *Return of the Jedi* after the production of the three prequels only serves to complicate matters. Instead of the old Anakin Skywalker, on whose vulnerable, dying face we looked with Luke, the force ghost takes the form of the young Anakin—the impulsive and unrepentant one who thought that women and children deserved to die. Although the redemption of Skywalker/Vader is cinematically compelling, it is theologically challenging. Redemption does not simply erase wrongdoing and put the pieces of our lives back together without it. In the hands of a master storyteller, however, the fragmentation of characters is a thread that runs through the whole narrative and drives the plot. In his trilogy, *The Lord of the Rings*, Tolkien reminds us that "more than one power [is] at work." Those powers do not clash (only) on the battlefield, however, but within each character, and the story hinges on their moments of triumph or of failure.

"What You Meant for Evil, God Meant for Good": Wrongdoing and Redemption in *The Lord of the Rings*

In Sméagol/Gollum, Tolkien gives us a character whose treachery ends up saving Middle Earth. More obviously than any other character in *Lord of the Rings*, Gollum is at war with himself; he helps, he fawns, and he plots destruction.

> Gollum looked at [Frodo and Sam, sleeping peacefully]. A strange expression passed over his lean hungry face. The gleam faded from his eyes, and they went dim and grey, old and tired. A spasm of pain seemed to twist him, and he turned away, peering back up towards the pass, shaking his head, as if engaged in some interior debate. Then he came back, and slowly putting out a trembling hand, very cautiously he touched Frodo's knee—but almost the touch was a caress. For a fleeting moment, could one of the sleepers have seen him, they would have thought that they beheld an old weary hobbit, shrunken by the years that had carried him far beyond his time, beyond friends and kin, and the fields and streams of his youth, an old starved pitiable thing.[14]

Tolkien shows here—as clearly as Luke asserts—that "there is still good in him, I know there is!" Whereas Darth Vader chooses, in the end, to save Luke, Gollum does not choose to save Frodo. At a harsh word from Sam, aroused by suspicion, "Gollum withdrew himself, and a green glint flickered under his heavy lids. Almost spider-like he looked now, crouched back on his bent limbs, with his protruding eyes. The fleeting moment had passed, beyond recall."[15] But Gollum's treachery cannot thwart the quest. His plans to steal back the Ring for himself are, in the end, turned to serve the quest; he, not Frodo, is the one who carries the Ring into the fires of Mount Doom. Middle Earth is saved from the power of the Dark Lord Sauron by Gollum's betrayal.

Yet Tolkien does not suggest that the role Gollum played justifies the harm he inflicted. Sméagol was an unsavory character before he obtained the Ring; then he murdered his friend to gain possession of it. Having the Ring helped Sméagol along the way of corruption, allowing him to sneak and spy. Frodo refers to him as "that vile creature" and Gandalf does not correct him. And Gandalf agrees with Frodo's judgment that Gollum "deserves death." He replies, "Many that live deserve death. And some that die deserve life. Can you give it to them? Then do not be too eager to deal out

---

14. Tolkien, *Two Towers*, 324.
15. Tolkien, *Two Towers*, 324.

death in judgement."[16] The indispensable role Gollum plays in destroying the Ring is inseparable from his treachery. Tolkien shows us not that Gollum is really one of the good guys, but that what Gollum means for evil, a power in Middle Earth turns to good.

Other characters, too, do battle within—Frodo sometimes resists the temptation to put on the Ring, and sometimes succumbs; in the end he fails to cast away the Ring and takes it for himself. Yet the evil power is not the only power at work in Frodo: he volunteers for the quest without willing it.

> A great dread fell on [Frodo], as if he was awaiting the pronouncement of some doom that he had long foreseen and vainly hoped might after all never be spoken. An overwhelming longing to rest and remain at Rivendell filled all his heart. At last with an effort he spoke, and wondered to hear his own words, as if some other will was using his small voice. "I will take the Ring," he said, "though I do not know the way."[17]

In Frodo's acceptance of the doom he dreaded, we perhaps glimpse the working of the power that put Bilbo's hand on the Ring in the dark, and stayed his hand when he could have killed Gollum. More than one power is always at work, not only in Middle Earth but in our own world as well. However meandering or twisted its course seems, the creation is bound inexorably for its telos: God *will* be all in all. It is time to turn back to the theological.

Grace and the Elusive Self

George Eliot's reference, at the close of *Middlemarch*, to a life "faithfully lived" raises questions about what makes a life *un*faithful. Our great temptation is to decide for ourselves what makes an apparently faithful life a sham. In this, we are bound to fail. The question whether Jean simply deceived us all is impossible to answer. Yet for Christian theologians wrestling with the legacies of fallen mentors and heroes, a fuller exploration of the question in all its awkwardness is indispensable. It will, likewise, be indispensable for the witness of L'Arche after Jean Vanier. Acknowledging that "there is still good in him" does not resolve the difficulty facing those individuals and institutions who owe something of their formation to Jean's influence. Now I turn to theological reflection to explore two aspects of reading a life. The first has to do with the impossibility of discovering the "real" Jean Vanier,

---

16. Tolkien, *Fellowship of the Ring*, 69.
17. Tolkien, *Fellowship of the Ring*, 264.

and the second considers the unfathomable work of God's grace in redemption, forgiveness, and healing. In this reflection I am helped by Rowan Williams's analysis of our modern concept of the self and the unfathomable character of Christian redemption.[18]

My theological reflection begins with a look back at Darth Vader/Anakin Skywalker. Who is the "real" Anakin Skywalker? The young force ghost reflects our cultural paradigm. The *real* Anakin is the one who has not gone over to the Dark Side. There is an impulse to associate the "real" person with either evil or goodness, however attenuated. Vader saved Luke in the end; therefore the good that was in him triumphed. That is the *real* Anakin Skywalker surfacing; having discovered the real Anakin, we can excise his misdeeds from the story. Those were not really his acts. Such an impulse to establish the real self and eliminate pieces that don't seem to fit stems from misdirected desire, which in such a case manifests as "a desire to possess or manipulate a power capable of obliterating part of ourselves and our past."[19] This is what a "cancel" culture is after: the power to erase the people we perceive as responsible for injustice in our world, for the wrong ways that we, as individuals and societies, are formed now. The temptation to erase those whose influence has shaped a racist, sexist, Eurocentric culture is great. But that is a hopeless gesture, based on a puritanical and Pelagian impulse to right every wrong ourselves—as if we ourselves are innocent. We are not. Who knows how future generations may judge us for the damage done to the earth, or for the creation of a soul-destroying meritocratic culture?

A cancel culture passes judgment on characters, erasing the wrongs in the one in whom the good is judged to be "real" and ignoring the good deeds of one whose "real" self is revealed in their wrongdoing. For a culture without hope of redemption, the only way to resolve the tension between the goodness Luke perceived in his father and the cruel deeds of Anakin Skywalker/Darth Vader is to obliterate the latter. Those acts were not committed by the "real" Anakin Skywalker. One might be tempted (in other cultural circumstances than our own) to narrate Jean's story analogously, to say that the "real" Jean Vanier is the man Nouwen described, the one who founded L'Arche and cofounded Faith and Light. But it will not do, just as the restoration of a pre-Dark Side Anakin Skywalker will not do. Obliterating the harm closes off the possibility of repentance, healing, and reconciliation. A cancel culture works on the assumption that the private sphere is of final, central significance.[20] Thus, the need to assert Anakin's good private self

---

18. Williams, "Suspicion of Suspicion."
19. Williams, *Resurrection*, 81.
20. Williams, *Resurrection*, 191.

that somehow persisted in spite of his apparent consumption by the Dark Side. Christian theological anthropology, on the other hand, holds that the human person is held together by God, from whom and in whom we and all creation have our being.

Although we are not capable of holding together our own fragmented selves, let alone making sense of the wholeness of others, God's grace remakes our stories, redeeming us without erasing our past. From a theological point of view, it is better to keep the old Darth Vader as the force ghost in *Return of the Jedi*. Why? Because if the good persisted in Anakin Skywalker, as Luke eventually proved, then he was never *fully* consumed by the Dark Side. Obi-wan stands, healed and whole—only one of Anakin/Vader's many victims, of course. On a theological reading, we might see Obi-wan not just as a single victim, but as a symbol of all those Anakin/Vader killed. The grace that redeems the sinner also heals the wounded, remaking them whole, restoring fullness of life without erasing their past. We are, on the whole, too mired in the pain and fear and resentment that pervade our fallen world to imagine that final restoration of all things in God. But Scripture tells us that we will *all* be changed, and we who believe will be like him—the One who was wounded for our sake and died and rose again. Rowan Williams reminds us of the hope that the resurrected Christ holds out to us: not the hope of innocence but the hope of redemption. In beholding Christ, we behold not just our own pain, but

> the all too recognizable face of the world whose suffering we have helped to make, and which we cannot therefore draw into ourselves. Grace deals with us whole: it does not simply console me as victim, for that would be to leave untouched the reality of my complicity in the hurt and damage of the world. Human beings long to be reassured that they are innocent. . . .
>
> The gospel will not ever tell us we are innocent, but it will tell us we are loved; and in asking us to receive and consent to that love, it asks us to identify with, and make our own, love's comprehensive vision of all we are and have been. That is the transformation of desire as it affects our attitude to our own selves—to accept what we have been, so that all of it can be transformed. It is a more authentic desire because more comprehensive, turning away from the illusory attraction of innocence that cannot be recovered unless the world is unmade. Grace will remake but not undo. There is all the difference in the world between Christ uncrucified and Christ risen: they speak of two

different kinds of hope for humanity, one unrealizable, the other barely imaginable but at least truthful.[21]

In Christ we see simultaneously our own pain and the pain we have caused. Williams urges us to recognize that the grace that saves us also saves those we have hurt and those who have hurt us. If we want God's healing for those Jean harmed, we have to accept that their healing is bound up with the redemption of the world—including Jean's.

The Paradox of Redemption

Jean presents a *paradox* for cancel culture because his good deeds and grievous misconduct sit together uneasily in any story we might tell of his life.[22] But Jean's good deeds do not justify him; only Jesus can do that. We (and here I include all those who have been touched by Jean's life and work) face the "barely imaginable." The culture that would cancel Jean longs for innocence, and cannot see beyond purgation as the way to cleanse our organizations and societies. Jesus offers a different way forward, a way that foregrounds the healing of hurts and promises a transformed life both to us as we are hurting and to those whom we have hurt. At no point does redemption erase the wrongs, or pretend they were not wrong. Rather, a redemptive vision hopes for God's transforming work that heals those who have been hurt, and the fulfillment of the promise of being a new creation in Christ, which is held out to the wounded. The old, broken, sinful person is made new in Christ.

Trying to work out how justice and mercy go together in God lands us in the realm of the unfathomable. God's grace and God's justice are intertwined in the redeeming of the world, and we cannot imagine how. But as Christians, that is the "barely imaginable" for which we are called to hope. The cultural knee-jerk reaction of rejection and cancellation runs counter to the gospel. Cancel culture does not have space for a justice that is simultaneously grace. There is no space for reconciliation in such a framework, either between the perpetrator and the victim of the abuse, or between the abuser and God. It is a *hopeless* response, one that locks the perpetrator and the victim in their violent relation for eternity. The hope for true repentance and full healing is nowhere to be found. Yet that is precisely what the Gospel

21. Williams, *Resurrection*, 81.

22. We prefer—it seems—characters that are easy to pigeonhole. We think Luke Skywalker is good and Emperor Palpatine is bad. Darth Vader is more difficult, despite his cruelty. A cancel culture requires characters to be heroes or victims, or villains. Yet Luke believes that there is still good in Vader, and is proved right in the end.

is about: freedom from the bondage of sin, redemption, the resurrection of the dead—going from being dead *in* our sins to dead *to* sin and alive to Christ. However much we might resist the redemption of those who have hurt us deeply, we must remember that when we ask God to forgive us, we also say "as we forgive those who trespass against us."[23] It is a hard saying, and painful. But it is essential to Christian love, and faith, and hope.

Let's return now to my first encounter with Jean Vanier, the anonymous hero of Nouwen's anecdote. Was Nouwen just deceived? Was I, therefore, simply misled? Although I do not believe I was, that does not change what I would have to do in any case. Christians forgive, but do not excuse. No papering over, no minimizing the sin and the hurt. Forgiveness means looking directly at the sinner, naming the sin, and forgiving. The only way that this is possible is in the hope of redemption. We can forgive, but we cannot undo the harm.[24] We cannot take away the pain and hurt. We must, of course, do all we can to care for those who have been hurt and be vigilant in our protection of the vulnerable to prevent future harm. I said at the outset that I would not make recommendations, and I will not, except to remind us as Christians that the brokenness of the world and of all of us in it should not be an occasion for despair or condemnation, but for hope.

Bibliography

L'Arche International. "Summary Report." February 22, 2020.

Billy, Dennis, CSsR. *Weeds among Wheat: L'Arche and the Tainted Legacy of Jean Vanier*. St. Louis, MO: En Route, 2021.

Church, Bernard, OP. "To Whom Shall We Go? Jean Vanier and the Loss of Hope." Dominican Friars, February 25, 2020. https://www.english.op.org/godzdogz/to-whom-shall-we-go-jean-vanier-and-the-loss-of-hope.

Dulle, Colleen. "Jean Vanier: Living Saint who Ministered to People with Disabilities Dies at 90." *America Magazine*, May 7 2019. https://www.americamagazine.org/faith/2019/05/07/jean-vanier-living-saint-who-ministered-people-disabilities-dies-90.

Eliot, George. *Middlemarch*. Oxford: Oxford University Press, 1986.

Girard, Jocelyn. "Les communautés de L'Arche après le scandale de leur fondateur." *Culture et Foi* January 31 2021.

Guth, Karen. "Doing Justice to the Complex Legacy of John Howard Yoder: Restorative Justice Resources in Witness and Feminist Ethics." *Journal of the Society of Christian Ethics* 35 (2015) 119–39.

Keenan, Marie. *Child Sexual Abuse and the Catholic Church: Gender, Power, and Organizational Culture*. Oxford: Oxford University Press, 2011.

23. Volpe, "Lord's Prayer."

24. Jason Greig's "Sitting at the Table with a Sinner" addresses the issue of forgiveness in more detail.

Mackie, Carolyn. "Sin, Grief, and Jean Vanier." Women in Theology, Feb. 24, 2020. https://womenintheology.org/2020/02/24/sin-grief-and-jean-vanier/.

Marlow, Tanya. "But His Books Are Still Good, Right?—5 Things Christians Must Stop Saying about Sexual Abusers." Tanya's Substack, February 16, 2021. https://tanyamarlow.com/5-stupid-things-christians-say-sexual-abusers/.

Nouwen, Henri. *The Return of the Prodigal Son*. New York: Doubleday, 1992.

Richardson, Sam. "A Statement Regarding Jean Vanier." SPCK Publishing, February 24, 2020. https://spckpublishing.co.uk/blog/a-statement-regarding-jean-vanier.html.

Study Commission Mandated by L'Arche International. *Control and Abuse Investigation on Thomas Philippe, Jean Vanier and L'Arche (1950–2019)*. Châteauneuf-sur-Charente, France: Frémur, 2023.

Tolkien, J. R. R. *The Fellowship of the Ring*. London: Allen & Unwin, 1966.

———. *The Return of the King*. London: Allen & Unwin, 1966.

———. *The Two Towers*. New York: Ballantine, 1966.

Vanier, Jean. *Our Life Together: A Memoir in Letters*. London: Darton, Longman, and Todd, 2008.

Volpe, Medi. "The Lord's Prayer in the Life and Liturgy of the Church." In *T&T Clark Handbook of Christian Prayer*, edited by Ashley Cocksworth and John C. McDowell, 617–30. New York: Bloomsbury, 2021.

Williams, Rowan. *Resurrection: Interpreting the Easter Gospel*. London: Darton, Longman, and Todd, 2002

———. "The Suspicion of Suspicion: Wittgenstein and Bonhoeffer." In *Grammar of the Heart: New Essays in Moral Philosophy and Theology*, edited by Richard H. Bell, 36–53. San Francisco: Harper and Row, 1988.

Epilogue

Needing Vanier
A Brief Confession

Stanley Hauerwas

Arriving at the end of this book the reader has witnessed many accounts of Vanier's abusive behavior and encountered many insights into what may have contributed to its occurrence. As said in the introduction, trying to account for what went wrong is necessary for the witness of L'Arche to be carried on in the future. That Vanier betrayed its witness has been established beyond doubt, but Vanier wasn't L'Arche, even when he was sometimes talked about as if he were. The foregoing essays have given me much to think about, such that I do not see the need to add to what insights and accounts they have presented. But I do feel the need to look back in an opposite direction, as it were, and reflect on my own role in this abysmal story. After all, I have applauded Vanier and my admiration was not lost upon him.

The revelations surrounding Vanier's life along with the earlier disclosures about John Howard Yoder profoundly depressed me. That is to put the matter too lightly. Their behavior came close to making me despair, and I am in general a person of hope. I was particularly troubled not only because of how their behavior injured the women they misused but also becuase of how their behavior raised the question of my use of them. And that is what I was doing; that is, I was using them. I ended up being used. Let me try to explain.

I believe we live in a time when it is by no means clear we know what Christianity is or what a Christian should look like. There are no doubt many reasons for the decline of Christianity in the industrial West, but the continuing loss of Christendom surely accounts for the increasing loss of adherents to Christian practice. I have not regretted the loss of Christendom, but it has meant there are fewer Christians and the ones left often are not well formed. I fear many who count themselves Christian know little about what makes Christianity Christian.

I have over many years tried to think through what Christianity might look like given its changed status. In particular I have tried to recapture the significance of the church as an alternative to the world. So understood the church might be capable of producing people of character. I needed examples such as Dorothy Day or Karl Barth and, I thought, Jean Vanier. I thought I was using Vanier, but it is obvious that I got used. My fault.

Vanier seemed to be exactly what I needed in order to show that Christianity is not some ideal struggling to be realized. L'Arche was the politics that I needed to counter any suggestion that the church was withdrawing from the world. On the contrary, in a world that increasingly has little reason to care for disabled persons, L'Arche was the witness that Christians had a different narrative about the way things are. And all this had been made possible by this strange man from Canada named Vanier.

I had read most of what Vanier had written before meeting him. I thought he was theologically thin but solidly in the bounds of the Christian faith. I thought his views were shaped more by psychological rather than theological insights, but most of the time they were good insights dealing with pain and the need for recognition. I found him a bit pious for my taste, but I thought a Catholic is a Catholic. But the most significant aspect of Vanier was how he related to his friends in L'Arche. He was not frightened by persons with cognitive impairments.

I also thought him to be a person of profound humility. He was particularly good in presenting L'Arche to groups that did not know what it was. I did wonder how he managed not to get bored by saying the same thing time after time. But I assumed that was necessary if he was to be a witness to the work that is L'Arche.

I had some vague sense that his relation to his mentor involved some controversy with Rome, but I had been around Catholics enough not to take that too seriously. I did hear someone ask him about the status of the Order that they had originally tried to start but he quickly dismissed the question. I assumed that was the "past." Again I was wrong not to investigate those matters but I needed him—and he needed me.

I did not see it at the time but he used my admiration for legitimacy. He took my description of L'Arche as an ecclesial reality as a general approval of his "church" rather than Rome. I just did not get the ecclesial politics that were in play. I was unable to see because I was blinded by the good I thought I saw in Vanier and even more in L'Arche.

I am, moreover, left with a deep challenge for how I have thought about the notion of character as essential to a good life. Deeply influenced by Aristotle, I have argued that morally good deeds cannot be accounted for as intelligible in themselves; they are produced by virtuous character. In this sense there must be a connection between virtue and knowledge. To be virtuous is to know what to do. Morally good persons cannot act different than they are. To be morally virtuous means nothing is hidden. What you see is what is there. If true, this means it is not easy to account for Vanier.

I am simply stunned by his ability to appear morally committed yet with a dark side almost beyond the imagination. What, I wonder, was the story he must have entertained about his behavior that allowed him to appear morally impressive? What categories are available that might help explain how he seems to be a living refutation of Aristotle's account of moral weakness. Given his behavior, he was not morally weak. It is more appropriate to say he was evil.

Without making too much of the difference, I think at least one of the implications of Vanier's duplicity is the contrast between rationalistic accounts of moral behavior and the theological category of sin. If you leave theological categories behind, it is very hard to comprehend what Vanier thought he was doing. He was rational enough to find a way to describe what he was doing as some good, which means he could only be drawn deeper into a morass of the terror he was perpetrating. Self-deception was surely at the door of Vanier's life.

I have spent a life arguing against the use of sin as an explanatory category. When the notion of sin is invoked to explain, something has gone wrong. Sin cannot explain because our sin is always parasitic on our conception of the good. Accordingly, sin is not just what we do but a power that possesses. It is an unsettling thought but I think it right to suggest that Vanier was so possessed. He was just enough convinced of his own virtue to be dangerous. He was just good enough to seduce many of us to forget critical issues that should have been raised but were lost amid our admiration for what we saw in L'Arche

Vanier remains a challenge to my moral imagination. I cannot imagine what and how he thought about his life. The pious bullshit he entertained I detest. Christianity can be quite dangerous when it is not tested critically by theological questions. I fear too many of us left those critical questions behind when confronted with what we took to be Vanier's insights. We rightly want L'Arche to have a future but it will have to be one whose narrative includes a confession of sin.

I remain stuck with texts I have written praising Vanier. I wish I could erase them but that would be cheating. What I can say is I believe Vanier was made possible by a Christianity that is coming to an end. I hope in some way what some of us have tried to do is help imagine what the alternative will be. That includes an honest acknowledgment of the failure to get Vanier right because we needed him.

www.ingramcontent.com/pod-product-compliance
Lightning Source LLC
Chambersburg PA
CBHW030112170426
43198CB00009B/597